PATRICK SHAW STEWART

Patrick Shaw Stewart

An Edwardian Meteor

MILES JEBB

THE DOVECOTE PRESS

199996
£22.00

I saw a man this morning
Who did not wish to die:
I ask, and cannot answer,
If otherwise wish I.

Fair broke the day this morning
Against the Dardanelles;
The breeze blew soft, the morn's cheeks
Were cold as cold sea shells.

But other shells are waiting
Across the Aegean sea,
Shrapnel and high explosive,
Shells and hells for me.

O hell of ships and cities,
Hell of men like me,
Fatal second Helen,
Why must I follow thee?

Achilles came to Troyland
And I to Chersonese:
He turned from wrath to battle,
And I from three day's peace.

Was it so hard, Achilles,
So very hard to die?
Thou knewest and I know not –
So much the happier I.

I will go back this morning
From Imbros over the sea;
Stand in the trench, Achilles,
Flame-capped, and shout for me.

PATRICK SHAW STEWART, 1888-1917
Gallipoli, 1915

First published in 2010 by The Dovecote Press Ltd
Stanbridge, Wimborne Minster, Dorset BH21 4JD

ISBN 978-1-904-34977-8
© Miles Jebb 2010

Designed by The Dovecote Press
Printed in Great Britain by the MPG Books Group, Bodmin and Kings Lynn

All papers used by The Dovecote Press are natural,
recyclable products made from wood grown in sustainable,
well-managed forests

A CIP catalogue record for this book is available
from the British Library

1 3 5 7 9 8 6 4 2

Contents

Acknowledgements

I AM MOST GRATEFUL to the family of Patrick Shaw Stewart for providing me with the archive of his papers and for much personal assistance. Patrick's older brother Basil was, like their father, a distinguished soldier. As an officer in the artillery he served first in India, and then fought in Gallipoli and Flanders, attaining the rank of Brigadier, before being badly wounded in 1918. His son Michael was a successful architect, practicing in Edinburgh. After his retirement Michael began a project to write a life of his uncle Patrick. But regrettably he was unable to continue with this due to illness. The initial chapter ('Childhood') is taken from his text. So my particular thanks are due to Michael's widow Grizel and his daughter Helen, and to Jack, his brother, who has resolved to ensure that this project should not wither on the vine.

I am also grateful to Viscount Norwich for permission to quote from the letters of his mother Lady Diana Cooper (formerly Manners). Also to Viscount Gage and Lady Cazalet, the two surviving grandchildren of Lady Desborough, for their encouragement for my use of her letters.

I acknowledge permission for the reproduction of the following illustrations: to Viscount Asquith for Edward Horner and Katharine Asquith; to Balliol College for Patrick Shaw Stewart at Balliol; to Artemis Beevor for Diana Manners and Duff Cooper; to Lady Bonham Carter for Violet Asquith; to Eton College for Cyril Alington and Charles Lister; to Lord Freyberg for Johnny Dodge; to Viscount Gage for Raymond Asquith, Cynthia Charteris, Winston Churchill, Ettie Desborough, Bernard Freyberg, Julian Grenfell, Archie Gordon, Rosemary Leveson Gower, John Revelstoke, Vita Sackville West, and Patrick Shaw Stewart as Robin Hood; to Peter

9

Jones and Tracy Wilkinson at the Archive Centre, King's College, Cambridge for Rupert Brooke (RCB/PH/263-7), Denis Browne (RCB/PH/148), for the group on camels in Egypt (RCB/PH/269-71); to Charles Maclean for Laura Lister; to John Rous for Arthur Asquith; to the Earl of Verulam for Hermione Buxton; to the Shaw Stewart family for the remainder.

INTRODUCTION

Patrick Shaw Stewart was the cleverest and most interesting of a group of friends who were nearly all killed in action in the First World War. The tragedy of their deaths was no greater than that of millions of others. But because of the privileges they enjoyed and the social prominence they acquired, they made during their short lives an impact that outlasted their deaths. Being in their mid-twenties at the outbreak of war, they were old enough to embark on the ladder of life after completing their education, old enough to relish the pleasures of upper-class living, in contrast to the youths who went to fight immediately on leaving school, and to the many who never had such luxuries. The shock of military danger, discomfort and discipline, was thus for them all the greater, but they unquestioningly accepted what a malign fate had in store for them.

The war brought the end of an era, and in particular it ended the dominance of the aristocracy. Eight years of a Liberal Government had certainly weakened the landed aristocracy, but it still retained its social superiority, and the possession of an hereditary title counted for much in terms of opportunities in political appointments, the acquisition of directorships, and advantageous marriages. The aristocratic circle in which Patrick moved would in earlier times have been designated as Whig, even though most of its members supported the Conservative Party. Being generally extremely rich and completely self-confident, its members could look down on more conventional and humbler Tories without having to associate themselves with Radical or Socialist politics.

They were more broad-minded, and included intelligent women who despised stuffy conventionality and encouraged intellectual conversation, in the manner of the famous Parisian *salonières* of the Ancien Regime They also respected academic brilliance, which at the time meant successes at Oxford or Cambridge, though still expecting their sons to be educated at Eton. It was on this basis that Patrick, the son of a distinguished Indian Army officer, was so accepted into the highest echelons of English society during those same eight years of Liberal ascendancy (English and England was the usual idiom for British and Great Britain).

From the age of ten Patrick displayed exceptional aptitude for competitive examinations. He was a brilliant classical scholar, from when he entered Eton at the top of the annual Election to College until he left Balliol with his Double First, followed by a Fellowship at All Souls, picking up all the most prestigious prizes on the way. By nature inclined to be dilatory, he rose superbly to a challenge and, by means of concentrating his razor-sharp mind and drawing on his superb memory, he was often able to beat off all competitors. The classical education he received, however restrictive in its subjects, did serve to foster extreme accuracy and precise deduction, and these he was able to apply in his profession as a banker. It was transmitted to him by excellent teachers, men who made friends with their pupils and gave them individual encouragement in many subjects outside the school curriculum.

When still at Oxford, and then at Baring's Bank (where he became a Managing Director), Patrick was taken up by a group of aristocratic families, and swept into an endless round of visits and parties. In particular he in time became a leading member of a young group known as the Corrupt Coterie, whose queen was Diana Manners, daughter of the Duke of Rutland, and whose antics were blazoned all over the popular press. But this fast living was short lived. When war broke out in 1914, Patrick was not yet twenty-six. From then on he was caught up in the dreadful war machine, which claimed the lives of a quarter of the Etonians who joined the forces, and specifically of four of the twelve Eton Collegers of his year.

His life was now changed utterly. His transformation into a brave and zealous warrior in the Naval Brigade proved that his social life had not rendered him effete. He was tough, able to withstand not only mortal danger but also extreme discomfort better than most, and to lead from the front. He raised the morale of others with his cheerfulness and caustic wit. He accepted the slaughter of most of his close male companions with stoical resignation.

His disregard for the danger of death is most apparent in his determination to return to the front-line in 1917. Having survived the whole campaign on Gallipoli, he was serving as a staff officer in Macedonia. Most men would have held on to such a posting, on the grounds that they had done their bit in the trenches. But Patrick was determined to get back to his old battalion, now in Flanders. This was partly fatalism. On the question of whether he wished to avoid death, his reply was ambiguous: 'I cannot answer if otherwise wish I.' But it was also because beneath his carapace he felt so lonely, and longed to be able to be with his friends again, to be in the circle in which he had shone so brilliantly. He nearly made it, dying on the penultimate day of 1917, after which the Hood Battalion incurred no further catastrophic casualties. He is buried in the British War Graves Cemetery at Metz-en-Couture near Cambrai.

It is through his letters that we discover Patrick. From Eton he wrote home every week, to his parents and to the nurse who meant so much to him. To her he related everything in an exceptionally honest and revealing way. To his two sisters he also wrote long descriptive letters. With manhood this letter-writing broadened into correspondence with several friends, the most notable being Lady Diana Manners and Lady Desborough. Other faithful correspondents were Edward Marsh and members of the Asquith family – Raymond, Katharine, Arthur, and Violet. Because he spent nearly the last four years of his life abroad, Patrick's letters were as from an exile preserving precious links with home, with long descriptions of his life as a traveller and a soldier. As with all letter-writers, what he wrote was geared to the recipient, and thus his accounts of events differed and were slanted. However, when a soldier, he in no way minimized the horrors he saw on Gallipoli or in Flanders. When in the trenches he had ample time for writing a diary, a memoir, or a novel, but only produced two fragments, of some five thousand words in all, the first about his time at Eton and the second about his voyage out to Gallipoli. As to poetry, apart from schoolboy attempts, we only know of one poem, albeit a masterpiece, printed at the front of this volume. Instead, in the trenches he read widely, never omitting the Classics, especially Greek. Herodotus and the *Iliad* were in his knapsack on Gallipoli: Achilles was beside him in the trench.

From the start Patrick's letters to Diana contained professions of undying love. She being only just sixteen when they began, such declarations were at first innocent of serious intent, and took the form of delightful stimulants to the replies of a budding enchantress. After she had 'come out' into society Patrick's love-letters became ever more serious, whilst hers were intent on fending him off, which she succeeded in doing throughout his life. She several times made it clear that she did not feel for him more than for her other suitors, but he ignored this warning. As with these others, she teased and tantalized him, and at the end he never realised that she had given her heart to Duff Cooper. The correspondence with Ettie Desborough was of an altogether different mode, she being twenty-two years older than he, the mother of two of his close friends. Here it was Ettie who set the pace, as she was able to do as a great lady in society, a hostess with two large country houses at her disposal. Her love for Patrick, though flirtatious, was platonic. This made their friendship easier, as with her Patrick would never have made advances or attempts at seduction. His unhandsome looks did not concern her. His able mind, his contrived delivery combined with his inner honesty, was what drew him to her. After the terrible blow of the death of two of her sons in action, she relied on him all the more for being a link with them, and to some extent a replacement for them, or at any rate a retention of youthful masculinity in her life.

A fortnight after Patrick's death a long obituary appeared in *The Times*. It dwelt on his 'effortless superiority' coupled with his devotion to his friends, his casual approach to work coupled with tremendous application when required. But in addition to an obituary those who had known Patrick best felt that some longer memoir should be written about him. Three of his closest companions in war had been commemorated in books. Edward Marsh had written a memoir about Rupert Brooke in *The Collected Poems of Rupert Brooke*. Lord Ribblesdale had put together a book about his son Charles Lister, in *Letters and Recollections*. And Ettie had commemorated her two sons, Julian and Billy Grenfell, in *Pages from a Family Journal*. It was at the suggestion of Ettie that Patrick's sisters persuaded Ronald Knox to write on Patrick. *Patrick Shaw Stewart* appeared in 1920. It is largely an anthology of his letters, with short introductions to the chapters by Ronald. The letters were predominantly those to his family – his parents, sisters, and his beloved nurse – but also some supplied by Ettie. Ronald made his selection from letters fed to him by Patrick's sisters, which did not include references to his love-life. Also he was ignorant of letters written to Patrick, or things subsequently written about him. For these reasons Ronald Knox's memoir does not present a truly rounded picture of its subject.

Other than those who are born great, or possess the spark of genius, the lives of those who die in their twenties seldom merit a full-length memoir. But Patrick's life is an exception because it was so intense and packed with action, and because it was set in the final flush of Edwardian aristocracy and its sudden immersion into the horror of the Great War. And in any case, in the stories of many eminent men and women, it is the early chapters on childhood and youth that are often the most appealing. Ambitious yet self-deprecatory, honest yet cynical, physically daring yet cool-headed, attractive yet unhandsome, socially charming yet cliquey, Patrick Shaw Stewart, in his short life, and in the contradictions of his character, provides a captivating insight into the age in which he lived.

The Principal Characters

First-name references most often used, for names appearing in the text. For full and subsequent names and titles, see the Index.

Angy	Angela Manners, daughter of Lord and Lady Manners
Basil	Basil Shaw Stewart, Patrick's brother
Betty	Betty Manners, daughter of Lord and Lady Manners
Billy	Billy Grenfell, son of Lord and Lady Desborough
Bunt	George Goschen
Charles	Charles Lister, son of Lord and Lady Ribblesdale
Cynthia	Cynthia Charteris (later Asquith), daughter of Lord and Lady Elcho
Cyril	Cyril Alington, Patrick's Tutor at Eton
	Cyril Bailey, Patrick's Tutor at Balliol
Dear	Elizabeth Reid, Patrick's nurse
Diana	Lady Diana Manners, daughter of the Duke and Duchess of Rutland
	Diana Lister (later Wyndham), daughter of Lord and Lady Ribblesdale
Duff	Duff Cooper
Eddie	Edward Marsh, Private Secretary to Winston Churchill
Edward	Edward Horner, son of Sir John and Lady Horner
Ego	Hugo Charteris (later Lord Elcho), son of Lord and Lady Elcho
Ettie	Lady Desborough

THE PRINCIPAL CHARACTERS

Hermione	Lady Hermione Buxton, daughter of the Earl and Countess of Verulam
Hester	Hester Alington, wife of Cyril Alington
Hoj	George Fletcher
Julian	Julian Grenfell, son of Lord and Lady Desborough
Katharine	Katharine Horner (later Asquith), daughter of Sir John and Lady Horner
Laura	Laura Lister (later Lady Lovat), daughter of Lord and Lady Ribblesdale
Letty	Lady Violet Manners (later Lady Elcho), daughter of the Duke and Duchess of Rutland
Margot	Margot Asquith, second wife of H. H. Asquith, Prime Minister
Marjorie	Lady Marjorie Manners (later Marchioness of Anglesey), daughter of the Duke and Duchess of Rutland
Oc	Arthur Asquith, son of H. H. Asquith, Prime Minister, by his first wife
Pua	Winifred Shaw Stewart, Patrick's sister
Raymond	Raymond Asquith, son of H. H. Asquith, Prime Minister, by his first wife
Ronald	Ronald Knox, son of the Bishop of Manchester
Rosemary	Lady Rosemary Leveson Gower, daughter of the Duke and Duchess of Sutherland
Rupert	Rupert Brooke
Tats	Katherine Shaw Stewart, Patrick's sister
Venetia	Venetia Stanley (later Montagu), daughter of Lord and Lady Stanley of Alderley
Viola	Viola Tree, daughter of Sir Beerbohm and Lady Tree
Violet	Violet Asquith, daughter of H. H. Asquith, Prime Minister, by his first wife
Vita	Vita Sackville West (later Nicolson), daughter of Lord and Lady Sackville

ONE

Childhood

PATRICK HOUSTON SHAW STEWART was born on 17 August 1888 at a house called Aberarto, near the village of Llanbedr, deep in the hills of Merioneth. Patrick's father, General Jack Shaw Stewart, had rented this remote house for the summer, where the embarrassing business of giving birth to his fourth child could take place in relative seclusion, away from the prying eyes of family and friends. Jack was in his fifty-seventh year, and his wife was in her forty-second. With their three other children – Winifrid (15), Basil (10) and Katherine (8) – it might be assumed that the family was complete by 1888 and that their child-bearing years were behind them.

Jack was the second son of a younger son of Sir Michael Shaw Stewart, 5th Baronet of Ardgowan in Renfrewshire. The Shaw Stewarts were an old family, and Sir Michael was the fifteenth in direct male succession to John Stewart of Ardgowan, a natural son of King Robert III of Scotland. Ardgowan was given to his son by that monarch in 1405, and it has been occupied by the family ever since. Like most younger sons, Jack as well as his father had to choose between the Church, the Army, or the Professions. Jack's father had been an advocate, eventually becoming Sheriff of Stirlingshire; Jack chose the Army and India, where he was to spend thirty-three years of his life. After training at Addiscombe College at Chatham, he joined the Madras Engineers in 1853, at the age of twenty-two. When he retired in 1886 Jack could look back with satisfaction on a worthy and distinguished career, during which he had held the post of Consulting Engineer for Railways, membership of the Madras Legislative Council, and Secretary to the Madras

Government. He was not directly involved in the Indian Mutiny operations in 1857, but in 1860 he had seen active service with Lord Elgin's Expeditionary Force in China, where he commanded the Sapper contingent. After the fall of Peking in October 1860, he witnessed the sacking of the Summer Palace by French and British troops, and was shocked by what he saw. All the same, Jack was to find himself in possession of some of the plunder, which included a unique milk-opal cup, gold-embroidered mandarin robes and throne covers, also a quantity of jade and Imperial yellow china. Ironically, his most memorable legacy to his family was to be the mysteriously-acquired plunder from the Summer Palace.

While home on leave in 1871, Jack became engaged to Mary, the only daughter of another sapper, Colonel George Collyer of the East India Company. Mary's mother had died of cholera in India in 1847 shortly after she was born. She was brought up, a precious and lonely heiress, by her grandmother at Shieldhill, Lanarkshire, where piety was encouraged as well as ignorance of the world and its ways. When Mary was thirteen her father returned from India, and with the help of his second wife, Rose Dillon, he had taken her under his wing at 61 Lancaster Gate, London.

The wedding took place in Edinburgh in September and was the occasion of much rejoicing in both families. Like many Victorian brides, Mary had a romantic view of the state of matrimony, and her sheltered upbringing had not prepared her for the realities of married life with a husband who was sixteen years her senior. The shock must have been considerable for this motherless, sensitive and spoilt girl, and the honeymoon spent in the West Highlands of Scotland and visiting her husband's relations must have been full of tensions and dissatisfactions for both parties. After the euphoria of the wedding, the gradual realization began to dawn on Mary that the day of departure for India was approaching, when she would have to leave her close-knit circle of cousins and female friends. Adding to her dread of that unknown land must have been the thought that her mother had died of cholera in India, when she was a baby. Her worries and fears began to affect her health.

Jack's leave was due to have expired in January 1872 but, owing to Mary's difficulties, his return to India was postponed. About this time Mary appears to have considered the possibility of abandoning her husband and letting him sail without her. The idea may well have been put into her head by Jack's old uncle, Admiral Sir Houston Shaw Stewart, who had taken a particular fancy to his young niece. When the time finally came for Jack to sail in March, Mary's nerve cracked and she refused to go with him. For the next six months she remained under the wing of her father and step-mother, blaming them for what had occurred, while being charming to everyone else, including Jack's mother and sisters. In October, in a state of exasperation, Colonel Collyer took his daughter to Marseilles, and put her forcibly on a steamer, accompanied by her maid, Knowles.

The Colonel was told by his doctor that if Mary had a child it would be the means of perfect recovery. Dr Luke's advice did not go unheeded. Mary arrived in India in the middle of November, and the therapeutic first child, Mary Winifred, duly arrived on 25 August 1873. For the time being the therapy seemed to have worked. Mary came to terms with her married state, and she settled down to the rigours of life in a strange land, far from her beloved Shieldhill. Three further children were born in India – John Archibald (born and died 1875), Basil Heron (1877) and Katherine Bedingfield (1880).

When she came home on leave in 1881, Mary decided to advertise for a nurse to help with her growing family. After much searching in and around Edinburgh, she engaged Elizabeth Reid, a stonemason's daughter from Cullen in Banffshire. This turned out to be one of the most important decisions Mary ever made. Elizabeth, or 'Dear,' as she was soon to be known, became the mainstay of the Shaw Stewart family. She was to become especially close to young Patrick, when he appeared on the scene in 1888. (His second name of Houston was used in the family because an ancester had married a Houston heiress.)

When Patrick was on his way to Gallipoli in 1915, he wrote

down his view of his family :

> My father was a man of great personal distinction, of
> exceptional abilities, of the most transparent sincerity
> and generosity, and of that earnest though latitudinarian
> religion which since his day has become exceedingly rare.
> His weaknesses were in worldly wisdom, in patience, and in
> humour. As he was nearly fifty-seven when I was born, it may
> seem that I am charging him with the faults of age; but his
> career makes it evident that they must early have militated
> against the success which his great qualities deserved. His
> utter inability to conciliate his superiors, or to do any time-
> serving action, would seem wholly a noble failing, had I not
> been the witness of its reflex action on my mother's ambition
> and my sisters' chances in life. For my mother was, like all
> spirited women, reasonably ambitious, but though a clever
> and delightful companion, she was not capable of dispensing
> with the solid masculine assistance, the lack of which she
> half-consciously deplored. She herself contributed further to
> depress the prospects of my sisters by too much monopoly
> of the foreground. At the same time her vivid, half-histrionic
> temperament, and her incapacity to abstain from the planting
> of pin-pricks had worked on my father's slightly irascible
> downrightness to bring about, shortly after my birth, one
> of those superficial alienations between two fundamentally
> virtuous and loyal souls which are, for the purposes of daily
> life, as tragic as the most complete and dramatic subversions.
> A brutal modern outsider might say that my parents had
> failed to make the always arduous transition from Anglo-
> Indian to retired English life with any real success, and that
> to this was added the internal scourge of a lack of humour on
> both sides.

> My brother in early years was a mere incident in my life,
> being at school and then at Woolwich. He was naturally
> bored with me on the rare occasions when I was accidentally
> left in his path, and I feared and disliked him as children will.

My sisters, then as always, spoilt me and I adored them; but above them, above my parents, above the whole world in the time of my first sentient decade looms the figure of my nurse, Elizabeth Reid. I know it is a common thing for men to retain a considerable attachment to their nurses long after any direct relationship has ceased, to speak of them with affection, to write to them, to visit them; but the clue to my childhood is contained in the fact that our mutual devotion was on quite a different plane . . .

Patrick's arrival stirred the maternal instincts of his two sisters, and it gave them a new objective in life. The family were much given to the use of nicknames: Winifred was known as Pua (pronounced 'poor'); Basil was Tom, or The Gunner; Katherine was Tats or Tatie (pronounced 'tarts' or 'tartie'); while Patrick was Pady (pronounced 'pardie'). Led by Dear, they lavished their pent-up love and affection on the new baby. He was a precocious child, and was encouraged by Dear to exercise his brain in the study of the animal kingdom, which he illustrated copiously in note books. Dear also introduced him to the Bible and Classical mythology; she had a copy of *Lemprière's Classical Dictionary* of her own, which was an unusual reference-book for a nanny. Dear was a remarkable person, full of common sense and humour, and strongly religious. Patrick's relationship with her was a very special one. As to his parents, Patrick was never close to either of them. The age difference made it difficult for the General to unbend and to enter into the world of his children. For them he was often a figure of fun. Patrick's mother on the other hand was over-dramatic, and tended to smother her children with love and affection, combined with self-pity. She did not enjoy good health and was neurotic and preoccupied with her frequent quarrels with her husband. It was in this situation that Dear came into her own, acting in loco parentis. She took complete charge of Patrick's early education and upbringing, and with her sensible, energetic, and downright attitude to life, she was obviously more fun to be with than his elderly parents.

Patrick's formal education began when he attended Miss Roth's kindergarten in Kensington Gardens Square, after which he graduated as a day boy to Mr Wilkinson's preparatory school in Orme Square. Mr Wikinson was one of those energetic and ambitious schoolmasters whose main objective was to win scholarships at public schools, thereby earning kudos for his own school. He was quick to spot a winner in Patrick, whose appetite for competitive examinations was awakened at this time, and was to remain with him throughout his educational years.

There was much debate in the family about Patrick's future education. Should he follow his elder brother to Marlborough, or should he try for an Eton Scholarship? The General, having more or less decided on Eton for Patrick, went to Eton with Pua to spy out the land. Patrick meanwhile was kept busy at Orme Square construing Livy and Thucydides, composing Latin verses, and generally honing his skills in preparation for the scholarship examination in July 1901. His studies were interspersed with football and fives, and with tea parties and dances during the holidays.

Since her marriage in October 1900, and setting up house with her farmer husband Alec in Rosshire, Dear by her absence had left a great void in Patrick's life, and he wrote a long letter to her each week. She spent the autumn and winter altering and improving the little farmhouse at Findon Mills on the Black Isle so that she could have her former charges to stay with her. Tatie was the first to sample the joys of Findon Mills, and Patrick and Pua went during the Easter holidays. Patrick took to life on the farm with an enthusiasm and an interest which was never to leave him. Its simple pleasures, and the joy of being with his beloved Dear, were a wonderful and relaxing contrast to his hectic existence south of the Border.

For the next two months he was fussed over and groomed and fed a diet of old Eton scholarship papers in preparation for the Big Race at Eton in July. On 8 July Patrick and Pua proceeded to Eton and set up lodgings. Patrick's struggle with the examiners was of absorbing interest to the whole family, also to his headmaster, who all scented victory on a grand scale. They were not to be disappointed. Four days after finishing his last paper the news came that he had been placed first on the Scholarship list. For Patrick, this was his first taste of fame and, as noted by his schoolmaster, he managed to avoid letting it go to his head. Letters and telegrams from family and friends poured in to his proud father. Besides the announcement of the election in *The Times,* there was also one of Patrick's victory in the local *Paddington Gazette.* The scholarship relieved Patrick's father from all Eton fees.

Up to this point Patrick had been the centre of attention in the family, doted on by Dear and his two sisters. He was not exactly spoilt, but he had come to rely on their love and affection, and on their applauding every scholastic and athletic achievement. At the end of July the family migrated northwards to Flowerburn Cottage, Fortrose, on the Black Isle, which the General had rented during August and September, and where they would be within bicycling distance of Dear at Findon Mills. His six weeks holiday at Flowerburn, where he was surrounded by feminine influences, marked the end of his childhood. He was shortly to enter a very different world at Eton, where influences were to be entirely male.

TWO

A Colleger at Eton

A t the beginning of the twentieth century the British independent public schools were at their zenith, and Eton was recognized as the foremost among them, due to its long-established attraction for members of the upper classes. Fifteen Prime Ministers had been to Eton, six to Harrow, and only one to Winchester. The school was one of the largest, with over a thousand boys, divided as between the seventy Foundation Scholars (the Collegers) who lived in the college itself, and the fee-paying remainder (the Oppidans) who boarded in adjacent houses. The great majority of the boys now expected to have to earn a living. Nearly half proceeded to universities, most of them in preparation for one of the professions, principally the Church, the law, or the Civil Service. About a quarter went to Sandhurst to acquire a commission in the regular Army, though some as a matter of form before inheriting country estates. The educational curriculum was still firmly based upon the Classics, with other subjects considered as secondary, though a system of specialization had recently been introduced for the senior boys. Games were mandatory, and highly competitive. Eton was an enclosed world, only tenuously connected to the outside by means of weekly letters home.

Patrick was brought to Eton by his father at the start of the Michaelmas Half of 1901 (the three terms were known at Eton as Halves), and deposited in his cubicle in the Long Chamber, together with seven other new boys of his year (the remaining four arriving later), and joining some of those of the previous year in the fifteen stalls. Of the twelve in his year, seven were the sons of schoolmasters or academics. The three front-runners in terms of dominance in the Chamber were Alan Parsons, Foss Prior and Victor Barrington-Kennett. All those joining with Patrick had boarded at preparatory schools and so were well adapted to the conventions of the communal life now imposed upon them. Patrick was thus at a disadvantage, but one which he could easily surmount as 'a healthy normal boy with a great zeal for the classics, a respectable though not notable aptitude for games, and an average social talent which placed me in the ranks of neither the ragged nor the raggers.' The junior Collegers, the denizens of the Chamber, were thrown closely together, not messing in separate groups but in front of the fireplace, with a Captain who kept order with a toasting fork. However, in his autobiographical notes Patrick delves into a deeper self-analysis:

> I was passing through the distemper of active-minded childhood – religious mania – in one of its less common forms, hypertrophy of the conscience. This hypertrophy manifested itself in me, both then and afterwards, in a highly specialized form, as a sanction of rigid formal honesty. Our world distinguished habitually between the honest and the honourable; never was there more need for this dichotomy than in my case. I have never been a punctiliously honourable boy or man, nor was I then, but honesty shortly after my entrance into Eton came on me like a storm.

This search for honesty required rigid self-examination, and was the thread that ran though his daily prayers. Several of the other small boys also said their prayers, but Patrick's were so intense that he found that the five minutes allotted to them at 9.55 pm in the Chamber before lights out, kneeling beside his bed, were insufficient, requiring a continuation when kneeling in bed. And in the morning he took advantage of the silence of the lavatory for further prayer. Dear, who had taught him to pray, urged him to restrict himself in what she called his 'concerts': 'Pady for the tenth thousand time say in the morning Our Father and Father thou hast heard us. I mean all your morning prayer to get into 5 minutes and the night one not to exceed 10 minutes.' When staying with Alan Parsons and his family in Scotland the following summer, Patrick shocked his friend's father, though himself a clergyman, by remaining for half an hour in the bathroom in prayer after lunch. However, during the following year his fervency abated, and he complained to Dear that 'even the reformed concert takes at least three valuable minutes.'

During this first Half Patrick constantly scored top marks among the collegers in his year. He won prizes for the study of selected passages of Homer and Virgil; he was commended for his Greek and Latin verses; and he won the Trials Prize. After his Christmas holidays in the bosom of his family at Inverness Terrace, he faced the Lent Half with assurance, though his achievements then were cut short after three weeks by chicken-pox, from which he recuperated in London and with Dear at Findon. But even in the three weeks of his attendance his form master, Henry Bowlby, signalled him out for praise: 'he was the baby of the division in years but certainly the oldest in mental grip and sureness of touch.' There followed the Summer Half, marred for Patrick by a persistent failure at cricket, which he had mistakenly regarded as his game. And he still felt homesick – 'still the day boy, still feminine influences, which were soon to disappear for some four years, and then return, never to depart.' He was still too young to hanker after field sports during the holidays, and content to be at a small house near Inverness that his father had taken for the summer.

The Master in College, who exercised paternal care among the Collegers, was Arthur Goodhart. But each boy was allotted a Tutor, responsible for his academic progress, and in Patrick's case this was Cyril Alington. Cyril Argentine Alington, now aged thirty, had recently come to Eton from Marlborough, where he had taught the Sixth Form. He was a scholar (of Trinity College Oxford and a Fellow of All Souls) and an ordained Anglican priest. He was a stimulating teacher, an inspiring preacher, and a clever versifier. His prodigious memory made up for any lapses in true scholarship. And he personified muscular Christianity with a handsome presence and ability to compete at cricket, fives or racquets with the most gifted of the boys. With all these attributes, he was also a sympathetic man, whom the boys trusted and liked. Each Tutor held court every day for an hour in their Pupil Room, and here Alington excelled, encouraging his flock with imaginative comments and readings, reciprocated by them.

Under the watchful eye of Alington, Patrick progressed at Classics under a number of first-rate teachers, such A. C. Benson (who 'encouraged us to express ourselves in English') and Hugh Macnaghten ('who opened the eyes of some of us to the true meaning of classical education'). In his report on Patrick in December 1903 Hugh Macnaghten wrote that he had come on amazingly: 'I am not afraid to say this, because I must honestly confess that I believe his progress is chiefly due to his Tutor, who combines with the inevitable weaknesses/graces of an Oxford scholar a gift of inspiring his pupils, which is all his own, and which no one else here possesses in anything like the same degree.' Another Classics master was Arthur Heygate, who was the butt of some derision by Patrick and his friends. 'He is unliterary, un-classical and un-scholarly, to the last degree,' but 'continually demanding quotations for everything, all day long and every day, which is really quite exciting,' and all for facts and brevity. 'A Heygate', in the slang of Patrick's contemporaries, meant something stuffy and timidly conventional. However, Patrick agreed with Arthur Heygate in his love of the poetry of Horace, whom Cyril Alington disparaged as 'a fat man sitting in the sun on his farm, reeling off disgusting lyrics.'

Patrick's second year at Eton (1902/3) was less happy than his first: 'The extreme cosiness of Chamber life was forgone, my contemporaries were more impatient of my idiosyncrasies, and those idiosyncrasies had as yet shown no trace of modification; and while making no further athletic progress, I was twice robbed of my very marked scholastic pre-eminence by Foss Prior and an Oppidan. I was at this time absolutely devoid of social prudence, a quality which suddenly developed itself in me at the turning point of my adolescence.' But a double-defeat for first place by Foss Prior served to stimulate him, and carried him to a sweeping Trials victory in the summer. And meanwhile he continued to receive prizes, such as two bound volumes of *The Iliad* for the Christmas Holiday Task. But the summer was marred by an ignominious start as a 'wetbob' on the river, allocated to the position of cox in a Junior House Four, at which he exhibited a degree of incompetence. He alternated this with occasional cricket (a 'drybob') at which he sometimes made reasonable scores. Sport was suspended in June, due to the chronic Thames flooding, the boys resorting to 'runs, walks, fives or stump cricket in a lake.'

Foss Prior had by this time become Patrick's leading contender in the race for the top place in his Election. The significance of this was that some time during the following year they would be promoted into the First Hundred, at which point their respective places would be frozen until they left Eton. Because of their near-identical ages, this would mean that, provided they stayed on into their nineteenth year, one of them would eventually become Captain of the School, and the other would not. Foss Prior's father was a Cambridge don and a cleric, as keen for his son as the Shaw Stewarts were for theirs. In February Patrick was erroneously told that Prior had been given a 'double remove', thus putting him way ahead; but next day 'Oh what joy, he's not out of my reach.' In March he rejected taking a long-leave for fear of jeopardizing his race against Prior. In December 'it doesn't matter so much about Morris [an Oppidan] so long as I beat Prior!' But, of course, they were close friends (though still addressing each other by their surnames) enjoying shared experiences, such as bicycling to Hampton Court with Cyril Alington on a wet day, losing the way on their return, all three returning coated in mud. On another occasion that same Half, Patrick and a fellow-colleger lost their way on a run and were stoned out of a village by the young villagers. Foss Prior often came to stay at Inverness Terrace.

Of his third year at Eton (1903/4) Patrick writes: 'My third year was for the most part supremely uneventful. I performed the normal functions of adolescence such as going into tails, and (still unusual then) joining the Volunteers. I played for Lower College at football, and continued to be incompetent and unsuccessful at cricket. I remember opening the season with seven successive blobs in Junior Matches, till my nerve was reduced to pulp.'

Academically the year started well, when he repeated his summer triumph at Trials in the Michaelmas Half, scoring 1270 marks out of 1450, 'which must have come near to making a record for these puerile and mechanical contests.' He scored 100 out of 100 for Greek translation, and 98 out of 100 for Greek extra, 'but, alas! 8 out of 34 for one part of Algebra.' He hoped that for the Lent Half he and a few others of his Election would now be promoted into the First Hundred, himself at the top, able to take things easier, and settle down to studying *The Iliad*. But this was not to be, and when the Lent Half's Trials took place, it was Prior who was first, and they entered the First Hundred with Patrick's chances of being Captain of the School seemingly gone forever.

Still, in the Summer Half he set to work hard on the Certificate Examination, which involved close attention to Greek texts ('becoming interested in the Colossians and enamoured of the Seven against Thebes'), and to everyone's astonishment carried off the Reynolds Scholarship 'not only over the heads of eminent seniors such as Daniel MacMillan, but also over the redoubtable Ronald Knox, one year senior to me with whom I now crossed swords for the first time. This surprising success gave me great self-confidence and a considerable reputation for precocity.' And the three precocious newcomers to the First Hundred (Prior, Shaw Stewart and Morris), now up to the veteran Henry Broadbent, during the Summer Half rose to the top of his Division, dubbed by him as the Three Graces.

Meanwhile the religious obsessions of the fifteen-year old Patrick were waning:

Sexually and socially I was still entirely undeveloped: religiously I was earnest but increasingly doubtful, to the extent of refusing to be confirmed after going through the course of preparation. This had the curious result that whereas if I had come up for confirmation the year before, I should have carried it right through with zeal, or if the year later from incuriousness, I actually was never confirmed at all, as it was left to my initiative to come forward in succeeding years, and that in my increasing scepticism I never had the assurance to do so: accordingly I missed the sensations of first Communion which many of my pagan friends assured me is both rare and exquisite.

Naturally, this withdrawal from the rite of confirmation was a disappointment to Cyril Alington. But he was broad-minded about it, telling Patrick that literal belief was not necessary so much as to 'feel that you want to be on the right side.' He also told Patrick, in one of his one-to-one chats, that cleverness in boyhood was not everything, and that purely scholastic men were like 'a diet of unmixed potatoes.' Two events now brought Cyril Alington into a closer relationship with Patrick. The first was that at the end of 1903 he took over from Arthur Goodhart as the Master in College, as well as continuing as Patrick's Tutor. The second was that in the following spring he married Hester Lyttelton. As Patrick described it to Dear:

> my Tutor has entangled himself at last in the matrimonial net, as wielded by the hands of the Hon Miss Lyttelton, half sister of *the* Lytteltons, Alfred and Edward: age about thirty, just a little younger than himself, looks plain, hair about my colour, smile broad, stature fairly mountainous, nearly as tall as her fiancé – about 5 ft 8, I should say. So much I gathered from a short interview on Wednesday evening, when I was presented to her as what he called a 'specimen pupil.' Her character must, I suppose, be charming, as my Tutor has gone completely daft ever since the afternoon when he proposed to her, and in the course of the evening informed first his pupils in Private and then the whole of the College at prayers. He even brought it into his little weekly talk with me, in words to

the effect that I would find it useful for the strengthening of faith, and then departed chuckling!

Edward Lyttelton became Head Master of Eton in the following year, and the Lyttelton family was at the heart of the Liberal establishment, Hester's father having been the brother-in-law of Gladstone (and indeed her daughter was destined in time to marry another Etonian Prime Minister, Alec Douglas Home). Patrick became a great favourite of Hester. One day Cyril took Patrick and Foss together with him in a dog-cart to meet her off the train at Slough, and on other occasions took them with him to visit the school at Marlborough and to see *Alcestis* performed at Bradford. During the subsequent Christmas Holidays Patrick went to stay with the Alingtons at their home, The Chantry, in Herefordshire.

Meanwhile in his letters home Patrick regaled his family and Dear with vivid descriptions of schoolboy life. The Chamber singing, when by acclamation boys were obliged to sing a song of their choice solo: 'the new lot were quite good on the whole, and no breakdowns: one youth sang a most ingenious song called "Jackdaws's Note", whose chorus began with two loud caws, in which the assembled College joined vigorously.' The Corps: 'I've learnt to salute, fix bayonets, order arms, ground arms, slope arms, trail arms, present arms, ready, and fire! And in fact I'm a most accomplished military man, and will be most useful if the Boers invade England!' The masters running along the tow-path in support of the house bumping-races on the river: 'the dear little new French Master, Monsieur de Satgé, tearing up and down in white shorts, and fancying himself, I'm sure, a fearful "sporman"; dear old Muggins panting along, almost totally last, cap in hand, with a sweet but weary smile, watching two boys being hopelessly walked over, of whom one at least, if not both, I think hail from his house; and dear Byrne, my German instructor, in an Oxford Eight cap and blazer, yelling directions through a microphone.'

He reported on painful moments too, as when being beaten by the Sixth Formers in College for alleged misbehaviour. In all he was beaten on nine occasions, which was probably more than most of his contemporaries in College, and indicative of his perceived bumptiousness. But it had no psychological effect on him: after one beating he wrote to Tats that he had been 'worked off for the eighth and I suspect the last time – it was such fun!' As someone who throughout his life suffered from bad teeth, Patrick undoubtedly experienced more pain from the dentists than from the prefects. Another setback was that a couple of valuable coins, ordered from Spinks to add to his collection, were stolen from his room. And he simply could not cure himself from his inveterate unpunctuality. He was always late. Late in meeting his father off the train at Windsor; late for classes; late in getting up in time for morning prayers, 'in a state of doing up my waistcoat in a sleepy unbrushed condition.' More than once he suffered the standard penalty for being late, having to sign the Tardy Book in the School Office before early school. This particularly distressed Dear: 'Darling do for heavens sake get up when you are called for it is so awful to be put on Tardy Book and I do not know what will follow if things go on like this.' As to the coins, she wrote: 'Well Pady I am thankful that it was some one that went off with your property and not you that went off with someone's.' In March of the following year the *The Eton College Chronicle* printed a piece on Punctuality, and Patrick may well have been in the writer's mind when he described a certain Agoraius: 'I used to be late for everything. My first two years here I never tried to be punctual for anything: I think I used to consider it rather a fine thing to be a quarter of an hour late for early school – it was bound to attract notice. I don't suppose I was ever off Tardy Book for more than a week during the Half.'

Now turned sixteen, Patrick was becoming discontented with the boredom of his home life, dominated by his elderly parents and adoring sisters. Once more at the house near Inverness in August, although he had Colleger friends to stay and played a lot of golf, he felt restricted and regretted that he was unable to go out rough-shooting. But relief was at hand. General Shaw Stewart's uncle, the 7th Baronet, had recently died, and his son, now Sir Hugh Shaw Stewart, had gone to live at Ardgowan, a large Georgian mansion on the Renfrewshire coast, with magnificent views across the water to the hills of Argyll – since obscured by the trees which Sir Hugh planted. Hugh, now a man in his fifties, had married Lady Alice Thynne, a daughter of the Marquess of Bath. In his letter of commiseration to Hugh on the death of his father, the General told the new Baronet about Patrick's successes at Eton and his exemplary character, his 'simplicity, honesty and humbleness of mind' combined with his ability and industry. This resulted in an invitation for father and son to visit Ardgowan.

Here was an entirely new world for Patrick, that of the grand Edwardian country house, one he was destined to thrive in and adorn. He wrote a meticulous account of it in a long letter to Dear, which expresses not only his concerns at avoiding social gaffes (or floaters, as he would have called them), but reveals something of his innate social sense. The former were at the fore to begin with: 'we drove up to a sort of barracks, hospital, and British Museum rolled into one. A butler who might have stepped out of a society novel assisted us in, and into the drawing room. I was so frightened that I hardly knew whether I was standing on my head or my heels.' After a desultory conversation, they were shown their rooms, and then asked what they would like to do: 'Pa wanted to rest. Sir H asked me if I was a fisherman (No), then would I like a spin on his bike (O-er-yes, with a bright smile) or a ride (I gasped) but no no; then a bright idea struck him: would I like a walk by myself? I thought this was the weirdest, but cheerfully consented.' During this walk he encountered Lord Bath, who responded to none of his overtures till asking about Eton 'and then we were quite comfortable.'

Dinner dress was white tie and tails, and at it Patrick was able to observe the other guests. These largely consisted of his hostess's family. There was her brother Lord Bath, 'tall, dark and amiable,' and her mother, Lady Bath 'a sweet old lady, with a funny little manner and a very funny voice, but a regular dear.' Then her two sisters, Lady Beatrice, the nicest of the three sisters, Patrick thought, though 'very fierce looking, with enormous black eyebrows, and too thick-set for her height; hardly beautiful'; and her other sister, Katherine, who had married Lord Cromer, a man twice her age – 'a sort of December and late June business' – 'the youngest and the best looking of the three: very tall and solid indeed a regular sort of stalwart young English matron.' Then the Earl of Cromer himself, formerly the all-powerful British Resident in Egypt, 'a terrifying old gentleman, the only one in the company who frankly treats me like a black beetle, and I feel like one with him.' At dinner, sitting next to Lady Bath, 'under the influence of a delicious champagne cup I expanded and beamed upon her.'

Next morning he was awoken by a valet who asked in respectful terms, 'Bath or bathroom Sir?': he chose the bathroom. Breakfast was 'a positive torture, as all the ladies seem to forage for themselves as a matter of course,' with self-help carried to such an extent 'that Pa had to hobble round and insert his arm over Lady A's shoulder to procure a boiled egg.' There then appeared Sir Hugh's brother, the Reverend Charles Shaw Stewart with his German wife. Patrick was detailed to go with Charles to supervise the local village children's sports, but in the afternoon was allowed to go out on the yacht. He found himself sitting next to 'Mrs Charles' at dinner, as at subsequent dinners, which was a trial, as he and his father found her most uncongenial. After dinner there was bridge most evenings, and the General was delighted by being asked by the great Lord Cromer to 'smoke a pipe with him'.

On the Sunday it was church services for all, some going to Greenock for the Episcopalian service, some to the nearby kirk. And on both the two remaining days Patrick went out rough shooting, bagging a few grouse and snipe. There was also another trip in the yacht to visit the Channel Fleet at Rothesay and seeing over the Admiral's ship – 'it bored me immensely.' For Patrick the most interesting fellow-guest, who arrived on the last evening, was Andrew Lang, famous for his translations of the Classics and Germanic childrens' fables, who offered to write a piece in *The Eton College Chronicle* at Patrick's behest. Throughout the visit the only floater was made not by Patrick but by his father. Instead of saying 'I hope you enjoyed your drive, Lady Bath,' he said 'I hope you enjoyed your bath, Lady Drive.'

Patrick returned to Eton for his fourth year (1904/5) and continued to advance by brawn and brain. The College fielded Upper and Lower teams for the school football (the Eton Field Game, a mixture of soccer and rugger), and Patrick was appointed the Junior Keeper of the latter, with the coveted right to wear shorts instead of breeches. At the readings of the Shakespeare Society he read the parts of 'the agitated old Duchess of York' in *Richard II*, and the Prince of Denmark himself in *Hamlet*. He won the Essay Prize with a paper comparing the policies of Henry VIII and James I. And he came a very creditable second in the King's Prize for German, especially since the winner was half-German. But already he had now set his sights on a far greater prize, the Newcastle Scholarship.

The Newcastle has been described by a subsequent victor as the Everest of Eton scholarships. Founded by the Duke of Newcastle in 1829, it consisted of ten papers, taken morning and afternoon over five days in late March. Most of these were in construing unseen Greek and Latin Prose, and composing Greek and Latin Verses. To these were added a general paper on Divinity, and detailed examinations on St Matthew's Gospel and the Acts of the Apostles in the original Greek. With few exceptions it had been won by Collegers, and in the previous year by Daniel MacMillan, with Ronald Knox as *proxime accessit*. It was generally expected that Knox would now get it, even though he was younger than several of the other contenders, and would be able to try for it again in the following year. The two examiners were Oxford or Cambridge Dons, though famously Mr Gladstone had once taken it upon himself to judge the Newcastle. Those sitting for it were cosseted and given the unique privilege of playing fives between the buttresses of College Chapel between their mental gymnastics. The result was published in *The Times* and the winner considered by many to be the cleverest boy in the country. The Scholarship was worth £50 for three years.

Patrick could look forward to two further Newcastle contests, but decided to go all out for this one for a special reason. It was the convention that the Newcastle winner, if not already in Sixth Form, would be immediately promoted into it. In his case this would place him above Prior and secure for him the Captaincy of the School in 1906/7. It was indeed a mountainous task, and several of the aspirants were two years older than he was. But, encouraged by the Reynolds victory, he set forth to climb it, or rather, to dig into it – 'to sap like a thousand devils.' He ploughed slowly and deliberately through the scriptural texts, reading every word of a book once begun, and refraining from annotating down the side, determined to rely on his memory. Although the Classical texts could not be prepared, he spent weeks studying the *Birds* of Aristophanes, without notes or cribs. The week of trial began. He rendered into English verse passages from Homer, Aeschylus and Aristophanes, and from Lucretius, Horace, Lucan and Martial; and into English prose passages from Thucydides, Aeschines and Plato, and from Cicero, Livius and Tacitus. He composed his Greek hexameters and iambics and his Latin hexameters, elegiacs and lyrics, from passages of English poetry. And he answered the technical questions relating to grammar and criticism in Classics and in Divinity. On 7 April the result was announced: Patrick had won. As Evelyn Waugh puts it in his biography of Ronald Knox: 'On hearing the result, Ronald sat down and read the *Book of Job* straight through; Shaw-Stewart gave up work for the next four years.'

Patrick had pipped Ronald to the post not through his clever translations and versifications but through his near-faultless performance in the Divinity papers. As one of the examiners told Cyril: 'His Divinity was the best by a good deal: it showed extraordinary grip of the real points in one so young.' This was ironical, because Patrick had by now shed his religious sentiment and held no special veneration for the sacred texts, whereas Ronald was already destined to be a man of the cloth. His father was the Anglican Bishop of Manchester, and Ronald felt a deep concern in religion, not in the erastian practices of his father, but in Christian piety and ritualism, concerns which were to lead him to convert as a priest to Roman Catholicism. He had bound himself to a vow of celibacy. He had composed a collection of verses. He was in place to be Captain of the School for the first two Halves of 1906.

Rather than Divinity, rather than Latin, what Patrick loved most was Classical Greek. To him it was more than just a dead language or a brain-test. He revelled in the syntax, the vocabulary and the poetry. Above all, he adored Homer. The original Greek, when easily understood and fluently read, sharpened the effect without any of the inevitable awkwardness of translation, and seemed to transport one into a primeval world. The stories of the capricious gods and doomed heroes, couched in the timeless hexameters and repetitive images, affected him just as Wagner's music affects others when applied to the Germanic sagas. Words counted for more than music for the unmusical Patrick. And the bite and brutality of the scenes of battle appealed to his masculinity and his personal bravery, identified around the central figure of Achilles in *The Iliad*. When it came to the canon of English Literature, however, Patrick was surprisingly dilatory. He now had plenty of time to delve deep into the English classics, but failed to do so, and regretted this in the last years of his life.

Back at Eton for the Summer Half Patrick was duly promoted to Sixth Form. This brought with it several distinctions. For formal dress he now wore a rather uncomfortable stick-up collar and white bow-tie in place of a turned-down collar with white tie tucked in. At Chapel the Sixth Form paraded in after all the rest of the school had taken their places, Patrick, as the junior, leading the way. In College he could sit with the other Sixth Formers in their room, and was allotted a fag to perform menial tasks for him. In Hall, the Sixth Form table enjoyed better food. He did his turn as Praepostor for a week, relieved from classes in order to summon boys to the Head Master 'and assist in the passing of sentences and (if any ensue) at executions.' But he was not at ease with himself. Set among the Sixth Formers he was somewhat distanced from his contemporaries (though he still managed to mess together with Foss Prior), and forced into the company of older boys such as Mark Young, a sharp-tongued eighteen-year old. At sport he was still a rather inept cricketer, playing in the Second Lower Club. He was also aware of a severe patchy baldness, an alopecia, extending on his head.

At the Fourth of June celebrations, to which his family came, he performed twice at the Speeches, at which members of the Sixth Form recited, in scenes from Sheridan and Plautus (and, in the next year, from Shakespeare and Dante). But by early July his alopecia had worsened, his bald patch 'as big as a tea-cup.' So he was taken by the College Matron to Harley Street to see a specialist, who pronounced that he was over-worked, a victim of the Newcastle, though actually it was probably due to a fungoid infection. He recommended a visit to an Alpine hotel, dismissing Patrick's preference for going to stay with Dear in Scotland. His father duly agreed to this, and Patrick left school three weeks before the end of the Half, not sorry to part from the dull Sixth Formers who were leaving, though sorry that Edward Somerville, in his Election, was also leaving. Accompanied by Pua, and after a journey which concluded with a mule-ride up a track, they arrived at the Hotel Pension Bel-Alp in the Valais, overlooking the great Alesch Glacier, the largest in Switzerland, at an altitude of 2,180 metres. Although not a sanatorium, the Bel Alp attracted otherwise healthy people who believed themselves in need of its therapeutic benefits, particularly for the lungs. As readers of *The Magic Mountain* will know, the chief interest in such places was the other people.

In Patrick's case these turned out to be mostly English, including no less than twelve Anglican clergymen. In a letter to Tats, he provides thumb-nail sketches of them all. For instance there was Mr Drake: 'He preached this morning, and as he has a very poor memory, he was rather embarrassing, sticking not only in a Browning quotation, but also in the Absolution, which he tried to do from memory.' There was Fairbanks, 'an oldish fat padre who simply runs the place. He has been here thirty-five years running, and is a "name to conjure with". He commands the expeditions and cracks low German jokes with the guides.' And an un-named 'curious large fat padre, who looks episcopal, and is rather out of the clerical "push" here. He is rather too Piccadillisome, and carried a top-hat into chapel today, to the astonishment of the natives.' Patrick reported more favourably on the non-clerics; one played well at bridge, another was a charming old-Etonian in his sixties. But there was also 'a very unpleasant deaf bronchitic old man with a portable spittoon, who sits next to me at table in stern silence.'

When it came to the ladies, two of them got full marks from Patrick. 'First and foremost, Miss Hunnybun, the life and soul of the party, a delightful old maid who has quite taken Pua, including me, under her wing. She is one of the oldest habitués, and wears very quaint and fantastic Alpine raiment. A keen Alpinist.' And there was Mrs Fothergill, 'the most amusing old lady it has ever been my lot to come across. Not so very old, that is, and very good-looking. She makes the funniest remarks quite unconsciously in a slow deliberate voice with a killingly funny look. She is also easily amused, and occasionally guffaws at a joke of her own with a guffaw which is quite her own.' Against them there was Mrs Bright, 'about the only unpleasant person here. She is large and square and aggressive and ruddy and rather like a pig, and fairly unpopular. She is very haughty and crushing, but her manners are not quite so. Pua wonders whether she's an actress or a lady's maid on the spree.' Critical though he may have been of the fellow pensioners at Bel Alp, it is clear that Patrick engaged himself actively in conversation at the communal table and elsewhere. But he was also sharp with those who bored or annoyed him, and also with his well-meaning sister, which he regretted subsequently.

Apart from netting butterflies, the only exercise at Bel Alp was to go on walks, long or short. Patrick joined some and shirked others. He does not seem to have experienced the thrill which some derive from mountain walking and scrambling, finding it boring on

40

the whole. There were several days of rain. Still, he did the usual walks, including one to the Marielensee lake, losing contact with their guide on the descent among the crevasses of the glacier; and he walked up the Sparrenhorn and the Furshorn. By the time he left Bel Alp, Patrick's bald spot, regularly scrubbed with carbolic, was shrinking, and the month in the Alps was pronounced a success. Then it was back home and on to Scotland, to a house his father had taken near Tain, to Dear in her new home at Blairdhu, and to Ardgowan for shooting, tennis and 'cut-throat bridge.'

Blairdhu was a small farm only a few miles from Findon Mills, but in a better position, and Dear and Alec had saved up enough money to buy it. But it involved unceasing hard work. Alec looked after the sheep and the joinery and the improvements of such things as the well and the coal house, while Dear occupied herself with the domestic animals, who figure large in her letters to Patrick – Teresa the cat, who chases the chickens, the new puppy who growls at Alec – as well as the garden with its gooseberries and the pears. But her letters are always concerned for her first love, for 'the darling wee boy who used to put his arms round my neck and tell me all his woes.' And when Patrick came to stay at Blairdhu, he helped manfully at tasks allotted to him, and Pua cheerfully helped in lifting the potatoes.

The Michaelmas Half of 1905, beginning his fifth year at Eton, started well. Apart from the fact that the new Head Master demanded some smartening up (Patrick could no longer shuffle in to early school in his slippers, and had to stand up when construing), and devised a new penalty for his tardiness (he must be in bed by 10.30), he could anticipate a leisurely existence, with plenty of time for the Shakespeare Society, German and French studies, and sport. He was now strong enough to expect to be included in the College Wall. The Eton Wall Game took place against the brick wall of the raised road leading out of Eton. The principal contest was between the Collegers and the Oppidans, held on St Andrew's Day (30 November). It assumed a much greater importance among the former, who had to produce a team of eleven from their total complement of seventy, than the latter, who had a pool of a thousand. But this inequality was mitigated by the fact that almost the entire game was spent in a series of scrums up against the wall, all on top of each other, held fast till someone shouted 'air' in danger of asphyxiation. The ball was from time to time released, scoring a shy, but its conversion into a goal was rare indeed. The previous three years had all been draws. The three heaviest of the team, known as Walls, were padded and helmeted, and the rest waded into the mud, emerging unrecognizable and often with damaged bones or muscles.

But fate now intervened; or, in Homeric terms, a goddess had it in for Patrick. On a Sunday in November, Edward Somerville, now at Sandhurst, visited Eton, and in the afternoon was settling down to a game of bridge in Patrick's room with two other Collegers, when Cyril Alington came in. A gentle warning might now have ensued. But 'The swansong of my hypertrophied conscience drowned the voice of prudence, and I quite unnecessarily (to the disgust of the rest) confessed to my Tutor that 1/- a hundred had been proposed just before the discovery, though nothing had yet been won or lost.' To play for money was in contravention of the School rules, and to do so on a Sunday was an added sin in the eyes of Cyril. 'My father was informed of this: it sounded like gambling (with a capital G) to him, and he was much distressed.' (Patrick evidently did not adopt the ploy once used by Arthur Villiers, an Etonian three years his senior – and a future Managing Director of Barings – who said to his tutor: 'Sir, I have been praying hard about this and know that God has forgiven me. I assume that under the circumstances you will also').

But worse was to come. St Andrew's Day dawned, and the *Chronicle* set out the two teams, with interviews with the Captains. Patrick was in the College Wall as a Second, being relatively light at 10 stone 8 lbs, and described as 'A very zealous and energetic second, most prominent in making progress in loose bullies. Charges with enthusiasm, but is rather too tall to hold.' He had his College Wall Colours (purple and white thin stripes); but, unless

College lost, he could expect to get his Mixed Wall Colours also (red and dark blue thick stripes).

> Then came St Andrew's day. The game (Wall Game) was a draw: in the evening there was the centenary Dinner of College Pop [a debating society for senior Collegers], and (feeling secure in my Mixed Wall) I got gloriously drunk on alternate glasses of Hock and Claret (how pathetic it sounds, but it is strictly true). My Tutor, vigilant man, discovered it, and I went before the Head Master, and was removed from Sixth Form for the remainder of the half, as well as being compelled to take an informal pledge [to abstain from alcohol] to cover the remainder of my time at school. Back I went to low collars, and solitary at the end of the row in Chapel I awaited the Sixth Form Procession. Two days later another got his Mixed Wall in my place. A very depressed youth.

Usually the Mixed Wall was awarded to the top players as listed before the match. But to be passed over in favour of the next Colleger, Julian Huxley, looks like a pointed snub against Patrick by the senior Collegers, especially Robin Laffan, the Keeper. But among the smaller boys he was considered a great dare-devil and quite a notability, and his lack of Mixed Wall colours was mitigated by getting his College Field colours (purple and white thick stripes) at the end of the Half, and thus a respectable 'two colour man.' A visit to Balliol also put him back on the road to success. He was awarded the Third Scholarship, although he was typically dismissive of the two above him, the first 'a man of straw, and the second one of nature's seconds' (Ronald Knox had been awarded the first scholarship in the previous year). The visit was a cheerless one since 'the cellar hospitality extended to all candidates was a mere mockery to the abstainer,' but the ovation he received from the Collegers in Hall on his return was heartwarming.

During the Christmas holidays Patrick once again went to stay with the Alingtons in Herefordshire, together with Ronald. They all went to a local dance, where Patrick's attraction in the eyes of

Hester was apparent: 'That dance was amusing, though poor Mr A didn't seem to find it so. He was terribly bored, and wanted to come away at 12, but as Mrs A and I went in to supper at five to twelve and didn't emerge till a quarter to one, he just had to wait, and he was pretty bored before he got away.' But the two seventeen-year-olds got good marks in working in the garden, chopping wood and damming a stream 'in good old Findon fashion.' A dance in London to meet young girls was not, however, a success – 'a *terrible* set of females, not only plain but ditchwatery.' Patrick had already begun to exhibit his preference for more mature women, though perhaps not consciously for, as he put it, 'I increased I think in sentimentality and the atmosphere coloured my holidays at this time, so that they were strangely clear of both the higher and lower feminism.'

The Lent Half flowed placidly by – 'Nothing to work for, nothing to play games hard for.' The study of the Classics was dropped in favour of History, French and German. An essay for the Essay Society, on the subject of 'Character in Homer,' was composed in the small hours of the night before and completed a quarter of an hour before the event. An account of a football match was written 'in the style of Seton Merriman.' There was running with the School Beagles and in the School Mile. There was Fives and Racquets. But when Henry Marten, the History master, found Patrick subversively doing other work in class, there was general discontent; and the Head Master concluded that he would never work without a definite challenge, and ought to leave the school at the end of the summer. Meanwhile Ronald Knox, now Captain of the School, was expected to have a clear run for the Newcastle, but was suddenly struck by acute appendicitis. Prayers were said for him in Chapel and the Bishop of London celebrated Holy Communion in his London hospital room on Easter Day. Patrick went to the Head Master and suggested that he should resign his own Newcastle Scholarship in favour of Ronald, an apparently altruistic action. But actually, in a letter to Dear, he confessed that it was also a ploy to provide him with a reason for staying on, and sitting for the Newcastle again in the following year, it being too late to 'sap' for it now.

Of the Collegers who were rough contemporaries of Patrick the one who was destined to become his closest friend in life was Charles Lister, a year older than him. By this time Charles had cut quite a figure in the School. He was a Member of the Eton Society (the self-appointed prefects) and, of course, a sixth-former. He was tall and slender, pale complexioned, with fair closely curling hair and eyebrows that went up when speaking. He was unworldly, unselfconscious, talkative and enthusiastic, clumsy, an eternal student, as sketched later in lines by Cyril Alington,

> To have laughed and talked – wise, witty, fantastic, feckless –
> To have mocked at rules and rulers and learnt to obey...

In early February Charles was seized with the necessity of protesting against the Russian Government's arrest of the St Petersburg Soviet, and of raising money for the prisoners in Siberia, as pleaded by an itinerant Orthodox priest, Father Gapon. For this purpose he hired the Conservative Club in Windsor and opened the proceedings with himself in the chair, flanked by two other speakers, and supported on the platform by his family and his fellow Collegers – Knox, Laffan and Shaw Stewart. To enliven the proceedings he had a family friend, Viola Tree, to sing in the intervals between the speakers. Due to lack of publicity, there were very few in the audience, though in the centre of the front row sat Cyril Alington. Patrick was overcome with hysteria at intervals but full of admiration at the initiative of 'that indefatigable boy.' As to Charles's sister Laura, and Viola, both of whom were to become very close to him, he hardly noticed them. But he could not but be impressed by Charles' father. Thomas Lister, Lord Ribblesdale, was a commanding figure, immortalized in Sargent's famous aggrandized portrait of him in riding clothes, and known in society as 'The Ancestor.' Ribblesdale's father had lost a fortune, but he himself had married Charlotte (Charty) Tennant, a daughter of the immensely rich Sir Charles Tennant, and sister of Margot, wife of H. H. Asquith, the new Liberal Chancellor of the Exchequer. Following this encounter Patrick received an invitation from Lady Ribblesdale to accompany her and Charles on a visit to France in the Easter holidays, together with Frank Walters, another Colleger of Patrick's year. They reached Tours by rail in one long day, then toured the chateaux of the Loire in a car brought over from England. But at Bourges Charles fell ill, and their tour was curtailed, Patrick and Frank returning in the motor. Charles pursued his Quixotic, or rather, Tolstoyan, search for socialism. During the vacation he became a member of the Independent Labour Party – an unheard of initiative from among the aristocracy – even organizing a tea-party for the ILP at Gisburne, the Yorkshire home of his tolerant parents.

The Summer Half of 1906 established Patrick as a leading figure in Eton life, beyond the bounds of the College. The Collegers were often disparaged by the Oppidans, thought of as too clever by half, and known as 'tugs' (from the Latin *togati* – gowned-ones). Some of the rich Oppidans despised them as being the sons of parents who could not afford the school fees. Success at school was defined very much in terms of sport. The twin pinnacles of sporting achievement were to be included in the Eton Eleven (cricket) or the Eton Eight (rowing), and during all Patrick's years at Eton only one Colleger was in either of these (George Fletcher, in the Eight in 1906). The Eton Society ('Pop') was dominated by sportsmen who were also considered to be good fellows. Of the twenty-four members in the Summer Half the Collegers were Laffan, Knox, Lister and Robson. Of these Robin Laffan got in as being a mighty performer at the Wall Game, and Charles Lister must have been helped by being the son of a peer – the only one in College in Patrick's time. Ronald Knox was the exception that proved the rule. He never obtained any sporting colours at all. As Captain of the School, and faithful to his vows, he never beat any of the younger collegers, leaving the Sixth Form room for someone else to administer the punishment. Patrick, by contrast, relished the spectacle of others being beaten.

The Eton College Chronicle was jointly edited by a Colleger and an Oppidan. This summer these were Ronald Knox and Julian Grenfell. Ronald was a brilliant versifier, and a volume of his poetry (in English, Latin and Greek) was published during the Half. Grenfell, a Sixth Former, wrote with exceptional clarity. These two editors conceived the idea of producing a weekly paper that would amuse the Eton community by breaking out of the staid and strict parameters of the *Chronicle*, which emulated those of *The Times*. They envisaged an editorial staff of six, themselves plus four others – two Collegers (Lister and Laffan) and two Oppidans (Horner and Gold). But, seeking further talent, they co-opted Patrick as well.

The result was *The Outsider*. The title page showed a photograph of the seven editors in ridiculous postures. The contents comprised a mixture of parody and gossip, with references to senior boys and masters, and making gentle fun of some of the hallowed traditions of the games-players, but in no way criticizing the School. Ronald wrote a parody on *Pilgrim's Progress*, Christian meeting the boys: 'Surely these must be they who are called Little-Faith, Ignorance, Sloth, Hopeless and such-like.' Patrick's principal contribution, and one which today holds its humour better than any of the others, was a serial story about a ghastly boarding school called St Mary's. Amongst the characters were Guy Bendall, 'an ingenious youth who has just arrived at St Mary's'; Ambrose Higginbotham, 'his devoted if not disinterested friend'; Pompey Desborough, 'a youth with an angelic countenance and penetrating eyesight'; Guy's housemaster, Mr Bimsay, 'a man of summary methods and nocturnal habits'; and a cast of dubious characters such as Bones, Smackworth, Hinch and Squawky (an Etonian Stalky). *The Outsider* ran for the six last weeks of the Summer Half, selling around 300 copies a time at sixpence each. Etonian (and Old Etonian) opinion was divided about it, and it fell foul of the Head Master because of a passing reference to him. Cyril Alington also got rather fed up with Patrick, who was rude to him, and suggested that he should find another tutor, but then relented. All the editors except Patrick left school at the end of the Half, and when he tentatively proposed the continuation of *The Outsider* in the next, permission was rejected. Meanwhile Patrick, though still an occasional cricketer, obtained credit for setting up a tennis net in College Field.

But Patrick's main ambition was to be elected to the Eton Society, known as Pop. Under recent reforms to the system, the Captain of the School got into Pop ex officio. Patrick had hoped to be Captain in the forthcoming Michaelmas Half, but then George Fletcher decided to stay on to enjoy that coveted status. The members of Pop were elevated among their contemporaries more than were the prefects at other schools, partly because they had been elected, rather than nominated by the Head Master, and partly because of the gorgeous clothes they wore – braided tail-coats, carnations in their button-holes, and bright waistcoats. Not all boys aspired to Pop, and the wiser ones ignored the distinctiveness it gave; but to someone of Patrick's ambition it meant everything.

I freely confess that the pondering of this question occupied me in the period between bed and sleep, and that I went as far as to make up lists of the electors and the dangers of blackballs potentially wielded by each. There is certainly a vital anxiety surrounding the entrance to Pop – an anxiety to which the proudest cannot be indifferent, an entrance which the most assured cannot take for granted. To judge by the amount of open courtship which takes place, the volume of self-questioning such as mine must be proportionately vast. Probably I was one of those accused of courtship. Certainly as the Half went on I emerged, to my own astonishment, from tuggish seclusion, and was admitted to the smiles and nods of the main body of Pop, and to the intimacy of its intellectual elite.

The election took place on the last Sunday of the Half. Although there would be another election at the beginning of the next, Patrick knew that most of his sponsors would have left by then. Six blackballs excluded, but a name blackballed could be proposed again, and a vicious contest took place, with factions mutually conceding. Patrick had to wait till half past four to be told he was in, but there was general disappointment in College that Eric Forbes Adam, a great favourite of Ronald Knox, had failed.

Patrick was now no longer a boy but a young man of eighteen who wanted to get away from home. He went to the house near Kelso which his father had rented for the summer, and had Knox and Fletcher to stay there. But he became aware of the gap between his family and his brilliant new friends, a gap that was never to be bridged. He had another wonderful time at Ardgowan and with the Lister family grouse shooting at a lodge on the Helmsdale, and reappeared at Eton for what he expected to be an 'Olympian year,' to become Captain of the School in the Lent Half and continuing as such till the eve of his nineteenth birthday. But when in November Patrick decided not to bother to enter for the King's Prizes for German and French, Cyril Alington questioned the point in this delightful prospect, and put it to Patrick that he should go up to Balliol in the New Year, and thereby gain a year on life. Typically, Patrick consulted everyone he knew, and delayed his decision as long as he could. Dear urged him to go, but wrote with prophetic warning: 'If you decide to go to Oxford I know you have a few boon companions waiting for you there already. But just you think twice before you let anyone of them influence you.'

The final week was one of exceedingly sentimental farewells to masters and boys. But at least a couple of minor achievements came right for him. He was assured of a commission in the Volunteers, which had been withheld from him earlier (even though, in leaving, he could not take it up). And he performed heroically in the Wall Game on St Andrew's Day from the padded Snout-like position of Wall. *The Chronicle* recorded his weight at 11 stone 2 lb, and in an interview with the Keeper of the College Wall the following appeared : 'At this point the door burst open, and College First Wall rushed in. "I say," he said, "I have just got to run down to Philpott's and have a tooth out, and then do the Latin Prose prize and then next week's leader: but I'll be down at the racquet-courts immediately: don't trouble to wait".' Charrington, the Keeper, then observes, '"We all have our own times for going to bed, from the Junior Keeper, who goes at 7.30, to the First Wall, who goes somewhere between three and four".' Anyway, the match was a glorious victory for College, and Patrick duly got his Mixed Wall.

The Alingtons suggested that Patrick should join them on a visit to Rome immediately after the end of the Half. This was at Hester's suggestion for, as she told Pua, 'she would miss him very much, in fact she was so fond of him that she didn't like to say too much in case people thought her silly.' Also with them was Cuthbert Blakiston, an Eton master who knew the Roman monuments well. In letters to his family Patrick described their sightseeing, but the principal personal touches which he recorded were Hester's steadfast refusal to let Cyril read a letter she had just written to her sister, and Hester's disturbed night from a dream that Patrick would go to the bad at Oxford. These was also a comic scene at the Post Office when Patrick was ordered to open a small box containing a false tooth, the officials convinced that it was made of gold and of great value. His release from his vow of abstinence while at school was celebrated in a tankard of Munich beer.

THREE

A Balliol Freshman at Brancaster

THE PRESTIGE OF BALLIOL COLLEGE, Oxford, established in the nineteenth century under the Mastership of Benjamin Jowett, had been maintained into the first decade of the twentieth. Balliol had succeeded in holding its position as the most academically distinguished college, with a lead over all others in terms of first-class honours as well as in the number of its members who had become fellows of other colleges. The Ireland, Craven, and Hertford Classical Scholarships were usually won by Balliol men. Balliol despised the over-emphasis on sport of some of the other colleges, such as Brasenose or Oriel, and the aristocratic snobbery of others, such as Christ Church, Trinity or Magdalen. Balliol's intellectual primacy at this time was also assisted by that fact that it awarded its open scholarships in November, well before those of any other Oxford or Cambridge colleges. This meant that it could cream off the highest flyers rather unfairly. By now it had shed its closed scholarships, which still persisted elsewhere, such as those for Wykehamists at New College or for Etonians at King's College, Cambridge. It was indubitably the right college for Patrick.

When Patrick arrived there, the three most prominent alumni were H. H. Asquith, the new Chancellor of the Exchequer and future Prime Minister, Edward Grey, Secretary of State for Foreign Affairs, and George Curzon, formerly Viceroy of India and about to be Chancellor of the University. Many Balliol men occupied prominent positions in Parliament, the Church, the Civil Service, and the Empire, and the college rested, in Asquith's phrase, on the 'tranquil consciousness of effortless superiority.'

James Strachan Davidson was about to be elected Master of the College, and of the twelve Fellows nine were regularly engaged in teaching undergraduates in a very restricted number of subjects. Most were resident bachelors, some of whom devoted their lives to the young men in their charge, receiving them in their rooms for informal talk in the evenings over drinks and tobacco, and arranging reading parties for the more serious during the vacations. The Fellow who is most remembered for this was Francis Urquhart, the first Roman Catholic on the foundation. But Patrick's Classical Tutor, Cyril Bailey, was equally approachable and relished his friendships with the young, although marrying in 1912 at the age of forty-one in a union that was 'unassailably happy.' Bailey was a highly successful lecturer, brilliant at his classical compositions, and deep in research on Lucretius and Epicurus. He was also an athlete, who walked with a springy step, and was one of the best-loved Oxford figures of his time.

Patrick was also tutored by H. W. C. ('Fluffy') Davis, a formidable classical scholar, who sparred with the young bloods when Dean of the College: 'I'm afraid I made rather a floater last night, Fluffy,' said one of them: 'If by "Fluffy" you mean me, my name is Mr Davis, and if by "floater" you mean making a beast of yourself, I heartily concur.' The lively undergraduates who responded to the scholarship and friendship of such dons also made great fun of them behind their backs.

The undergraduates were still very largely public-schoolboys. Of the fifty-four who had come up in Patrick's year, seventeen were Etonians (including five Collegers). Twenty had scholarships of various kinds (five of them the newly-established Rhodes Scholars): the normal scholarships were worth £80 a year, covering about half of an average man's expenses. On leaving Balliol, twelve became academics or schoolmasters, ten commercial or financial businessmen, six became Civil Servants, five lawyers, two priests, one a physician, one a journalist, and several who did not take up any profession. Seventeen of these fifty-four freshmen were destined to be killed in the War. But what is more remarkable is that nine of the seventeen Etonians were killed.

Most of these undergraduates were studying Classics, either the four-year Literae Humaniores ('Greats") or the three year Classical Moderations. Their personal lives were closely controlled. They had to attend morning chapel, or a roll-call, on a number of days. The college gate was closed at 10 pm. They were expected to dine in hall most days. The wealthier among them got their scouts to bring them breakfast and lunch in their rooms, messing together for lunch, though they had to walk across the quad in their dressing-gowns to the newly-installed bathrooms and lavatories. But on days when they didn't have to attend the roll-call they could simply lie in bed: (unsurprisingly Patrick missed a number of roll-calls and was compelled to stay up for three extra days at the end of his first term in penalty). By contrast the academic lives of the undergraduates were very loosely controlled. As he described it to Dear: 'No lectures are compulsory either, and even compositions for one's tutor can be shirked at will. In fact the whole system is based on the idea that you are working hard by yourself the whole time....' Actually, the regular lectures he attended in his first two terms were those given by Cyril Bailey on Lucretius and Homer, Pickard-Cambridge on Greek Religion, and Clark on Theocritus.

Unlike the appealing fifteenth-century architecture of Eton College, the appearance of Balliol was not beautiful. It was dominated by heavy Victorian buildings. The two rooms (a sitting-room and a small bedroom) allocated to Patrick were in the Brackenbury Building overlooking the Front Quad, up sixty steps on the top floor. Opposite him was Hastings Tavistock, son and heir of the Duke of Bedford. Given that there was no set placing in Hall, it was inevitable that the Etonians should band together. It was so much easier to do so than to go out of one's way to make new friends. But among the Etonian freshmen was a boisterous inner circle consisting of Charles Lister, Julian Grenfell and Edward Horner, to which Patrick now attached himself.

Julian Grenfell, the leader of the pack, was a strong handsome man with a cherubic face, fearless, pugilistic, and brimming with energy and aristocratic self-confidence. He could delight his friends with his originality, and express himself beautifully in prose and verse. Like Patrick, he had as a small boy been extremely pious. But he was also subject to fits of frustration and melancholy that led him to break into violence, and then he could become a bully, and one who liked to see his victim squirm. He was in the habit of cracking his horsewhip in the Quad on Saturday nights. He had been a prominent figure at Eton, Captain of his house, and in Pop. Edward Horner, a close friend of Julian when schoolboys, was also remarkably good-looking, very tall, with fair hair and luminous eyes. But he traded on his charm. His career at Eton had been something of a disappointment. He did not perform well at exams and was haunted by a feeling of failure, disguised behind his ebullience and his appearance as a social butterfly. This was the 'Eton push' about which Patrick had been warned, and he recognized that 'the other people here must simply loath us.' They attracted further attention by 'dressing down', wearing ancient shooting coats, prehistoric grey trousers, and blue shirts, rather than the traditional suits worn by the other undergraduates. No wonder when, as he wrote, 'It always delights my oligarchical soul to feel that I'm really and truly disliked by the Balliol proletariat.'

Patrick initially messed with Ronald Knox, George (Hoj) Fletcher, and Edward Horner. Among the prominent second and third year Etonians at Balliol were Archie Gordon, Lawrence Jones, and Douglas Radcliffe. Archie Gordon, a grandson of the Marquess of Aberdeen, at that time Lord-Lieutenant of Ireland, was, according to Lawrence Jones, 'the most irrepressibly high-spirited young man I have ever known.' Many of these belonged to the Annandale Society ('the Anna'), Balliol's smart dining club, at which 'high spirits, humour, sociability and easy manners were all that was necessary.' So was drinking a lot although, in his memoirs, Jones likes to distinguish between 'drunkenness' and 'buffiness': 'buffiness breaks into song and dance; promotes reconciliations; dissolves prejudices; is positive, hopeful and affirmative, and leads to high jinks.' Small wonder that Patrick, now released from his vow of abstinence, and possessive of all these qualities, was gloriously buffy from the start at Balliol, and was elected to the Anna in his first summer.

Harold Nicolson, now in his final year as an undergraduate, had been educated at Wellington, the military public-school. He was one who did seek to establish friendships across the board at Balliol, and disapproved of the incoming Eton push. But he considered Patrick to be tolerant and affectionate, and both a distinguished scholar and an avowed hedonist, of the sort loved by the Greek gods. To Francis ('Sligger') Urquhart, who was travelling around the world on a sabbatical and, like himself, had an acute eye for good-looking youths, he reported that Patrick was 'most delightful, with a face curiously ugly and unattractive – which destroys your theory of people's appearances being an index to their character.' Several of the Etonians at Balliol also decried the Eton push, among them Robin Laffan, who went on to be President of the Oxford Union. But across the wall in Trinity College, there were admirers of the Eton push at Balliol, notably Guy Benson, Denis Anson, and Alan (Tommy) Lascelles, who stuck up a great friendship with Julian and joined in the Balliol rags.

The Eton push may have propelled Patrick at Balliol, but he was also pulled back to Eton. During this first term in 1907 he went there three times. The first was in early February when he and Ronald Knox decided to bike there and back. Ronald had toothache, so armed himself with a large 'respirator' and a woolly muffler. They left at 7.15, breakfasted in Dorchester, and then pedalled up to Nettlebed on the ridge of the Chilterns:

> There in the midst of all the icy winds that blow, what should R's respirator do but burst its chord – and there for about 20 minutes we had to stand up and shiver, with all the juvenile population of Nettlebed (3 in number) looking on at one of the best shows they had seen for a long time, while I had to do up the beastly thing with a great coarse piece of twine, which of course broke the rest of the thread and then had

nothing to catch on to – and I never was a great one for that kind of a job! At last we fixed it up on a sort of loop and pulley system, which made conversation with R quite out of the question, and breathing fairly perilously, and down we rattled to Henley.

They then took a wrong turning before reaching Maidenhead, and got to Eton by 1.0 pm, just in time for lunch in Hall. In the afternoon Patrick played a vigorous game of fives, had tea with his old messmates, called on the Alingtons and, with Ronald's toothache worsening, returned by train, so tired that they fell asleep and had to be hauled out forcibly at Oxford. In mid March he went to Eton again, staying there over a weekend, playing racquets, and reflecting that 'I might have been no end of a God if I hadn't been such a fool as to leave.' Then at the end of March, being offered a lift in a car, he lunched with the headmaster and went to the School Concert: 'I am frankly unable to keep away from Eton when I have the slightest excuse for being there.'

Meanwhile in February Patrick went out to skate, bagging Ronald's bike without his permission. 'A judgement accordingly descended on me and one of my skates got entangled in the front wheel, so that it turned round and looked at me. I thereupon described a beautiful parabola on to the road and gave myself up for dead.' Carried to the house of a doctor, and fortified by brandy, it was found that no bones were broken, but his left knee was bruised, Cyril Bailey helping to bandage it up. But a few days later he decided to go boxing (probably at the instigation of Julian Grenfell), at which his knee naturally stiffened, and a doctor encased it in an immense bandage. The next few days were spent lying in bed in the morning, getting up to receive his mess for lunch, and 'from then onwards I sit and sprawl about in graceful postures, alternatively receiving company and devouring mental pabulum, till at last I drop slowly into bed.' His intention of playing rugger against Eton had to be abandoned, and he had to give up his position in the College Second Eight preparing for the Lent Term bumping races, the Torpids. Later in March he injured his hand by putting it through Ronald's window, presumably when 'buffy'.

During this interlude of inability to participate in sport, Patrick attended meetings of the University Debating Societies. At a meeting in Balliol he spoke in opposition to the Labour Party: 'I went completely off the point and tried to be funny, which I think they found rather refreshing in an ocean of seriosity.' He attended a joint meeting of the Canning, Chatham and Palmerston Clubs to hear a long lecture on Socialism. He went to a debate at the Oxford Union on Land Nationalisation. With the new Liberal Government the issues of reform were on the mind of everyone. In contrast to Charles Lister, Patrick's feelings from the start were suspicious of change and supportive of Conservative principles.

Julian was rowing in the First Balliol Eight in the Torpid Races in February, and his parents came to see it make a bump and so go Head of the River. After the race, Patrick had tea with the Grenfells, meeting for the first time the woman who was to mean more to him than any other, Julian's mother Ettie. Ettie Desborough (her husband had recently been enobled), now aged forty, produced an electric effect on lively and intelligent men, stimulating them to conversational heights and soothing them as the recipient of their innermost confidences. Her charm rested on her elegant figure, her exquisite manners, her witty and spirited talk, her imaginative sensibility, her delicious humour, her consideration for others, and her optimistic nature. She was established as one of the leading hostesses of the day, an heiress in her own right and married to a rich man. She held court at Taplow, on a hill overlooking the Thames above Maidenhead, and there entertained constantly, most especially with Saturday-to-Monday house-parties at which the guests, young or old, were all required to be bright and provocative and to participate in games, whether physical or intellectual. She was one of the stars of a group of aristocrats who had become known as the Souls, who despised the philistine rich and were well-read and liked nothing more than talking about ideas. They cut across political party loyalties and rejected the traditional subservience of women in conversation. They valued quick wit rather than deep expositions. However this did mean that Ettie in particular was dismissive of perfectly nice people of her class whom she considered to be slow or insignificant. She liked to control her family and friends and required sparkle from her guests, which some felt exhausting: as one once remarked to another, 'You have to be damned nippy in this party not to be left out.'

Ettie had led her very conventional husband into this exciting world, and he provided a perfect foil for her. He was reticent and dependable, conscientious in public duties, a great sportsman and athlete. He was about to preside over the London Olympic Games in 1908. Amongst other things he was Chairman of the newly-formed Thames Conservancy, and cut a magnificent figure as he propelled his punt on the reach below Taplow. Patrick noted: 'His Pa is a rather heavy man, with absolutely nothing in his head but sport, I should think, but Lady D is charming and exceedingly good looking.' A few days later a bump supper was held in hall to celebrate the Balliol victory. It was followed by a dance, men dancing perforce with men. 'It was a very hilarious occasion and everyone was to say the least of it merry, including the dons.'

Although Patrick had been unable to run along the towpath beside the boat, he was evidently well enough to go for a long walk next day to shake off the effects of the bump supper. The week was a busy one. On the following evening he dined at Vincents, the University sporting club, and then went to a meeting of the Canning Club. And next day came a big Union debate on a vote of no-confidence in the Government, with F. E. Smith proposing and Winston Churchill opposing. In conclusion, on the Saturday he went to see the Balliol Steeplechase, one of a number of horse-races that day. Julian, who was a competitor, hired a coach and horses to get there, and drove it himself. 'The party included F. E. and Winston, and as we were photographed by Hills and Saunders at the start, I had the felicity of being photographed with the great Winston sitting on my knee!'

The Easter vacation loomed. Patrick began it in Malvern in the company of his father and Tats, seeing Worcester Cathedral and Tewkesbury Abbey, then moved on to stay with the Alingtons in Ross-on-Wye, and thence to Sherborne with Foss Prior, now Captain of the School at Eton. After a few days in London, watching the Public Schools Racquets Competition, he went to stay with Dear at Blairdhu. But whatever his plans for the final week of the vacation, they were changed when he received an invitation from Ettie Desborough to stay at Taplow for a Friday-to-Monday. This first visit made a deep impression on Patrick, and he wrote a description in a long letter to Dear.

This house-party was entirely of young people, friends of Julian and Billy Grenfell. Among the girls were several who were to become great friends of Patrick – Violet Asquith, Cynthia Charteris, Laura Lister and Venetia Stanley. Most of the young men he knew from Eton or Balliol, and among them was Archie Gordon. At dinner Patrick sat between Laura Lister and Lord Desborough, whom he intolerantly dismissed as 'a sadly stupid man'. After dinner came some desultory dancing, and then male chat into the early hours. Patrick was delighted to find that the card on the door of his bedroom bore the name 'The Hon Patrick Shaw Stewart'.

Saturday was about the most strenuous day I have spent since I left Eton! In the morning I played one game of clock golf, one of croquet with golf clubs, two sets of lawn tennis, and one of a sort of semi-real tennis in a covered court which they have. Then after lunch we mostly went out on the river in parties of two and upwards (I having first by the way played another set of tennis). On the river I was assigned to Laura Lister, and we first tried a canoe, but as we neither of us had the slightest idea of its management, and it threatened momentarily to capsize, we drifted gracefully back to the raft and took a large safe flat punt, which we proceeded to work with paddles – a brilliant success if it hadn't blistered my right thumb so. Anyway, we got safely to tea. After tea there was a great game of hockey in a casual field with curious implements such as golf clubs. At dinner I took in mine hostess and was between her and her daughter – a considerable strain – but as Lady D insisted on playing on the spot an intellectual game I told her about, and enlisting all our neighbours on both sides, the matter was rather taken out of my hands. After dinner we had a more regular dance with a professional piano banger from Maidenhead which went on until about 1.30. I think I danced with everyone including several boys. Lady D spent patient hours and got badly kicked in trying to teach me to reverse.

On the Sunday Patrick accompanied Ettie and a few others to church. Before the sermon she tried to make a quiet exit but knocked down all the umbrellas with a resounding crash, and Patrick was obliged to stay till the end. Before lunch Winston Churchill arrived to join the party, rather surprisingly in view of its juvenile nature, though he was himself only thirty-three and was greatly admired by Violet Asquith. He was now a Member of Parliament and Parliamentary Under Secretary of State for the Colonies, and about to be appointed a Privy Counsellor.

After lunch, as it was still pouring, a peculiarly heathen entertainment was devised. We all put on old clothes (all that is except Winston, who had London clothes and a high bowler hat on, looking like a statesman, as Lady D said) and went out on to the river in punts, and there indulged in a water-fight with oars etc – watched from the bank by the good citizens of Taplow under umbrellas! Winston did great execution with a large baler till he dropped it into the Thames, but afterwards got badly punished – I don't think I ever saw anyone wetter. Finally Julian and he had a tussle on the raft and both plunged in bodily into the Thames. Anything more ridiculous than the statesman swimming in his bowler hat you can hardly imagine.

After dinner came the charades, one team led by Winston and the other by Rex Benson.

First Winston's company performed – their word was DRAG and accordingly they first came in suitably clad hallooing across the stage after a red herring. Then they did the letters:

D was Dante in hell, which was most realistic. I have never seen anything so creepy as Winston as the leading devil, clad entirely in red table cloths, torturing Guy Benson with a pair of tongs. R was Rizzio: enter Florrie Chaplin and Archie Gordon to a tête à tête supper, the latter a hideous Rizzio in kilt and Tam o'Shanter. Suddenly bangings at the door. Mary hides Rizzio very obviously behind a curtain and in hurredly enters Winston, a perfectly fiendish Ruthven, followed by his minions, who do the bloody deed chiefly with pokers before a perfectly impassive Mary. A was the Alps, a lurid climbing scene in which Winston was an inimitable guide: and G was the Gorgon; the Asquith girl took the title role, and most of the others turned to stone, till Julian enters, a very fit looking Perseus with cushions on his feet as wings, and decapitates her. Then Rex B's company took the field. Our word was SOAP, which was done by a 'dirty boy' scene in which Beb Asquith scrubbed little Alastair Leveson Gower, who had been corked phenomenally black and dressed in pyjamas. S was a stalking scene in which Billy G was the stag and I the hind, who vainly warns him with frantic barks to flee from the approaching party, with Lord D and Rex B perfectly beautiful stalkers with purple noses who talked a wonderful Gaelic. O was the outsider, not the paper, but the real life, a dinner party in which Beb Asquith as the outsider got tight and behaved himself disgracefully. A was an Antedilivian scene in which I and three other people, horribly attired and painted, formed a pre-historic bridge party which ultimately resolved itself into a caricature of 'The Cheat' picture, and was interrupted by a prehistoric serpent consisting of three people dovetailing onto one another and serpenting across the floor, of which Lady D was the tail. P was Pandora, represented by the lovely Cynthia, who let out the rest of the party in the guise of horrible diseases, who pranced about and moaned. After the charades, with the paint still wet on our faces we danced two or three dances and then retired.

The Summer Term held no challenges for Patrick, though he decided, rather as a matter of form, to sit for the Hertford Classical Scholarship, intending to try to win it in the following year. Meanwhile there was a beguiling round of activity. He attended the annual Encaenia, at which Curzon was being installed as Chancellor. He dined at All Souls. He spoke late at night in the Union to empty benches. He was swept from his punt by a willow-branch and lost his trousers ('running three times round a meadow to get warm, clad simply but elegantly in a pink shirt'). He attended the installation of the new Master of Balliol and the dinner at which the loving-cup was passed round. In Ronald's rooms he listened to the conversation between 'what are supposed to be the two cleverest clerics in England,' Bishop Gore and Father Waggett. He had his first dinner with the Annandale, arrayed in the club tail-coat with silver and grey facings, and getting through nine courses. It was held in a private room ('separated from the common herd'), after which one of the members shied two bowls across into the adjacent Trinity College, inflicting much damage to someone's rooms there. Besides this, Patrick joined the Caledonian Club, whose members wore 'a perfectly fascinating green dinner-jacket with purple facings representing the thistle.' And he went to the Balliol Commem Ball, dancing till 7.0 am.

He also made pleasurable day excursions. One was with Julian to Taplow, where a large house-party was of course assembled, hiring a car because of missing the train. The afternoon river expedition nearly ended in disaster when he and Lord Lovat came close to sweeping themselves and four ladies over the weir. The return to Oxford was 'the most exciting ride I ever had, as the driver, who I think was fairly full of Taplow ale, was absolutely reckless and nearly cut short our young careers times without number. Also petrol ran out at Henley and kept us there for some time. Finally we got into Oxford safe and sound at ten to twelve, much pleased with ourselves.' Another was to Sutton Courtney, the Thames-side house of Norah Lindsay, a great friend of the Horners. Here he found Katherine Horner and Raymond Asquith deep in love, 'spooning and rather bored than otherwise with us.' Naturally he went to Eton for the Fourth of June, with Charles. He heard Speeches, lunched in Hall, perambulated 'meeting people every two inches,' and after the procession of boats had dinner with Charles and his family in a pub: 'So like Charles – it was very amusing, the sort of meal where caterpillars fall off overhanging trees onto the mint sauce and mangy cats prowl around for morsels.' But they had to miss the fireworks to be back by midnight.

The Hertford involved six three-hour papers spread over three days, one of them in semi-darkness in the midst of a violent thunderstorm. He felt despondent, particularly about the Latin papers, and regretted there was no Greek paper, but he didn't do at all badly. It was won, gratifyingly, by Ronald, and Patrick was rated as 'distinguished' (in the top six). There were also Collections to be written, which posed no problem for him (he got alpha minus for each of them), except that he 'was in the novel but extraordinary position of having to do a little work.' At the end of term came the interview at which the tutors assessed the progress of their charges in front of the Master of the College, sitting at the high table in Hall, a process known as 'handshaking'. The new Master misunderstood what Cyril Bailey had to say about Patrick:

CB: Mr Shaw Stewart has been very satisfactory; he was distinguished on the Hertford exam, did good Collection papers, has done some nice compositions for me, and some particularly good papers on Homer; however I should like to recommend him to be a little more regular in his work, and consult the times of others more than his own (this I suppose meant shirking lectures). As it is I suppose he has some mysterious time of day when he works, but I have never been able to discover it; I fear he has other interests than his work.

Master: Oh, is his time taken up by societies?

CB: Well, I think he is a figure not unknown in societies and Society.

Master: (not fully understanding) Well, Mr Shaw Stewart, of course these societies are excellent in their way, but you must remember you have all your life to devote to philanthropy, or whatever you are keen on (I smiled at that; I suppose he thinks I am a Socialist) whereas your four years at Oxford are your only chance of making yourself an educated man.

So I said I would be sure to make myself one, and bowed out. Quite satisfactory, and I did like the philanthropy touch – I nearly told him I rather thought of devoting my life to the pursuit of bread and butter.

There followed a couple of weeks in London, during which he watched the cricket at Lords and the boat racing at Henley, and now, for the first time, attended some of the dances that constituted the season. He wrote to his sister, 'I've been asked to a dance on the 1st by a woman called Lady Stanley of Alderley, whom I've never set eyes on, but whose daughter (Venetia) I believe I met at Taplow. However, brave as a lion, I have greeted the unseen with a cheer and accepted.'

The next item on Patrick's agenda was to go on a reading party for two weeks in the company of Charles Lister, Edward Horner, and the two Knox brothers – Ronnie and his brother Wilfrid who was at Trinity. Charles' father Lord Ribblesdale had decided to take the vicarage at Brancaster, on the north Norfolk coast, for a few weeks, thought to be particularly good for his wife (known to her friends as Charty) and his daughters Laura and Diana. He had been encouraged to do so by his friend Sir Beerbohn Tree, the famous actor-manager, who had taken a large house in the village. So it seemed convenient that the reading party should go there also. They stayed in the Manor Farm, just over the way from the Ribblesdales, and close to another reading party, one of Alan Parsons and fellow Magdalen men.

Brancaster is built at the edge of an area of marsh that becomes partially flooded at high tide, and beyond this is a wide expanse of sandy beach, sloping very gently into the sea. This gives for magnificent bathing, especially at high tide when the water has been warmed. Although a railway had been built along the coast, there were few opportunities for staying in Brancaster, and so not many others around on the beach. The other attraction was a golf course right on the edge of the dunes. In theory the mornings were sacrosanct for reading, but the four friends found themselves talking so much that little reading was done. And the rest of the day was available for pure enjoyment by the eight young men and the half-dozen or so even younger girls. The great excitement was the bathing; they do not seem to have gone sailing from the little creek at Brancaster Staithe.

Patrick slipped away from Brancaster to participate in the annual Taplow water-party, performing well in a pair canoe. He also went London to attend the wedding of Edward Horner's sister Katharine to Raymond Asquith, son of the Chancellor of the Exchequer. This took place in St Margaret's Westminster, on 25 July, followed by a dance at the Chancellor's official residence at 11 Downing Street that evening. Next morning, bleary-eyed and in his dressing-gown, Patrick gave an account of these events to Tats. Raymond Asquith had arrived late for the wedding, so that the bride burst into tears, as did all her family, and the sobs of her rejected suitors made for a very watery wedding. In the evening Patrick had danced steadily till 4, except for a short interval when Ettie took him up to see Margot Asquith, who had retired early and was eating supper dressed in a kimono. Tats reported that he was now going to Roehampton, 'where the Arthur Pagets are giving a dance and he's evidently going to meet all his friends again.'

A letter to his father from Brancaster on the last day of July announced a change of plan: 'Dear Pater, I'm afraid the temptations to which I am exposed have proved too strong for me. In other words I shall stay here like a dutiful Balliol scholar and continue the reading, with which I am making such excellent progress, into next week.' In support of this he added that 'our life has been peaceful and studious and I am making up almost indecently for arrears of sleep.' Of course, the unspecified temptations of Brancaster were not the bracing air and healthy life, but the girls who were there too. Besides the two Lister girls and Viola Tree, there were now two daughters of the Duchess of Rutland, Marjorie and Diana Manners, staying with the Trees. And since the Magdalen reading party had broken up, and Edward Horner had also gone, Patrick and Charles were the star male attractions. Viola had a fine voice, and was to train as a professional singer, and Marjorie also sang well. So the evenings resounded with piano and song, not much appreciated by the tone-deaf Patrick who wrote home that Viola 'discoursed sweet music to us yesterday afternoon, while everyone else was enchanted and Charles and I smiled on bravely and patiently.' However, he must have joined in the refrains of such favourites as 'Juanita' and 'Maud': 'Maud,' they joked, 'is not yet seventeen, but she is tall and stately.' A week later he wrote to his mother:

> The last week at Brancaster was much like its fellows – quiet studious reading, with a slight fillip of female society. We bathed nearly every day – frightfully rough sometimes but extremely salubrious – I feel quite offensively healthy as a general result of the place. Viola Tree is the strongest swimmer I ever saw. I bathed in pyjamas at first till I could raise a bathing dress: pyjamas are elegant enough in their way, but have rather a drowned rat appearance after the bathe. The Trees had two of the Manners girls staying with them – first Lady Marjorie, who is a great songstress and competed with Viola, and afterwards Lady Diana, who is still a flapper and rather podgy, but promises to be very pretty, which Lady Marjorie certainly is: in fact I think I never saw anyone better looking, but she is rather a half-hour person, and tiring after a time – I liked the little girl better.

Amongst the other people staying with the Trees was Alfred Lyttelton, brother of the headmaster of Eton and widower of Charty Ribblesdale's sister Laura ('I liked him awfully'); and Hugh Godley, a lawyer who had earlier been at Balliol ('a very jolly Irishman with a sort of interesting melancholic pose'). But the one who had the greatest effect on Patrick was Edward Marsh. Eddie Marsh, now aged thirty-five, was Winston Churchill's Private Secretary and a very social figure. With his tufted eyebrows, his monocle, his sharply chiseled features and his laconic mode of speech, he could hold forth on many subjects with authority, particularly on art and literature. He was a confirmed bachelor. He had fallen in with the present Eton push at Balliol through his friendship with the Horner family. Eddie struck up a close friendship with Patrick, discussing the rival merits of Theocritus and Wordsworth, and sharing an extravagantly affected sense of humour. 'Beloved Patrick,' he wrote, 'Do also write and tell me the Brancaster news, if you can spare the time from the Alexandrine poets.' A piece of Brancaster news that reached Patrick after he had left was that Alan Parsons had returned there to stay with the Trees, being 'so much *épris*' with Viola. This 'makes me laugh till I cry. Dear Alan, he always had a soft heart,' wrote the harder-hearted Patrick.

From Brancaster Patrick went to stay with the Horners at Mells in Somerset. Edward's parents Sir John and Lady Horner were a popular couple. Frances, his mother, had been brought up in political and artistic circles. Her father had been a patron of the Pre-Raphaelites, and Rossetti and Burne-Jones had both admired her and painted her when a girl. As a married woman she was also much admired by members of the Liberal ascendancy, notably the Asquiths and Sir Edward Grey. The Horner's mansion was Mells Park, set on an eminence in the midst of a large park, overlooking a lake. Although they still used it on occasions, they had themselves by now moved into the Manor House at Mells, for reasons of economy. This was a much smaller house, one of medieval ancestry, having been the residence of the prior when Mells had been a monastery. It only had four bedrooms, apart from servants' rooms in the attic. The enchanting ensemble of this gabled house, its walled garden, the church with its great perpendicular tower, and the adjoining village street, captivated all visitors, and within the house they found a delightful profusion of books and paintings, seen though the light of the latticed mullion windows. Prominent in the drawing room was a piano painted all over with floral and figurative designs by Burne-Jones, a wedding present for Frances.

Patrick's visit coincided with the arrival of the newly-married Raymond and Katharine, back from their honeymoon in Italy. The purpose of their visit was the celebration of their marriage with a tenants' party. This took place in a marquee outside Mells Park, with the family and their guests, including Patrick, at the high table. There were rustic games, the house was illuminated, and there were fireworks. They had hired a car and, together with Edward and Patrick, drove into Somerset, setting eyes on Montacute and Barrington. But the lachrymose Katherine found the strain of being with her new husband amongst her own family so much that she and Raymond left to stay quietly at Lord Manners' house at Avon Tyrell. For the rest, Patrick went riding, bathed in the lake, and was taken to see the Manor House. Eddie Marsh also made an appearance.

Raymond Asquith was ten years older than Patrick but, as the new brother-in-law of Edward Horner, he was attracted to the bright young Etonians of Balliol. And to them he was an awesome figure, greatly to be admired, for he had climbed the pinnacles to which they aspired. A Wykehamist, at Balliol he had won the Ireland Scholarship, got a First in Greats, been President of the Oxford Union, and then been elected a Fellow of All Souls. He was now a successful barrister, and had been adopted as the prospective Liberal Candidate for Derby. But he seemed to take his professional duties lightly, with plenty of time for society, and was noted for his sharp wit, cynical turn of mind, and studied irony. In turning his attention to Patrick, he described his visit to Mells in a letter to his sister Violet, reporting that Ettie had 'abandoned herself' to Patrick 'without reserve'.

Patrick's next port of call was Ardgowan, arriving there after a complicated train journey, then straight out on to the moor for grouse shooting on the 25,000 acre estate. When at Ardgowan, on his birthday on 17 August, a parcel arrived from Eddie Marsh. It was preceded by a spoof letter supposedly as to a prostitute, pining for her with coy endearments, and with allusions to 'a bumptious red-headed youth who got on my nerves.' The parcel contained a pair of blue pyjamas, and the accompanying letter began with three appalling verses, of which the first read:

> To celebrate the day
> I send you deevy pyjies –
> Fitting (I hope) array
> To celebrate the day
> Which leads you on your way
> Towards manhood's privileges,
> To celebrate the day
> I send you deevy pyjies.

Why Eddie Marsh should have chosen these as a birthday present is not clear. There must have been some camp banter between him and the strongly heterosexual Patrick, perhaps originating in the bathing at Brancaster. Patrick, wrote Eddie, was 'the first person who has stirred me to invoke the Muse since I left Cambridge,' and his lines concluded 'Patrick is just nineteen, But he is tall and stately' (shades of Maud). In due course Patrick acknowledged the gift, deciding not to go to the trouble of composing a poem in thanks. Eddie's letter had concluded, 'Please put me flat on my stomach before Lady Alice.' But when Patrick had passed this on to her she had said 'Who? Marsh! Oh yes – clever little man, isn't he' – 'as who should discuss the merits of a performing flea.'

From Ardgowan Patrick went to stay with his family at Nigg, in Ross-shire. This remote Scottish county had become a fashionable place for members of the society into which Patrick was now admitted, whether or not they had taken estates for the shooting. The Desboroughs were at a house called Poyntsfield on the Black Isle, and Patrick went over to stay for a Saturday-to-Monday with them. He found them alone with their children, and was charmed to find Ettie in quite a different guise: not the great hostess, but the adoring mother, surrounded by her adoring children and devoted to organizing sport and games for them. They strolled out after dinner one evening, and one said how good summer nights smelt in Scotland: 'Yes,' said Patrick, 'of tired cow.' Julian came to stay some days at Nigg, disconcerting the gamekeeper by insisting on coursing rabbits with his greyhounds, rather than shooting them. And the Asquiths were at Highfield on the Muir of Ord, also in Ross-shire. The Ribblesdales were now in Nairn. Eddie Marsh was on this social circuit, but about to accompany Winston on a great Colonial tour, sailing to Mombasa and then travelling by the new railway up through East Africa to Entebbe, and thence into the Sudan and back through Egypt.

In September Patrick received an invitation to stay with the Asquiths at Highfield. He had been unable to come to a dance held there, and Violet now wrote to 'Dear Mr Patrick' to ask him to come anytime: 'Don't reply that you are staying at home or anywhere else. You are impossible to get – so fashionable or domestic, and poor we fall between these two stools. Please come,' and concluding 'No "party" – undiluted Asquiths, 2 young and 2 old spinsters in the bush – and several fishfaces in hand.' On the way there by train, Patrick stopped off for an afternoon with the Desboroughs, where Julian now was, recovering from a high fever when staying at Dunrobin and about to go to a crammer for the Army examination. Unfortunately, when he reached Highfield, Violet was not feeling well. But Patrick had some shooting and played golf with her father, still the Chancellor of the Exchequer, who was pleased to have beaten him in spite of giving him a handicap. Patrick reported to his father that 'Mrs Asquith is most delightful – the most wonderful talker I think I have ever met, but then all the family are that.' This admiration was mutual, for Violet in a letter refers to 'the jokes such as only you can make.' From there Patrick also bicycled over to see Dear at Blairdhu.

His short year as a freshman at Balliol had established Patrick as a meteoric figure, much noticed and discussed by his new friends. Above all, Patrick was a good conversationalist. If good conversation is defined as cleverly returning the ball served to one, as in tennis, he excelled. He was inventive and could be very amusing. He had a fine voice, strong and low. His rather contrived manner of speech (as if in inverted commas) was extremely effective. The Balliol College Record attempts a succinct summary of his character. He had 'a singularly honest mind, sometimes disguised by a superficial cynicism'; he also had 'an ungrudging loyalty in friendship and was intensely critical of himself.' This summary is endorsed by Edward Marsh, who writes, 'He was deeply devoted to his friends, and they to him; but to make his surface he carefully polished an authentic vein of hardness and cynicism in which we all rejoiced.' Not everyone who knew him rejoiced in his cynicism, however. Viola Tree wrote of his 'charm and genius for understanding,' but added that 'most people did not understand him, and took his bluff for conceit. They thought he had no heart.' He could be very intolerant in argument.

It was in matters of the heart that his honesty gave way to complexity. The girls admired him, and he was fun to be with. He was attentive to them, and deeply susceptible to feminine charm. He exuded boyish enthusiasm. Violet Asquith found him always to be 'on the crest of a wave.' They liked him as a friend, but were cautious about emotional ties. They responded to his warmth and affection, but somehow thought him insincere (Diana Manners was to award him 0 out of 10 for sincerity), an insincerity revealed in emotional complexity rather than smooth flattery. They found it hard to probe inside his carapace. When Viola accused him of complexity, he replied that he was unable to write sweet simple letters, but nevertheless alleged 'I am not very clever (except superficially), but I am very very nice (not only superficially) and I am passionately fond of you.' In saying this he certainly understated his cleverness and rather overstated his niceness.

But these characteristics served him well with older women, the mothers of his friends, whose matronly hearts were stirred by the attention he lavished on them. And their husbands were generally enchanted with him too, pleased that, in contrast to the prevailing style among the upper classes, he addressed them as 'Sir'. Likewise, his tutors at Eton and Balliol relished his receptiveness to their pedagogic guidance. All were impressed by his exceptionally honest mind, his self-deprecation, his lack of duplicity. It is a tribute to his charm that he was not a handsome boy or man, of the sort who so often turned the heads of the bachelor masters and dons. Viola found him 'comparatively ugly', though, she thought, he would have looked good in an Elizabethan ruff. He was tall and had a 'dead white face, pale red freckles, and red hair, straight and shiny. For the most part he laughed, but his eyes were extremely expressive when he was quiet.' Patrick's laugh was rather nasal, and his engaging smile revealed his gums: he blushed readily when embarrassed.

It would be unjust to deplore Patrick's immersion into the fast set at Balliol – the 'Eton push' – or to suggest that he should have acquired less arrogant or boisterous friends in the college. There is no reason why he should have resisted association with his pre-existing school friends, wild though some of them were. Besides, in some ways his closest friend at college was Ronald Knox, the antithesis of roistery. By nature, he needed stimulus as much in life as he did in work. He was never cut out to be a dry academic, such as many of his fellow Eton Collegers became. And these wild friends, particularly Charles Lister, Julian Grenfell and Edward Horner, opened the door for him to enter the exciting world of high society. Without them he would never have been able to enter Barings with such high prospects, arranged for him by Julian's mother Ettie. Nor, as an officer, would he have been allotted to the Hood Battalion and become the companion of Rupert Brooke without the arrangements of Edward Marsh, met through the Horners; nor been selected for liaison with the French without the patronage of Sir Ian Hamilton, also met through Ettie. He would never have consorted with the political titans of the day, such as Balfour, Asquith, Curzon and Churchill, in the ambience of large house-parties in great houses.

All the same, when at Balliol Patrick was aware that he was at times demeaning himself in keeping up with the 'Eton push'. Once in their society his frank social ambition became evident, and by some he was considered to be oleaginous. He made no secret of his single-minded aim to make money. Against this, most of the young men he met could, unlike himself, rely on private means, or the expectation of them; and the girls were extremely conscious of who was worth what. He had to contend with a latent snobbery among the upper classes, critical of his social success. This criticism was to broaden into the public domain when the revelries of the so-called Corrupt Coterie were blazoned about in the popular press a few years later.

FOUR

A Balliol Scholar among the Souls

BACK FOR THE MICHAELMAS TERM OF 1907 at the beginning of his second academic year at Balliol, Patrick's main aim was to try for the Ireland Classical scholarship. But a letter from Lady Alice Shaw Stewart was his first concern:

> My Dear Pat, I am very glad to hear you have settled down to work and you have our very best wishes for your success. Don't waste your time now as it will make all the difference to your future. Basil says you are going to work for a scholarship. Which one is it? Do let me know when you have finally settled what you are going to do after leaving Oxford. Should you want to take up a profession for which it would be necessary to have some real help for a few years Hugh says he will be very glad to help you, of course on the understanding that you really mean to take life seriously and to work hard at whatever you go in for.

Patrick consulted his father who recommended acceptance, particularly because he believed he himself had not long to live. With the termination of his pension there would be very little money available for Patrick. Patrick was inclined to play it long, so as not to commit himself immediately to reading for the Bar, or even entering the Diplomatic Service. Besides, the offer appeared to apply from the moment Patrick left Oxford, so no money would need to be forthcoming till then. The offer was accordingly accepted with 'plain if vague gratitude', and because of subsequent decisions, never materialized. Incidentally, although it was Lady

Alice who wrote, and who had probably suggested it, the offer was from Sir Hugh. As a childless couple they were both ready to give some help to young relations, although Ardgowan was entailed to the baronetcy, and hence would go to his young nephew Guy. Lady Alice had already resolved to leave her own money and possessions, which were considerable, to the infant son of her sister Katherine Cromer, the four-year-old Evelyn Baring.

Patrick was once more plunged into the active undergraduate life. He went rowing every day in a four ('Life is simple and stern – rowing and work, work and rowing'). His boat was eliminated early, but he resumed rowing later in the term in an eight. He went over to Eton to play football, and to watch the wall game on St Andrew's Day, on the first of these staying with Hester in the absence of Cyril – 'If you feel disposed to be guest, Master-in-College, and Captain of the School in one, you will be most welcome.' At Balliol revelry predominated. There was the dinner of the Caledonian Club, arrayed in the green dinner-jackets, eating haggis and later dancing reels and 'schottisches': 'There is much to be said for exclusively male dancing I think – though steering is not always perfect, and I have seen quite 16 men on the floor at once. I am rather a good "lady" myself.' There was the Morrison Dinner in Hall, where during the longest and most trying speech someone acted as if incapable, and Patrick and others 'carried him out amid scenes of indescribable enthusiasm, returning with a suitably solemn air at the end of the oration.' More dancing followed, with the dons joining in. Philip Sassoon gave a champagne dinner. Raymond Asquith, up for the annual dinner at All Souls, was taken on to the river in a dinghy which capsized, but Patrick and Raymond managed to bestride the keel unwetted. On Guy Fawkes Night, fireworks being prohibited in the college, a little black pig was introduced, which ran like a hare into the Senior Common Room: 'We had a most hilarious evening, and made an enormous temple of crockery in the quad, where we worshipped with due ceremony – that pleased the dons a great deal; they are really very good chaps in that way. They (represented by the Junior Dean)

75

merely made a little oration to us afterwards about examples, etc, in the course of which he said we were all "prominent men", which pleased Edward tremendously – he said he had never been called that before in life.'

This hilarity was made all the more immediate for Patrick because he had moved from his rooms in the Brackenbury Building to Staircase 14 in the Basevi Building, looking on to the Garden Quad. The others on the staircase were Julian, Charles, Lawrence ('Jonah') Jones, Douglas Radcliffe and Jasper Ridley. The latter three were third-year men. Julian did not take kindly to their imputations of seniority. On one occasion he burst with indignation and dragged an unwilling Patrick to eat across the way in Edward's rooms for some days. Julian's intemperance had been matched by that of Archie Gordon, who a couple of years earlier had had a fearsome row with Jonah and Alexander Cadogan by refusing to take off his cap at lunch.

Meanwhile Patrick attended the lectures of Pickard-Cambridge on Demosthenes, Clark on Theocritus, Bywater on Aristotle, and Blount on Lucretius. He joined in debates, and wrote a paper for the Canning Club at short notice, the time made shorter by not beginning it till the previous day and completing it at the last moment. The subject was 'The next Hague Conference' and, knowing that the members of this Conservative club disapproved of the recent peace conference in The Hague, he let fly with 'fine old jingo invective on Peace in general,' with the result that 'some of the audience got hysterical in the first minute or two and were ready to laugh at anything.' In the light of his fate ten years later, it is interesting to find him arguing in favour of war. In the first place, war is inevitable: 'The fallacy which needs to be controverted is that war is a relic of barbarism, a savage, primitive, and uncivilized condition out of which mankind is destined to grow. Nothing could be further from the reality.' Then, it is also cathartic: 'to the trained soldier war is his *raison d'être,* his *apologia pro vita sua*: to the volunteer it is the opportunity for the most splendid self-sacrifice that it commonly falls to the lot of mankind to make. To the nation at large it is practically the only influence which can shake the average citizen out of his self-absorbed tranquillity.' This benefit is felt even in times of peace: 'It is the possibility of war, though it may be as remote as we are assured that it is today, that fosters the national spirit, the spirit of independence, the spirit of competition which is the animant spirit of the human race.' Such sentiments by Patrick in 1907 certainly provide an intelligent explanation for the craze for war in 1914, a craze which in the event he did not himself share. But since the essay was written in such a hurry, and for such an anti-Liberal gathering, it is questionable whether Patrick truly did believe in this piece of 'fine old jingo invective.'

By now a correspondence was flowing between Patrick and Ettie, she constantly affecting ignorance in the face of his superior knowledge. In a letter asking him to keep an eye on Billy, who was coming to Balliol to sit for the scholarship exam, she wrote, 'It is a dreadful curse to know the mother of your friends, poor Patrick – my eyes fill with tears of pity as I think of all the boring, floating, yellow-jarring losers I said to you in life.' She confided to him about her family, and her letters, written from such addresses as Sandringham or Eaton Hall (and liberally sprinked with 'heygates' in true Eton slang), sometimes opened with 'CF,' for 'Close Friend,' though he commenced with 'Lady Desborough' for another year yet. And his cosy exchanges of letters with Dear continued, the fate of her pets being a recurrent theme; Cullicudden the cat was ill, and Roy the dog had died: 'My goodness, Dear, I am so sorry for you all.'

The date of the Ireland approached. Patrick settled down to his usual last-minute concentrated cramming. Once the ordeal was over he was far from confident, writing to his father that he had done 'the six worst papers man has ever done.' On 12 December the result was announced: Patrick had won – both the Ireland and the Craven Scholarship that went with it! Letters of congratulation from friends expressed astonishment; 'Your daily half-hour of work seems to have been very efficient'; 'I shall never again believe that you are not an extremely hardworking early rising and sober-minded person'; 'a very great performance – and yet I don't believe you did a stroke of work for it.' And Raymond Asquith wrote, 'You have now joined the distinguished body of men from Charles Fox to myself, who have earned the right to the glorious title of a scholar and a drunkard.' But Hester Alington wrote: 'My dear, I am so dreadfully glad; you know how much I wanted you to baffle them, and I somehow felt you would! Go on and be everything that heaven means you to be.' The victory (the Ireland was only very rarely won by a second-year man) seemed to justify Patrick's decision to leave Eton a year before. It also immeasurably raised his standing with his new aristocratic friends, and inspired confidence in Lady Alice. For the two scholarships he was to receive £80 for two years and £30 for a third.

Within a day of the announcement in *The Times*, Patrick went to stay with the Stanleys of Alderley, in Cheshire, asked by Venetia. There was a large gathering of family and friends, and among the young women were Violet Asquith and Clementine Hosier, who was to marry Winston later in the year. There was shooting and golf and a tenants' ball. Meanwhile the Ribblesdales had decided to spend some weeks at Davos, helpful to Charty Ribblesdale's deteriorating consumption, and asked Patrick to join them. The cost of the journey deterred his acceptance, but then a telegram from Lord Ribblesdale arrived offering to pay for it and, after due consultation with his parents, Patrick accepted to go there for a week over Christmas but stayed for nearly a fortnight. He gave Tats an account of a typical day:

At 9.15 I hear a noise as from a bath descending a staircase rapidly to my room: which indeed it is. 'It all comes on from him to me, though it was hers before.' That is literally true of the bath (the minor bath, the large one being reserved for 'Altern' etc in this establishment). I get it last, after Charles, and consequently appear at breakfast last, about ten. After breakfast there begin uneasy movements among the skaters which generally culminate about eleven, when a brisk little party consisting of Lady R, Evan Charteris, Diana, Charles, and 'Zella may be seen trooping icewards: his lordship also goes to curl, and Laura and I, unless we feel especially lazy or correspondence is especially pressing, look on and apply Homocea and consolation to the fallen, and laurel leaves to the successful. Lunch reunites us, and generally introduces a stranger or so (nearly always tuberculous!) and much phthisical shop is talked over the hospitable board. Lady R has a morbid curiosity on the subject, and as most of her interlocutors have an equally morbid love of expatiating thereon, there is little or no place for what is officially called 'Gesunde.' After lunch renewed activity is displayed. The girls and I invariably ski, occasionally with Evan C or some stranger, the vigorous skaters skate again or walk. After tea various people disappear for mysterious tête-à-tête lessons. Laura has a charming Italian professor with whom she discusses amore and begli occhi on the Berlitz system, and Lady R a still more fascinating Teuton for the consideration of schwärmerei and the Dichtungsgeist. So considerable tact has to be exercised in approaching any of the public rooms. After that, something extremely intellectual such as reading Shakespeare, with whose works the house crawls. Dinner is brief and dirty, and is followed by somnolent chess between Lady R and Evan, perusal of sweated Blue-Books by Charles, and K G mods work by me. About 10.15 (it's now 10.35) bed is de rigueur, as the soporific tendencies of this climate are a thing apart.

For such an active man as Patrick this routine does seem rather subdued, though, of course, the skiing meant trudging uphill, there being no ski lifts. But here he got to know the Lister family even more intimately.

In the New Year of 1908, Patrick returned to England, spending the following weekend at Taplow and the next at Avon Tyrell, Lord and Lady Manners' house on the edge of the New Forest. Connie Manners was a cousin of Ettie's, and her husband a country gentleman who led a rather quiet life. Together they presided over a happy family of two sons and twin daughters, Betty and Angie, all of whom had become great friends of the Grenfell family, as well as of the Asquiths. On this occasion all the Grenfells, as well as Evan Charteris, were assembled.

The Lent Term now followed. It concluded with the next exam hurdle – Classical Moderations – which Patrick jumped with ease, getting a First, although not one of exceptional brilliance. Nevertheless he despised the Mods exam, telling Eddie Marsh that it was 'the most degrading and uninteresting exam ever created – the paradise of plodders, crammers and Heygates.' Ronald, to everyone's dismay, only got a Second, which Patrick attributed to Ronald's having 'so many side issues like religion and politics that he can't turn himself pro tem into a mechanical device for the absorption of facts.'

At a dinner for Old Etonians at Oxford, the Balliol push added to their unpopularity by dressing down: 'they [he really means 'we'] sat together very distinctively in a corner which they had secured beforehand, and were, as usual, arrogant noisy and uncompromising, also they were all wearing old clothes as a protest against the fashionable departures of Magdalen and New College.' Afterwards came the dancing, with Patrick 'considerably in request in a female role.' (Desmond Coke's *Sandford of Merton* amusingly describes such Oxford scenes at the time: 'Think of it, reader! Try to imagine what it means. When men dance together, one must perforce perform the movement of the Lady. Think of a sodden brute, clasped by a worthy partner masquerading as a Woman!'). At the Anna dinner, by contrast, Patrick decided to be quiet and abstemious, drinking only lemonade. This was just as well, as after it Charles Lister threw a croquet-ball into a window of Trinity, and Alan Lascelles (though a Trinity man, an honorary member of the Anna) uprooted the pet sapling of the Master of Balliol, with the result that the Club was suspended. Patrick gave one of the principal speeches in the Union (of which Ronald was now the Secretary) on another debate on confidence in the Government. He discussed Nietzche at the Orthodox Club, and in sport abandoned rowing for golf.

The Easter vacation was of nearly six weeks. It began with a busy time in London. But, as with the Christmas vacation, Patrick's plans were a disappointment to his sisters. He wanted to go to Florence under the aegis of Cyril Bailey and in the company of Hoj Fletcher and Edward Horner. Although his Ireland money would help, he needed more from his father, which was granted with 'subdued financial groans.' In addition to the attraction of being able to see Florence, Patrick had a further interest in mind. He told his father: 'I don't quite know how much I love Cyril, but I'm inclined to encourage him, as it's a good thing to have one don attached to one' in preparation for Greats in the following year – a sentiment supported by Dear who wrote, 'I would certainly nurse that inclination of Mr Bailey to love you.' Additionally, Patrick had in mind combining this visit with one to the Lister family, who were leaving Davos to be in Italy. But this progression prevented any chance of joining his sisters and Dear on a visit to Paris over Easter – in Dear's words, 'the first Easter I have been separated from you since you were born.' His inability to fit visits to his family into the schedules of his exacting social life was to become a chronic source of regret to his family. And he was generally unable to introduce his sisters into the brilliant circles in which he now moved.

Patrick set out to Genoa to join the Ribblesdales as their guest. Characteristically, he was a forgetful traveller. On arrival in Calais, when asked if he had anything to declare, he replied *'rien de chose, absolument rien,'* at which the douanier extracted from his bag two tins of tobacco and two boxes of cigarettes, and fined him. At Genoa he found he had 'parted company' with his case, which turned up next day. The Ribblesdales had abandoned Davos in favour of the Italian Riviera in a perennial search for healthy air for Charty, whose consumption was now worse, for although said to be better, she was coughing terribly and confined to her room: she died two years later. That left Patrick and Charles and Laura and Diana to wander around the city by themselves sightseeing, cementing further Patrick's unspoken love for Laura. They then moved on to Rapallo, to a palatial though uncompleted hotel in which Patrick slept in a curtained alcove off their sitting room. One day they took a cab to Portofino. From Rapallo Patrick and Charles went to Florence to join Cyril Bailey's art-studying party.

This was an eminently successful visit. The famous monuments and masterpieces were examined and intelligently discussed, and Patrick loved the small compact city that Florence then was. All the same, with Patrick and Charles and Edward there together, the ten days were never going to be merely for serious study. Edward picked up a beautiful Italian woman who he found painting in San Marco. Charles led them all to a German beer-hall where he drank quantities of beer and discussed politics and theology with all and sundry. Viola Tree was staying in Fiesole, and Hoj Fletcher lost his heart to her. From Forence they went to Assisi for a couple of nights, walking up from the station under a full moon in a mackerel sky into the silhouetted town, and kneeling down on the dusty road to say a prayer – 'even our rough hearts were touched.' He paid the piazza of San Francisco the compliment of putting it in the same class as the Eton School Yard, but thought the hills around the Hermitage of the Carcere 'all very well in their way, but I think Scottish mountains come first.' The party having broken up, Patrick resisted rejoining the Lister family on the grounds of cost, and returned, via Milan and a stop-over in Paris, some days sooner than expected.

The vacation had begun with another visit to Taplow, and the correspondence with Ettie had become more intimate: 'Goodbye, beautiful angel,' she wrote, in inviting him, tempting him with a Beagle Meet, 'where we could Beagle very peacefully and conversationally.' Patrick's long thank-you letter (or 'Collins') for this visit is extremely contrived, and appears to be an apology for some trivial gaffe or oversight, probably during some intellectual game. It is an example of maximizing small things and minimizing great ones that was such a feature in the conversation of the Souls. Practical efficiency is desirable he writes: 'The Super Patrick of your mind has it, and apparently the earthly copy is at present lamentably deficient in it, but it shall be seen to.' He pretends that he will be banished from Taplow. But, of course, he was welcomed all the more. In fact the vacation ended with another visit to Taplow, preceded by one to Panshanger, the great house in Hertfordshire, now owned by Ettie but with her widowed aunt, Lady Cowper, residing in it. In inviting him Ettie wrote, with pardonable exaggeration, that he would find 'much better pictures than at Florence.' The Taplow party included Winston Churchill and Lord Hugh Cecil, and also Archie Gordon, back from working in a bank in Berlin, 'very pleased with himself and "Oh-to-be-in-England"-ish.' On the evening in which he was bidden to take his hostess in to dinner Patrick kept them all waiting, clearly deficient in practical efficiency.

For Patrick the main focus of the Summer Term was for a second attempt at the Hertford, encouraged by the fact that Ronald, the previous year's victor, was standing aside. When he duly won it there was less surprise than there had been with his triumph at the Ireland six months previously, as he was now widely recognized as a champion exam-taker. The result was announced before he went to the Fourth of June. He paraded around Eton with Laura beside him, wearing his features in a 'hideous fixed grin'. But as he received 'the somewhat frigid salutations of usherdom' he reflected 'they don't like me much, you know – funny isn't it? Cyril [Alington] does though.' Indeed, a very merry lunch with Cyril and Hester Alington crowned the day, 'Cyril talking nineteen to the dozen, Hester burbling, and self lifting my elbows freely,' oblivious of the strictures about drink of eighteen months before. (Cyril Alington was about to leave his position as Master in College at Eton and to become Headmaster of Shrewsbury.) As to the Eton masters, it was perhaps natural that their interest in Patrick should have waned. Anyway, not all of them had been his admirers: the veteran Henry Luxmoore later wrote that 'his amazing cleverness, wit, cynicism, defiance, kept me off.'

Meanwhile he also had to begin his work for Greats. 'I now

go to a lecture on Moral Philosophy with a cleric at New College called Rashdale who talks about "the form of the moral law" and "the concept of conscience", and to one on the Republic, also at New College, where I am told about "customary virtue being inadequate" and that as a rule "ontogeny [history of the development of the group] follows phylogeny [history of the development of the individual]".' He attended the Master of Balliol on Roman Constitutional History – 'frightful hair-splitting about the exact status of the client and the manumitted slave in Early Republican times.' He also had to study for Collections, telling Eddie Marsh: 'I have got to get up the Ethics (of Aristotle) in the next 24 hours, and feel rather like Psyche – I wish some modern homosexual Eros would come and explain about ακρασια [lack of self control] and θηριοτγς [having the nature of a beast].' Patrick again made a principal speech in the Union, opposing a motion that the house would deplore the return of a Unionist Government. All his speeches at the Union had been in criticism of the Liberals, but they somehow lacked conviction and he admitted to his mother, 'I'm bound to say I don't harbour any very strong convictions.' The fact is that he was not deeply politically minded, or interested in what Violet Asquith called 'the great theatre of life.' Her father, now Prime Minister, celebrated his arrival at Number 10 with a ball for Violet, to which Patrick went: indeed, she urged him to visit her there any time, and 'I will show you Pitt's blood and Gladstone's ghost and all the relics of the great shades.'

The Eton push was pulled up short in May when Charles Lister was sent down for the remainder of the term. After a bump supper at Trinity a bonfire had been lit in the garden, and Charles and some other 'buffy' Anna men from Balliol went to join in the proceedings. To enliven things Charles seized a small young man and began to waltz him around, despite his protests. Unfortunately he proved to be the Reverend the Junior Dean. The Balliol authorities decided to make an example of him. But Charles, besides his wild eccentricities, had also a serious aspect to his character. He was still a member of the ILP and active in political affairs in municipal

Oxford, as for instance organizing support for the women on strike at the Clarendon Press and arranging an exhibition about industrial evils. He said afterwards that his expulsion was the best thing that had happened to him, and he went and worked at the Trinity Mission in West Ham.

But Charles' friends decided to stage a protest. They carved a mock memorial on the headstone above the entrance to Staircase 14, and it was Patrick's witty idea that it should include the quotation from Acts 23 verse 4: 'I wist not, brethren, that he was the high priest.' The unveiling ceremony involved Patrick, wrapped in a crumpled sheet taken off Julian Grenfell's bed, delivering a Ciceronian oration. Tommy Lascelles and two other Trinity men attended, in formal clothes with crepe-covered top hats, holding arum lilies and bearing a wreath, and joining a crowd of about a hundred. Thirty years later he recalled Patrick's oration as being one of the most brilliant he had ever heard. It began with praise of Charles, moved on to the time-honoured feud between Balliol and Trinity, and then launched into a diatribe against the Balliol dons, collectively and individually. The Balliol dons were angry, but took no further action other than presenting the bill for having the inscription scraped out. (Incidentally, Lascelles had earlier achieved a sensation by suspending three chamber-pots on a rope across the quad in Trinity, the central pot being that of the same unfortunate Junior Dean).

Sutton Courtney was on the Thames only a few miles south of Oxford, and Norah Lindsay was a warm-hearted woman who was generous to the young. During Eights Week she had Betty and Angie Manners to stay, and also Laura Lister. So on the Sunday the Balliol bloods came over, encouraged by her effusive letter to Patrick asking them all: 'I love a huge crowd of Irish, Scotch, Bessarabians, Mesopotamians, Girondins, Jacobins, Extreme Rights, Extreme Lefts, Vagabonds, Itinerant Musicians, scallywags, but no motor malmaison lovers who dine in Park Lane and eat paté de foie gras inlaid with plovers eggs, for they bewilder me, dazzle me, tire me, and make me sad.' (This last was a dig at Philip Sassoon, the rich

Jewish undergraduate at Christ Church, who was a particular butt of the Balliol bloods.)

After dinner it was hide and seek in the garden, and Patrick and Laura – she in a beautiful dress lent her by Norah Lindsay – ran to the boathouse and jumped into what they took to be a punt, but turned out to be a canoe: 'to the feverish hilarity of everybody else we appeared looking like river-gods, more or less.' Another acquatic amusement took place at Oxford when Ettie came with her daughter Monica to give a dinner for Julian and his Oxford friends, staying with the hospitable Master of the College. Eddie Marsh had sought unsuccessfully to be invited. Next day they were taken out in the punt that Patrick shared with Julian and Ronald, and she wrote to thank him. Even on the punt there had been intellectual games, including the favourite one of marking each other for various qualities, for she wrote: 'Please tell me exactly how you mark Eddie Marsh? Our pathetic bits of wet paper are still in my green bag ready to be played on.' For good measure, the Anna dinner was held on a steam-launch.

In these and other escapades Patrick's attraction is abundantly evident. On the one hand was his zest for physical activity. At school, though never achieving the highest renown, he had played football and racquets energetically, and thrust himself into the muscle of the Wall Game. At Balliol he slogged away at an oar in the Second Eight. He took to the saddle on awkward horses. He was a keen shot, if not a noticeably accurate one. He played golf. He loved swimming and water-fights, as well as heroic bicycle-rides. He was an excellent and enthusiastic dancer, an accomplished waltz-reverser. He was tireless in working in his old nurse's garden. On the other hand, he also shone in intellectual games, taking the lead naturally, fortified by his exceptional memory. He could 'write in the style of,' or compose definitions, epigrams, paradoxes, syllogisms, analogies, palindromes or acrostics, rapidly and well. He was a keen bridge-player and addicted to poker. With all this, he was a hedonist, a lover of high living. He drank far more than was good for him, especially when at Balliol. He gambled heavily at cards.

Patrick's father died of a stroke on 6 July. There was uncertainty about where his mother should now live, but an offer came from Lady Alice that seemed an admirable solution. Before Sir Hugh had inherited, they had for many years lived at a house called Carnock near Larbert in Stirlingshire, and had fond memories of it. It was, as described by Patrick, 'a perfectly proportioned old house with no visible front door, and two funny breakneck winding staircases.' They now proposed that it should be the home of their widowed cousin and her family. All four children pressed their mother to accept. It had so many advantages. It had a small estate, with some shooting. And it was near to Ardgowan and to the lady they now referred to as 'the Benefactress'. But Mary was unwilling to commit herself. She complained of its remoteness from London and its proximity to the coal mines, and went and installed herself, together with Patrick's sisters, Tats and Pua, in Folkestone. Dear was loud in her protestations. She doubted if Sir Hugh and Lady Alice would continue to be interested in their cousins if the offer were refused. She felt that the old family place would be just right for Pua and Tats. 'Isn't that infinitely better than having to follow about a Will-of-the-Wisp like Ma, who I am sure (I know her well) would never settle anywhere in peace.' So the lease was arranged, though Mary continued to grumble, finding nothing good about Carnock. Taking possession was easy, as the house was fully furnished and staffed.

Patrick's summer-vacation programme reads like a society gossip column. The principal progression was to Panshanger (Lady Desborough); North Creake (Lord Ribblesdale); Clovelly (Mrs Hamlyn); Mells (Lady Horner); Brancaster (Mrs Tree); Ardgowan (Lady Alice Shaw Stewart); Stanway (Lady Elcho); Rowsley (Duchess of Rutland); Gosford (Lady Wemyss); Gisburne (Lord Ribblesdale). Of these, the visits to Clovelly, Stanway and Rowsley were particularly appealing to him.

Clovelly in Devon was the home of Mrs Hamlyn, a sister of Connie Manners, a magical place with the hidden village descending steeply to the Bristol Channel. A large party of young were assembled, including Laura and Diana Lister and Lord and Lady Manners and their children – their daughters Betty and Angy, and their son John, at Eton and intended for Balliol, whom Patrick thought 'a really delightful boy with a most original mind, very handsome, very good at games, and a *parti* into the bargain.' The house party also included the three young daughters of Lord Curzon, and the great proconsul himself turned up for a few days. Lady Manners drew Patrick aside, and accused him of 'usurping the youthful heart of Laura'; 'I told her it was quite the other way round.' Patrick scored points with the devout Mrs Hamlyn by saying the psalms by heart at the daily morning prayers.

Patrick had been invited to Stanway by Cynthia Charteris, the daughter of the house. Stanway lies among the woods of the escarpment of the Cotswolds, a romantic manor house with a church and small village nestling against it. It had a magic similar to that of the Manor House at Mells, though larger and with a fine Jacobean hall. And Lord and Lady Elcho, Cynthia's parents, were themselves rather like the Horners, having aristocratic friends who were also artistic and bohemian, deriving particularly from the friendships of Mary Elcho's family, the Wyndhams. Like the Horners, the Elchos were not really rich, suffering from the agricultural depression of the times, and Stanway had a reputation for discomfort. But Lord Elcho was the heir to the Earl of Wemyss, an immensely wealthy Scottish aristocrat so, unlike Sir John Horner, he had great expectations. Patrick found Lord Elcho rather frightening, 'he is always throwing things at his wife's head,' but he thought Cynthia charming. Cynthia's older brother Hugo (known as Ego), a popular young man with a reputation for quiet humour, was home at the time, on leave from his position as an honorary attaché at the British Embassy in Washington. Evan Charteris, who had been with Patrick at Davos, was Cynthia's uncle.

The invitation he wanted most of all was for Stanton Woodhouse near Rowsley in Derbyshire. This quite small house had for some years been a summer home for the Duke of Rutland and his family.

He had succeeded to the dukedom and the ownership of Belvoir in Rutlandshire in 1906, but still went to Rowsley, which was close to his other property, Haddon Hall, now in ruinous condition but, under his direction, being restored. Marjorie must have hinted at it in a general way, but Patrick undoubtedly pressed for a definite invitation. It only came at the last minute, and he postponed his arrival to join his family at Carnock in order to accept:

but oh Dear, I simply couldn't resist it, they are such a fascinating lot of people. The mother of all three girls was there, each better-looking and more charming than the last, and the only other person in the house was Pamela Lytton, who is the flower of the flock, so you can imagine the rate of my pulse while I was at Rowsley. The Duke is an amiable old man though a terror to his family who are always having to 'amoose' him – my heart went out to him because he reminded me of Pa. Young Granby [Diana's brother] is a queer fish, not a conceited ape like Stafford and not a bit ostentatious, but a crank and a recluse and rather selfish, caring only about manuscripts and the history of his family and the repairs at Haddon Hall, which is the most lovely place I ever set eyes on.

Henceforth he referred to the ducal daughters as 'the Hothouse,' a name coined to describe their exotic affectations and the heady climate that distinguished them from the ordinary flowers out in the garden. The Hothouse clearly approved of Patrick, and he called in there on his way south in October. This time he found 'old Harry Cust hanging about and practically living there.' They went over to look at Haddon Hall by moonlight. He also stayed a few nights at Gisburne in Yorkshire, the seat of Lord Ribblesdale, with Sargent's famous portrait of him on the wall and 'a fairly large undulating park with timid deer battening for the Ribblesdale Buckhounds.' For some nights Patrick was alone there with the two girls and 'Zella, but this alarmed Lady Ribblesdale, who ordered the land-agent to stay in the house until her husband's return.

In terms of joy and fun, Rowsley was certainly the highspot of his summer, but in terms of society it was Gosford, the palatial house of the Earl of Wemyss overlooking the Firth of Forth. Ettie had arranged for Patrick to be included in a house party that included both the new Prime Minister (Asquith) and a previous PM (Balfour):

> I found Evan and Ego and Cynthia and Lady Elcho and Ettie and Raymond and Mr and Mrs Asquith and Arthur Balfour and Sir Edgar Vincent, and today Violet A and Venetia Stanley and Archie Gordon and Ribblesdale. Ettie is not on speaking terms with Evan at present which is no doubt unfortunate for him but pleasant for me, as she and I had two walks while Evan was philandering with the Prime Handmaid [Violet Asquith]. Cynthia has been more than usually accessible because none of her normal admirers are here. We bathed yesterday and she let down her hair – a remarkable sight I must say – down to the knees, very thick golden brown. With my venerable host I have had the most lively political discussions. He has warned me against excessive smoking and given me three anti-socialist tracts of his own authorship.

Several of them, including Ettie and Evan, bathed in the sea: 'can you believe it? In Scotland in mid October. Our costumes were slightly heterogeneous – Archie in a zephyr and shorts, Ego in grey flannel trousers, and I in a complete outfit of Forsyth's hygienic underwear.' On the Sunday, Ettie and Lady Salisbury, accompanied by Patrick and Archie, went to the kirk, arrived late, were reduced to laughter outside the porch, and were 'looked on with the gravest disapproval when we finally entered, and had to sit through a 45-minute sermon.'

The visits to Rowsley sparked the lifelong correspondence between Patrick, now turned twenty, and Diana, just sixteen. The initial reason for their letters was that Patrick had left some books behind, and had sent her a handkerchief, which she acknowledged. She began: 'Pattariga, Your letter overwhelmed me with pride, at being the receiver of such a one. You *are* a letterary bloke. It must be fun to write essays instead of a short scribble with the style and matter of an Otto's German exercise like mine.' At Rowsley she had presented him with a bunch of white heather for luck, and he had spent time with her in the schoolroom where, he wrote, 'I left my heart.'

Diana was still a schoolgirl and did not officially 'come out' in society till the summer of 1910, when she was nearly eighteen. But with her two sisters and their admirers she was quick to enter into the confidences of those several years older. She was already conducting a lively correspondence with several others, mostly women, but including Alan Parsons, and expected to receive several letters daily. Diana wrote in an intuitive style, very loose on grammar and spelling ('golf-linx,' 'fotographs'), and offended Patrick by writing his name as 'Shore Stewart'.

From the start, Patrick was constantly pressing for her replies, but when they came they were long and wildly descriptive. He was always urging her to visit Oxford, as her sisters did in the Michaelmas term, but 'What's the use of the Glorious Sisters to me, surrounded by a horde of Julians, Guys, Charleses, Edwards, Bunts etc?' Diana was curious about Patrick's relationship with Laura: 'L flabbergasts me, and it is never intensely gratifying to be looked down on as very much less than the weed that groweth at her door. Are you still ham on the sideboard, or beef on the fork?'

Patrick distanced himself from love of Laura, writing that she was to him as 'the shadow of a dream,' and that she and George (Bunt) Goschen cared greatly for each other. Diana expressed an interest in the novels of Meredith, and Patrick sent her an expensive edition. They met, with others, in London once or twice during the Michaelmas Term. Once he had to write an essay next day, but she provided pen, ink and paper, and he wrote it in the train back to Oxford.

But meanwhile for Diana it was back to the schoolroom in London, from where she expressed the inner uncertainties that never left her throughout her long life:

the new regime is schoolroom tea, no Oxford friends, stiff music lessons from snobbish masters, days at the Berlitz, and perhaps even solitary confinement at Belvoir, the which "bijou maisonette" is in my mind like the ultima thule. There is also the depressing idea that I know that what I want I get without even trying, that therefore for all the strivings of the experienced, I shall always continue to be a rotter as I have no strength of will to do that which I dislike, also the disillusion of finding that you are incapable of everything you had imagined yourself a genius at, music, drawing etc, is, to say the least of it, wretched. These and many worse subjects, morbid ones, made one feel that the misery of 1000 centuries were laid on my shoulders. Then to make it worse the heavens are wide open and the gods themselves do weep. I hope in sympathy. Do be sorry, wherefore I don't quite know.

Patrick's enthusiasm for the great world of country house parties soon became a source of amusement to his friends, as well as censure from his critics. After his visit to Stanway he received a letter from Cynthia written to 'The Hon'ble Patrick Shaw Stewart' (though beginning 'My Duckie') and continuing: 'I suppose this envelope with its modest and unassuming contents will greet your blasé eye in company with at least half a dozen more. I can visualize you extending a limp hand to grasp the mountain of coroneted envelopes lying on your breakfast tray in provocative suggestiveness.' And after his visit to Gosford she wrote, 'I suppose even you are by this time sheltered behind the walls of Oxford,' and went on to describe her visits to Whittingehame with A. J. Balfour (where 'crowds of adoring frumpy females gyrate round the central figure constantly coming into violent and feline contact with one another'), and to Archerfield, alone with Margot and Violet, ('an elysian life, breakfast in bed, symposium on wind-swept rocks, and hours of languidly transcribing Brahms [heavy] poems into our commonplace books'). Later Connie Manners wrote: 'My dear Patrick, it was very delicious hearing from you even though it was to tell us how much the ducal homes of England are to you.' And Eddie Marsh made much of a remark of Patrick that displayed his 'heroic snobbishness'. He asked Eddie about a certain duke's son, and when Eddie said that he wasn't up to much, Patrick declared, 'I've yet to meet the duke I couldn't like.' The epigrammatical Raymond Asquith said of him, 'All Shaws are charlatans and all Stewarts are pretenders.'

In her memoirs Cynthia wrote perceptively about Patrick. According to her 'Patrick's mind was so astonishingly quick that whatever you said to him was answered almost before it was spoken. Every ball was half-volleyed.' Lacking good looks 'he took infinite trouble to make people like him.' This he achieved by his 'amazing verbal memory, extreme candour, dislike of false enthusiasms, disarmingly frank and successful social ambition,' and 'an engaging trick of always trying to make one think the worst in him.' She also writes that 'he seemed to look on life as both a race which he intended to win, and a banquet which he intended to enjoy.' But she concludes, 'what I liked most in him – his intense appreciation and affection for his friends.' Raymond Asquith was another who relished his bouts of verbal sparring with Patrick, and Patrick was influenced by the style of the older Raymond, particularly in his use of irony. Raymond on first acquaintance had considered him to be 'a mad Irishman, wholly unprincipled but quite good company,' but soon amended this to the effect that 'he is Scotch, and egregiously, horribly, diabolically sane.'

During the autumn Ettie's letters to Patrick became more intense. She had been reading Gilbert Murray's translations of Euripides. The *Hyppolitus* and the *Trojan Women* had struck her deeply: 'Do you think in the controversy between Hecuba and Helen Euripides is really on the Hecuba side? I do.' She was concerned to know why Nietzsche was so dismissive of Euripides as compared to Aeschylus? Then she turned to Jowett's translation of Plato's *Republic*, ending her letter, 'by the fire, uncomfortably and unreadably,' with 'Bless you, Matron'. Patrick sent her the poems of the recently deceased Walter Headlam – 'it arrows to one's heart, thank you' – and a skit on Meredith done in the style of a leader *The Eton College*

Chronicle: 'Do send one on Prejudice, or Paradox, or Tradition, or Custom, or Lies, or Pride, or Mugwumps, or Screws, or Secrets, or Hobbies, or Calf-Love.' And then 'I am batting to see you, and have hay-ricks to say. Is this approximate Hot Bed terminology? How were (was?) the Hotbed? Blessings.' She is glad he looks upon her as a 'Hotbed confessor': she looks upon him 'as its duvet.' But her most explicit words of affection were in a letter of 25 September, inscribed to VDP:

> You are a very delightful asset in life. This sounds bowdlerized hot-beddish, but is crudely true. One of the drawbacks of Age is a certain lack of confidence, and nothing restores it so illusively as the friendship of the hungry generation, and of all the *very* hungry, beyond my very own, there is no one who contributes anything like so much as you do. It is especially happy that it should be so, for you have plumbed the depths of all my echt matron blue-faces, and on that side there can be no undoing stocks of crabbedness to discover! I do often feel as if there were a bed-rock of foundation, as if we are really friends, beyond the articulate – "The only things supremely worth knowing are those that never have been and never will be expressed or proved".

FIVE

Balliol Triumphs and the Aura of Diana

PATRICK'S third academic year at Balliol began with the
Michaelmas Term of 1908, and it brought a few setbacks.
At the Union, despite opening a debate on the Government's
Unemployment Proposals, he failed in a bid to be elected Librarian.
His speech was considered too light-hearted, 'an after-dinner
relaxation'. He had been relegated to a minor part in the University
Greek play. On the river, despite heroic efforts, he was in danger of
being dropped from the Balliol Second Eight. And, of course, there
were visits to Eton, for football and even the wall-game, 'I soon
realized the difference between playing it once a year and playing
it every day – after ten minutes I could hardly stand up.' For the
rest, it was 'golf, poker, edifying conversation and just a tinge of
work.' For the first time, there were no exams. But he decided to
take the first step towards a future career by reading for the Bar,
as likewise did Edward Horner. So on a Friday in mid November
he and Edward went to London and enrolled as Students of the
Honourable Society of the Inner Temple. The only requirement at
this stage was to attend a set number of dinners in Inner Temple
Hall, which they began on three consecutive days.

Patrick crammed as much as he could into this brief visit to
London. There was a farewell concert by the Australian soprano
Nellie Melba at the Albert Hall in the Rutlands' box. There was
a play and suppers with Eddie. There was tea with Viola Tree.
And there were Cousin Alice and Cousin Connie to be buttered
up. On another visit to London he went with the Rutlands to hear
Viola singing the leading part in a performance of a German piece,
'Paulo et Francesca,' at the Royal College of Music, where she was

a student, though 'for my own unmusical part I can only say that she made pleasant noises and acted remarkably well.' Patrick was, by his own admission, completely unmusical, indeed tone deaf. This was not perhaps so surprising since music, confined to live performance, was far less appreciated than now. England, despite its excellent choral tradition, was contemptuously referred to by the Germans as 'the land without music.' Music likewise meant nothing to Ettie. All the same, several of Patrick's friends were musical in the sense of being moved at classical performances. Likewise there were among them those who were knowledgeable about pictorial art. But there is no evidence that these things meant anything to Patrick, who in this context must be judged the philistine that he often proclaimed himself to be. Fortunately for him, although some of the girls played the piano or sang (Viola professionally), or sketched, the cleverness that really attracted them was related to words, whether in conversation or public speech or literature in prose and poetry. Patrick loved his poetry, from Shakespeare to his contemporary Georgian poets.

Shaking 'the dust, or rather mud, of Oxford rather prematurely off my feet,' Patrick went to Stanway, and paid for his bed and board by attending the Cotswold Spinsters Ball as the escort for Cynthia, in default of Herbert (Beb) Asquith, who was now her favourite, but who had been banned from Stanway by her father. But more stimulating was the presence of Arthur Balfour and George Wyndham. With Balfour, 'to my delirious joy I got in one or two words edgeways and found him perfectly delightful.' Wyndham, his hostess's brother, he thought 'the most amiable and confidential-mannered man in the world.' His mother and sisters, now awaiting him at Carnock, must have then read with some dismay that he had been asked by Evan Charteris to go with him to St Moritz to stay 'in the most luxurious palace in Switzerland, to ski, eat, drink and read,' as guests of the Duchess of Marlborough, though he decided not to accept this offer. But before going to Carnock in the New Year Patrick did stop off at Gisburne. Rather to his relief, a spell of icy weather prevented the hunt from going out, and he could pose as 'the disappointed frozen-out sportsman.' And also, after some other guests and Charles himself had left, Patrick found himself alone there with Ribblesdale and Laura. Consequently, as he put it in a letter to Dear, 'I wasted no time'. But any suggestion that this induced a budding romance is contradicted by his next sentence: 'She was extremely beautiful and quite gracious, and his Lordship as charming as ever. We went for long walks in the snow and felt very hardy.'

'My goodness I was exhausted after dancing at Hatfield till 6 on the Thursday, Stanway till 5 on the Friday, and Taplow till 2 on the Saturday,' Patrick told Dear in mid January of 1909, a trio achieved only with close attention to *Bradshaw's Railway Guide* and a few snatched hours of sleep. And these balls had been preceded by a large house-party at Belvoir. Here he found the Rutlands in ducal grandeur, very different from Rowsley and less appealing to him. At Rowsley it was 'three people in a room and loud shrieks echoing through the walls.' At Belvoir 'I spent most of my time trying to find my way about, failing, and being preceded by bored retainers to my destination.' He managed to strike up a relationship with the awkward John Granby, who 'insisted on doing strange things with me at 2 am, such as going to Grantham in the motor (with prodigious danger to life and limb) and looking at the 15th century manuscripts till 4 am, which he knows a good deal about and are rather thrilling.' But, together with the Hothouse trio, there were Cynthia Charteris and Betty Manners, and so much was going on, including going out shooting every day, that 'it is almost impossible to get a moment off duty.' At Taplow, so he told Diana, he spent his time 'fleeing from Laura, in whose eyes from tongue on the sideboard I have become cold pork, no more, no less.'

Back at Balliol Patrick painted a pretty picture of his daily routine in a letter to his mother:

At 7.25 I arise, fling myself into shorts and sweater, and GO FOR A RUN. Back at eight, bracing cold bath, breakfast at 8.20 (food carefully selected). Then work – there being

nothing else to do at that appalling hour – from 9 to 1 !!
Lunch at 1 (again all muscle building in accordance with the
latest principles), then down to the river at 2.30 and tug my
oar till 4. Then run round Christ Church meadows. Then tea.
Then work till 7. Then a dinner consisting mainly of toast and
lettuce and brussels sprouts. Then more work. Then BED AT
10.30. Do you recognize your son? And yet I assure you it is
the solemn truth.

Hoj Fletcher was coaching the boat, and in it with Patrick was
another ducal figure, but one of whom he did not approve – the
Marquess of Tavistock, 'the most absolute corpse-like creature
on God's earth' (and destined to survive the War by being a
conscientious objector, to the fury of his father, who attempted
to disinherit him). He told Diana: 'Row! Do you realize the full
inwardness of it. To sit for two hours with nothing on but a sort
of fig-leaf which Adam would have thought inadequate, on a
small piece of board, pulling away incessantly with hands like an
Alpine sunset at an oar from which icicles hang, and cursed by a
despot from the bank for minute faults of style. Why I do it I can't
imagine.' Patrick's boat, the Second Balliol Eight, lay at ninth place
in the First Division of the Torpids: after the six days of races, it
had dropped to eleventh place. Writing from the Balliol Barge,
Patrick admitted to Dear that 'boredom and a general uselessness
and consciousness of work undone and life misspent and floaters
made and friends lost and opportunities missed, descended on me
like a pall, which is only gradually lifting under the narcotic of this
daily rowing and inevitable work.'

But before and after the few weeks of this regime Patrick's
life was not so Spartan. Just before it he had been to London,
staying with Eddie Marsh in his rooms in Raymond Buildings in
Gray's Inn, taking another Inner Temple dinner: 'Eddie was quite
delightful – the most thoughtful and attentive host. He positively
studded my shirt and warmed my pyjamas with his own fair hands
– action which I have known left undone by ducal footmen who
hadn't so many capacities to fulfill!': he was 'host, hostess, groom

of the chambers and valet.' On one such occasion Patrick, before leaving next morning, tentatively put a cheque for £50 on Eddie's plate, for 'board and lodging', though knowing that Eddie would never accept it. Probably at Patrick's commendation, Eddie had read through *The Iliad* over Christmas, 'which I am proud of. Wouldn't it be awful not to know Greek?'

The races over, it was back to late mornings and late evenings and heavy drinking. But he still applied himself to hard work, the mountain of the Greats Exams now not more than a year away. He sat for the Jenkyns Exhibition ('the Jenks'), an examination on classics and philosophy, but without expectation of doing well in it. He composed Greek comic iambics for the Gainsford Exhibition. The Lent term also meant writing for Collections again, 'and what with wrestling with their inquiries on the Distinction between Real and Unreal Pleasures, and doing an essay for J. A. Smith on Aristotle's Conception of Happiness viewed in the light of Mill's "Utilitarianism", I really have lived among dogmas for the last few days.' 'Oh Dear,' he wrote, 'I do hate work.' He felt he was getting stale, his tutors were criticizing him sharply, and he felt destined to get only a Second in Greats. Dear had been at Carnock over the New Year, and had seen Patrick there for part of the time. She was beginning to view his hectic social round with concern, worried that he might slacken in his work. In contrast to the rich young men he lived among, 'it is just as well you have to work for your living, if things came too easy you wouldn't enjoy life half so much as you do.' For herself, she doesn't really like work either, 'but what can one do – one must get a living somehow and I have such difficulty keeping my 19 chickens alive in this terrible cold weather and the puppies are sick in the cold too.'

The alcoholic escapades of the Balliol bloods got their mention in the gossip columns of the press, and so came to the eyes of Cyril Alington. From The School House, Shrewsbury, he delivered a stinging rebuke, mortified that his star pupil should have lapsed so far in his private conduct, and that his strictures of 1906 had been so disregarded. He called him a knave and a fool, and that his health and his character was being put at risk: 'I'm inclined to think that, in the name of a good many things and people, it's time you decided to find out what's right and did it.' It says something for Patrick that he sent this letter to Dear to read. She approved of it, and felt grateful to Cyril for issuing this reproof. Patrick must learn to control his drinking: 'I would like a man to be master of himself and be able to say I'll take so much and no more.' But she has no doubts about his future, for he has 'that divine spark that sets some men and women above their fellows.' Meanwhile Hester Alington still sought his company, writing from Shrewsbury, 'Come here incessantly please, though it's most undesirable that I should talk often in that strain: you make me singularly wicked somehow.'

Diana's letters at this time get longer and longer. Patrick, who always suffered from bad teeth, would have been particularly struck by her lurid descriptions of dental treatment. First, a visit with her mother to the 'nerve shattering, knee collapsing chair, hung with decorative napkins and surrounded by picturesque jets of gas.' Next, 'after three hours of pain bearable only because of the operator's wonderful personality, I dawned upon the composed world with a mouth full with as many gold bars as the Armada held. I haven't spoken, eaten or smiled since.' And a few days later: 'At this moment I am suffering the paradoxical tortures of the early Christian martyrs. Blast the souls, nerves, roots, gaps of my bloody teeth and as for ten year offers they're as much use as ices in hell.' In the light of her later success as the statue of the Madonna in *The Miracle*, it is interesting to learn that 'I have cultivated a wonderful crying where perfect pear-shaped drops drip silently off an uncontorted face like a Virgin by Memling.'

Diana fed on flattery: 'It's fearful to feel oneself stooping to the lowest weaknesses of my sex and loving flattery and adulation, but it is fun, Patteriga. I believe everyone loves it. Doesn't it please even you to be told you're brilliant and clever, a tigsie of promise etc – it would elate me beyond words, as even to be told I'm liked makes my bones rejoice.' She ends a letter by saying that 'yours are everything to me'. This evokes his enthusiastic reply:

It is flattering and therefore (as you wisely admit) delicious to be told my uncouth, pretentious, pedantic letters are "everything" to anyone – and to *you*, it sends my pulse up to 72 to think of it. Understand once and for all that your letters are like the morning star and eggs and bacon and the Daily Mail rolled into one. "Dark and cheerless is the Morn, Unaccompanied by Thee", as in fact how should it not be, considering the *matter* of your letters is easily the best I get, and the *handwriting* the only one I know that gives me any pleasure in itself – why I don't know, but I *adore* it, it seems to me so like you, somehow, and not to be self-conscious as everyone else's is.

To this she responds:

Patteriga dear, you laid it on pretty thick last letter. Not that I don't like it. Some people take flattery as Hugh takes say a razor or a nail file, but to me its *drink*. There was only one trivial detail that lowered my spirits to the depth of the bottomless, and this was the comparison of my letters to morning stars, eggs and bacon and the DM. Was this complimentary or only a sort of whited sepulchre? I read it first as flashy overbearing, lying and libellous, but I quickly passed to that novel excitement, the sensation of rapture caused by anyone dwelling for more than one unwelcome moment on the subject of my handwriting.

But all this teasing and tantalizing letter-writing with Diana did not yet imply any serious yearning on either side. To Diana Patrick was one of several who delighted her. To Patrick Diana was a fascinating sixteen-year old with whom he could confide in his successes or failures with older aristocratic girls. Indeed, at this time he was exchanging letters with her sister Letty. After his January visit to Belvoir Letty wrote that her father was grumbling at her horsey life, saying she was becoming a hard-hunting fast woman. 'But Patrick, it isn't true, is it? I am depressed, so please quickly write to me again; your last letter has been my only support for a week!!! I think I am ill, I'm off my feed!! All these ills will be cured on receipt of a letter from you.'

The summer term proceeded with the usual punctuations – essays, lectures, debates, dinners – Patrick was by now a member of the Bullingdon Club. He was also now secretary of the Balliol debating club, the Dervorguilla (and was to be so of the Arnold also). The Fourth of June at Eton was a wash-out, and he began to realize that old Eton faces and old Eton places meant less to him, or he to them. But on Staircase 14 the Eton push continued to live it up. Poker was played regularly and seriously: Eddie Marsh was made to join in, though hating it and always loosing, but Patrick, in rasping and ruthless accents decreed, 'Eddie must pay for his keep.' Patrick's rooms had this year been on the first floor, and messing together with him were Julian and Charles.

Although Charles was now sitting for his finals (he had opted for the three year Classical Moderations course, and was to get a First), Julian was often moody and silent, given to melancholy but also to violent altercations. He was a bully, and his targets were usually other upper-class men whom he detected as too smooth or too timid. He notoriously chased Philip Sassoon out of the college, cracking a horse-whip around him. He tried to debag Hastings Tavistock in the street. Even within their mess Patrick later recalled 'a great buffy party which ended in a free fight, and I gave Charles a black eye and Julian knocked me down twice.' Next day all this was forgotten, and Julian and Patrick enjoyed such energetic outings as riding on horseback to Sutton Courtney, getting through two bathes in the river, two games of tennis, two of golf, and riding back. But Julian was heading for a nervous breakdown, seemingly caused by his intense love-hate relationship with his mother. He eyed Patrick suspiciously for his bond with Ettie, and most of all he hated Archie Gordon, her favourite. His younger brother Billy had in April won the Newcastle Scholarship at Eton (though less dramatically than Patrick, as he had already just turned nineteen), and also the top classical scholarship to Balliol, and was due to come up in the Michaelmas Term.

Diana had been to Italy, and Patrick only heard of her return in May by reading an account in the *Daily Mail* of her occupancy of the box of Lady de Grey at a performance of *Traviata* at Covent Garden. Soon after he was granted an audience at Arlington Street 'after five thirty' one day, which did not seem very encouraging. But, as always, she wove her magic, so that Patrick wrote from Balliol a letter more passionate than ever before:

> I wrote in a hurry this morning to say it was a bore not seeing you properly. Now I write at leisure to say so again – and to say that I love you more than anybody in the world and I'm dying to see you and come to Oxford quick quick. This is Saturday night and I'm just a little drunk so don't mind if my phraseology isn't as accurate as usual. But what I mean is that I love you (as I said before) and that you were looking your best yesterday and that you're more beautiful every time I see you, and more wonderful and delicious. And do love me a little, because I love you so much.

But this only brought a reprimand about his drinking, Diana being on higher moral ground because of being prepared for confirmation, even though feeling insincere about religion, a sentiment which she felt Patrick would never understand, 'never having come into contact with that arch-bore sincerity.' So Patrick felt obliged to defend his drinking record. Rumours of the Balliol excesses were greatly exaggerated, often fed by the Balliol bloods themselves, and in his case it was only in his first year that he had drunk too much. Diana accepted this, but remarked 'Do I laugh or weep at you and the world? I leave you to guess.'

The Summer Term concluded with the Commem Balls, Patrick's party amalgamating with that of Tommy Lascelles for a dinner forty strong in Balliol before the Trinity Ball. The summer vacation began in London with balls every night, Patrick nearly always among the clique of girls composed of Marjorie and Letty, Betty and Angy, Cynthia, Viola, and Mima Cecil. Thence to a visit to the Trees at Rottingdean on the Sussex coast, and from there to the summer reading party. This, with Greats on the horizon, was taken seriously, held under the aegis of the austere A. D. (Sandy) Lindsay (the future Master of Balliol) at a farmhouse on the edge of Dartmoor. There followed a progression to Mells, Panshanger, Rowsley and also to Knebworth, the Hertfordshire seat of the Earl of Lytton and his beautiful wife Pamela (who Winston Churchill had once wanted to marry). Then came Scotland at Carnock and Ardgowan, and in September he stayed at Beaufort Castle in Invernesshire, the seat of Lord Lovat. Simon Lovat, Chief of the Clan Fraser, exemplified all the most romantic ideas about a highland chieftain. He was immensely handsome, and had himself raised a regiment, the Lovat Scouts, to fight in the Boer War. Patrick shot a stag, and the house-party attended the Highland Gathering in Inverness. At Rowsley Julian and Billy had also been staying, Julian in vague attendance on Marjorie, and Bunt Goschen on Lettie. But Patrick felt unhappy, convinced that Diana was avoiding him, but 'I kept on loving you more and more.' To this she replied in words that he would have been wiser to remember better:

> I am too miserable, Patrick dear, to have the loathsome thought of your not having been happy here, confirmed. What can I say? Nothing can possibly justify me, except that I was fairly unconscious of being anything different from my heartless 'umble self, and that I've got one of those new marble hearts (which I feel the years will grey and harden, but which I know must finally be melted by a sigh), and that I like you as well (not an atom more) as anybody, and surely you must realize that I'm not so good a woman (I looked pretty plain in the hope that you'd think so), and please you mustn't love me because I am only one of those "Children of Illusion"

Back at Balliol for his final year Patrick now lived in digs outside the college, sharing rooms at 8 Longwall with Julian, Edward, Victor Barrington-Kennett and Paul Methuen. Julian was now becoming impossible, his mood-swings more alarming, and Patrick often had to do his best to keep the peace. In consequence he was more mellow and restrained in his own behaviour. He went over to Taplow and a walk in the woods with Ettie, discussing once again his future. He went to London, seeing Laura (with talk comprising 'simple little jokes') and Katharine Asquith (who wanted the 'Schopenhauer – Machen – Newman – Aristotlesque' level). And he continued to take Inner Temple dinners, usually staying at Eddie's, his host sometimes away, but looked after by his devoted and motherly housekeeper, Mrs Elgy. Eddie similarly entertained other favoured undergraduates, notably Rupert Brooke from Cambridge, who turned up unexpectedly one evening, 'beau comme le jour, αμουοικωτατοζ [a special guest for me] – he once read Paradise Lost at a sitting!'

But now two deaths affected Patrick's life. The first was that of Archie Gordon, who died a lingering death following a car crash. Ettie was heartbroken, and went through the ordeal of sitting at his bedside at the hospital in Winchester, determined to maintain a façade of happiness, and Violet Asquith even became betrothed to the dying man. From now, Patrick was Ettie's closest protégé, a substitute for Archie, and a consolation for what was going wrong with Julian, who had to leave Balliol in December, lying comatose at Taplow for two months, sunk in a severe depression, having composed a series of essays in which he crudely criticised the inherent falsity of Taplow society. He lay for hours on a sofa in his mother's boudoir, gazing into space. The other death was that of Mary, Patrick's mother, who died suddenly of a heart attack in December. It is true that she had played a less important part in Patrick's life than had Dear or his sisters. But he had been a good son to her, and her death affected him.

The Michaelmas Term of 1909 ended in Collections, in which Patrick did well but not brilliantly. He got a qualified alpha in the Logic Paper, considered to be his weakest subject, and in Greek History found that the examiner disagreed with him on almost every point. At the handshaking Sandy Lindsay reported to the

Master: 'Of course, Mr Shaw Stewart thinks nothing of philosophy, but I think he will be very good at it all the same.' So Patrick went into conclave with Edward and Ronald at Mells, cramming in eight hours a day, assisted by the wines from Sir John's cellar. Numerous invitations to stay were refused. It was sickening to have to do this, especially since his friends all said 'Oh, absurd! *You* could do it all in six weeks.' But he did go to Gisburne, once again alone with Lord Ribblesdale and his two daughters, plus 'Zella and a Bohemian music mistress. This time he went out with the Ribblesdale Buckhounds, though missed a pheasant shoot because he overslept. And once again he adored Laura: 'I love her more and more and her beauty is beyond all imagination.' But, of course, he was still ham on the sideboard, virtually part of the family, and next year the nineteen year-old Laura would be married to the thirty-eight year-old Lord Lovat.

Diana was now turning her attention to Greek, the literature that so obsessed her intelligent masculine friends. In June she told Patrick that 'We've practically read Plato [in Jowett's translation], and have voted him, roughly speaking, a failure.' In August she read Homer in Andrew Lang's translation: 'I got so excited, absolutely lived it.' And in September she expressed her determination to learn Greek, though 'it won't last because it's too much for me.' Eddie Marsh spent an afternoon teaching her the Greek alphabet.

Meanwhile the hot-and-cold correspondence with Patrick continued. In November he ended a letter 'I do dislike you – but still.' To which she replies, 'It's a bit uncomplimentary to find you no longer care for me that much, but I always told you that I was a dull and plain as a potato.' Patrick: 'My dear you depreciate yourself most unduly. You have only got to raise the extreme joint of your little finger and at once I am steel to the magnet, rabbit to the rattlesnake, flint to the lodestone, the earth to the sun, the penitent soul to Christ – all that there is of the most helplessly and powerfully pulled.' In December she sent him her judgement of him, though probably not so carefully thought out, since complete insincerity is hardly compatible with absolute sympathy:

Looks, 5; sincerity, 0; loyalty, 8; joie de vivre, 7; company, 9; intellect, 10; figure, 7; capability, 8; endurance, ?; manners, 8; courage, 9 ½; grace, 6; sympathy, 10; cleanliness, 9; eloquence, 10; letter writer, 10; humour, 10; snobbery, 8.

Ettie continued to pour her matronly love over Patrick. In August she wrote: 'How clever you are and how I adore cleverness, and how very golden you are (this ironfounded conviction is all the more valuable in that it is in some quarters regarded as disputable!). For intuition and sympathy, the infallible kind that helps and doesn't jar, you break the thermometer!' But in November came a scolding from the matron:

Now I shall begin with my preoccupation. It is this. Do in the name of anti-young-ass-hood give up SEX conversation. Let us leave all aesthetic and ethical grounds high and dry – there the subject is discutable and we disagree – and let us stick to cynical commonsense material expediency. It does you the most active and irremediable harm. The other day John asked me about it, adding, 'of course, it isn't true?' and that was all right, but who's to answer for next time? (and of course, it's a bore, though this is a negligible issue, that everyone who knows one likes you should think one either a Moll Flanders or an assish dupe) . . . This is the last time I am ever going to utter one word about it, and you don't know how I hate doing it. It is only from a fixed idea that you have no notion how that aspect of you is getting fixed, how materially harmful.

It is hard to equate this with Ettie's evident pleasure at being the recipient of Patrick's confidences in his pursuit of 'the does'. But it seems that her friends were becoming dubious about her exact relationship with Patrick, and that the rumour-mongers were at work. Unlike Pamela Lytton, who received Julian into her bedroom at Knebworth, all the evidence suggests that Ettie was platonic with her young men: she was a flirt, but did not want to go further than that. We do not have Patrick's reply to this stricture, but we may be sure that it was grovelling, begging forgiveness, as was so often the response from all Ettie's men, young or old. All the same, he didn't really mind being the subject of gossip, and in the summer had asked Ettie with pleasurable curiosity: 'How goes my character? don't please be discreet about the identity of the detractors.'

The deaths of Archie Gordon and of his own mother concentrated the minds of Patrick and Diana on the subject of death, when resuming their correspondence in the New Year of 1910. Patrick was firmly of the view that death was succeeded by nothing, and he could only feel 'the lack of those that are gone, and helpless anger that we must follow them into nothingness.' He quotes the sentiment expressed in *The Odyssey* by the shade of Achilles in Hades, that to be the meanest serf is better than to 'rule over all the legions of all that ever died.' All the same, he admits he would like to believe, to 'make a tremendous leap in the dark, the prodigious mental gymnastic, of hoisting one's belief to a nail such as a Personal God.' But this is a feat that he finds himself unable to perform. Nor does he see God in the universe. Diana disagrees completely. She firmly rejects Christian theology, and has no wish to be persuaded of it, but sees immortality in the infinite: 'As to not being capable of grasping the Universe as God and life and love and beauty, well one either knows it instinctively or being faithless resolves to cultivate some creed. Of course one can't explain, but one's understanding cannot possibly have reached its zenith, so why should one want to? Anyway we are not Children of Chance, we cannot go out like candle flames, that I know and you know and therefore it's true.' To this Patrick responds: 'I give up God: it is impossible to continue Him indefinitely on paper: only two things (1) it is precisely the dependent, un-strong man part of one that needs religion – the rest one can take to philosophy, or Paganism like Henley's "Out of the Night" (2) Of course our blessed little intellects aren't fully formed: that's why I distrust mine so utterly: am prepared to wait, suspend judgement on everything that matters, and so am left without a spiritual walking-stick, and the prey to every disaster.'

Mumps now laid Patrick low ('that odious disease whose very name is a laughing stock'). From the first symptom, of his left cheek swelling 'like a mushroom' on 25 January, to the diagnosis a couple of days later, he lay in his room at 8 Longwall, and then learnt that he would be confined there in quarantine for three weeks, followed by a further week's recuperation. Edward evacuated the house, on his mother's insistence. Tats and Pua were in London, and prepared to remain there until his recovery, but he urged them to return north. He grew a beard, which came out auburn, different from his red hair. He continued with his studies on Kant and Tacitus, and read Henry James, Pater, Yeats and *l'Oiseau Bleu*. His bed was surrounded by flowers – pinks from Ettie ('to remind you of out-of-doors sun and summer and sea and pinewoods and sun-grass smells and joys'), lilies of the valley from Ronald, hyacinths, daffodils in pots – and he munched plums and grapes. Diana had had mumps, and was able to give him a graphic account of it: 'The first catch in the neck felt when turning hastily, put down to common stiff neck, then the finding of a walnut just below the jaw, which one fingers untiringly in the belief that it will go in five minutes, and at last the shattering realization of the fact that one's face, that one loves like a mother loves her baby, must rise like yeast for a week, and triumph into zenith for another, and finally sink slowly like a pricked airball for interminable days.' Patrick was soon recovering and, as he told his sister, 'there are no signs *elsewhere*, which is the great thing.'

The question of where to convalesce then arose. Dr Waterhouse recommended the South Coast, the sisters Carnock or Blairdhu, but that was too far for a week. So Patrick opted for a hotel in Brighton. Fearing loneliness, he had an inspiration. He wrote to Eddie Marsh: 'Now look here: of course if you abominate it, and of course you are booked for several Homes – but if you by any chance evade the latter, you would be doing a wonderful charity if you could overcome the former and consent to sharing my salubrious exile.' Eddie extracted himself from a previous engagement in order to accept. He banned a stay at the Metropole, 'which is by all accounts a mere sink of vulgar lechery,' and Patrick suggested they might reduce the expenses by sharing a room 'unless you dislike that and think it compromising.' Much of their conversation was about the Greek verse which Patrick was composing for the Gainsford, and when he submitted it he reported to Eddie: 'I am sorry to say that αλλοτον τινα φγμι [speaking of other things] stood: now that it is irrevocable I know that it will ditch me. The agony of the accentuation (which took me *all* yesterday) was inconceivable.'

Diana's enthusiasm for learning Greek had hardly survived the New Year. Now it was Milton who entranced her, as she read *Paradise Lost* aloud to her sister Marjorie, 'an admirable poem, teeming with Bartlett's quotations.' But

as to the language of the Greeks (if you have tears to shed, refrain till you hear the end) – I've chucked it, not with boredom, or the fact that I have no living soul to help me – nor that because of piano, health and world of household matters overflows the short day – with all this I were practically content – but on thinking it over a whole night long, the conclusion was against it. To begin with I was shunned by most, from the dread of the brain of one who might even tamper with such a scholarly subject as Greek. Then who cares for a girl to know it, except herself. But I shall know it, not now, when I'm young and life is so overbrimming and crowded that there isn't room for a pause or a comma. When a youngish married woman however and désoeuvréness sets in which I imagine it must do, when my husband is conducting his orchestra, or unconfused among dispatches and budgets, or contemplating another picture or ode, or better tilling the earth, then I, after having made a fresh bed of young leaves and herbs, and having mended his bow, or having in the former cases seen the cook and answered begging letters, bending over First Steps, will wait without impatience his return, so absorbed and happy as to be almost unconscious of his absence. Now are you comforted, or do you honestly care a damn either way? Bless you said D.

Patrick was unable to produce any arguments for Diana to persist with First Steps, though he contested her future vision: 'nothing could be more glorious than the vision of a breathless brim-full Bandersnatch sort of youth; nothing on the other hand more hopelessly "of all things cured" than your relentless outlook upon the unemployment of the jeune mariée. I should call it a French novel point of view, were it not that the heroines of French novels don't generally find it necessary to fall back on Homer for the solace of the husbandless hours.'

The remaining weeks of the Lent Term were centered around a serious effort at the Jenks. It was won by Ronald, but Patrick was one of the named top five, so was not disheartened. He was told that the standard of the candidates was the highest in recent years, and that the top five were all very close together. His weakest paper had been for the General Essay, on the subject of the relationship of Art and Truth. Although developing the concept that art, for the beholder, explores the region between experience and ideals, he was deemed to have been too flippant. His best paper (second only to Ronald) had been on Philosophy. Sandy Lindsay believed he was now 'quite safe for Greats.'

The final reading party, again under Sandy Lindsay, was in a farmhouse at Budleigh Salterton in Devon: study throughout the morning, golf and riding in the afternoon, and plenty of good plain food and beer. Patrick shared a room with Edward and talked late into the night, so much so that they were habitually late for the 8.45 breakfast and had to move to another house. They also infuriated a farmer by riding over his crops. This stint in Devon was preceded by a visit to Taplow and parties in London which included a 'political lunch' with A. J. Balfour, at which the conversation was entirely literary and not at all political. The reading party was followed by visits to Gisburne, Belvoir and Carnock. Edward had preceded him at Belvoir and had made advances to Diana, about which she regaled Patrick, pleased to be adding Edward to her 'scalp collection,' which for her still happily included Patrick's. This incurred Patrick's mock despair:

As far as I can interpret, you want Love (love, love, all on an indrawn breath: you are responsible for the introduction of that grave and awful word) to bring to you pure fun and to your victim a sort of spurious gaiety that you can see and enjoy, and an inward misery that you can secretly gloat on. I think it is a delightful programme, and wouldn't rob you of any illusion it contains for the world: but I warn you that unless you put out a little more of yourself you're always liable to produce neither the one nor the other, but only an agreeable titillation. However I think you have (with reasonable care) an excellent chance with me. I may add that I have broken with Laura, floated irrevocably with Viola, and incurred Ettie's wrath. These have all happened simultaneously – how or why I couldn't quite say.

To the concern of her friends Cynthia became engaged to Beb Asquith, whom they considered unworthy of her. In a letter to Patrick responding to his congratulations, she reveals that he had been close to her affections. She wrote that in her friendship with Patrick there had been 'a tacit agreement that I should ultimately make what is called a "good marriage" so that I might be able to provide you with glittering gîtes, good shooting and tiarared routs.' But in now marrying someone who was as impecunious as Patrick, 'your splendid letter made me happier as from it I gathered you were not as angry as you have a right to be.'

In his letters Patrick gives scant attention to the political upheavals resulting from the rejection of Lloyd George's budget of 1909 by the House of Lords. As he told Dear: 'I am, as you know, one of those vulgar people who aren't much good at the subtler issues of politics.' But naturally he was caught up in the universal passion about the General Election of February 1910. The death of King Edward in May at least enabled him to witness some of the drama, for Ettie got him included in those watching the funeral procession from the terrace and windows of Lord Revelstoke's house in Carlton House Terrace. In a letter to his sisters he described the line of terraces packed with figures

RIGHT Patrick aged six with
his mother Mary.

BELOW Patrick's father,
General Jack Shaw Stewart,
spent his army career in
India and was a veteran of
Lord Elgin's Expeditionary
Force in China in 1860. The
General was 57 when Patrick
was born, and remained a
distant and remote figure.

BELOW RIGHT The only
surviving photograph
of Elizabeth Reid, a
stonemason's daughter from
Banffshire. Known as Dear,
she was Patrick's devoted
nurse and he remained close
to her all his life.

The Shaw Stewart children: Basil, Katherine, Winifred and Patrick.

Patrick at Eton in 1902, aged 14.

ABOVE Cyril Alington, Patrick's tutor at Eton and later its headmaster. As well as playing a crucial part in Patrick's academic success, Alington's friendship – and that of his wife Hester – continued long after Patrick left Eton.

ABOVE RIGHT Charles Lister, Patrick's contemporary at Eton and destined to become his closest friend. Charles was the only old friend to serve alongside him at Gallipoli, where he was killed in 1915.

BELOW The editors of *The Outsider*, a light-hearted weekly paper for the Eton community. From left to right: Patrick, Julian Grenfell, Ronald Knox, Robin Laffan, Edward Horner, Charles Gold and Charles Lister. Ronald Knox was later to write the only previous biography of Patrick, published in 1920.

LEFT Patrick whilst at Balliol College, Oxford.

ABOVE The poet Julian Grenfell, a close friend both at Eton and Balliol, who died in France from a wound in 1915.

BELOW LEFT Archie Gordon, another Oxford friend, and who died following a car crash whilst still at Balliol.

BELOW Edward Horner, a friend from Eton and Balliol, killed in action in 1917.

Lady Desborough in her twenties. After Dear, and despite being 20 years older than Patrick, Ettie Desborough was probably the most important woman in his life. Ettie was one of the great Edwardian society hostesses, and Taplow, her house overlooking the Thames above Maidenhead, became Patrick's second home. She was the mother of Julian Grenfell.

Patrick met many of the girls who were to become part of his group of friends whilst staying with Ettie Desborough at Taplow, including: ABOVE LEFT Cynthia Charteries, later Lady Cynthia Asquith; ABOVE RIGHT Laura Lister, Charles's sister and later Lady Lovat; BELOW LEFT Violet Asquith, the daughter of the Prime Minister and later Lady Violet Bonham Carter; and BELOW RIGHT Rosemary Leveson Gower, later Viscountess Ednam.

Lady Diana Manners, aged 20 in 1912, and of his contemporaries the one great love in Patrick's life.

Raymond Asquith and Katharine Horner, who married in 1907. The brilliant eldest son of the Prime Minister, Asquith was killed in action in France in 1916. Diana Manners believed that if Patrick had lived he might have married Katharine, who was Edward Horner's sister and who he had known since Balliol.

ABOVE John Baring, Lord Revelstoke, chairman of Barings and responsible for Patrick's employment in the bank.

BELOW Duff Cooper, Patrick's rival for Diana Manners, who she was eventually to marry.

BELOW RIGHT Winston Churchill aged 33. Patrick first met Churchill at Taplow when he was a junior minister in Balfour's government.

ABOVE Ardgowan, the Renfrewshire home of Patrick's second cousin, Sir Hugh Shaw Stewart. Patrick's visits to Ardgowan marked his initiation into the world of the grand Edwardian country house.

BELOW Vita Sackville West, who Patrick courted in 1912, unaware that she was secretly engaged to the young diplomat Harold Nicolson.

BELOW RIGHT Hermione Buxton, described by Patrick as 'a delicious creature with large melting eyes' and with whom he had a brief affair when a Junior Fellow of All Souls.

Fancy dress balls were a feature of Edwardian country house weekends. Patrick is dressed as Robin Hood with Lady Massareene and Ferrard.

Patrick in the uniform of a Sub-Lieutenant in the Royal Naval Division in the autumn of 1914.

Three of Patrick's fellow officers in the Hood Battalion of the Royal Naval Division, to which Patrick was transferred in the autumn of 1914.

LEFT The composer and musician Denis Browne.

BELOW LEFT The Australian Frederick 'Cleg' Kelly.

BELOW The American Johnny Dodge.

All three served alongside Patrick at Gallipoli, but only Johnny Dodge was to survive the war.

LIEUT. F. S. KELLY,
.V.R. The famous Eton and Oxford man, who won the Diamond Sculls three times. Awarded D.S.C.

Rupert Brooke, photographed in February 1915 at Blandford before the Royal Naval Division sailed to Gallipoli. The author of 'The Soldier' ('If I should die think only this of me') was the first of Patrick's circle to die in the war – from septicaemia following a mosquito bite, and Patrick was amongst the group of friends who helped bury him in an olive grove on the Greek island of Skyros.

ABOVE On leave in Egypt in 1915. *Left to right*: Arthur (Oc) Asquith, Aubrey Herbert, Patrick, Mary Herbert, unknown, Rupert Brooke.

RIGHT Patrick (standing) and Rupert Brooke on board the *Grantully Castle,* the small Union Castle steamer that carried the Hood Battalion to the Dardanelles.

LEFT Bernard Freyberg, the New Zealand born commanding officer of 'A' Company of the Hood Battalion. Freyberg later won the Victoria Cross on the Western Front, ending the war as the youngest general in the British Army. He served with equal distinction in the Second World War. In 1946 he became the first New Zealander to be appointed Governor General of his home country.

RIGHT Arthur (Oc) Asquith, the second son of the Prime Minister, in a Brigadier's uniform in 1918. Asquith was one of Patrick's fellow officers in the Royal Naval Division, serving alongside him both at Gallipoli and on the Western Front, and was one of only a handful of Patrick's group of close friends to survive the war.

all in black, shaded but not obscured by trees, and then after a long wait, the procession, and all the dignitaries preceding and following the coffin, upon which the Crown and Orb glittered and shone. Patrick then went along with Alastair Leveson-Gower to Stafford House (now Lancaster House), where they gobbled down a late lunch, and then walked up St James's Street to 16 Arlington Street, to find the Rutland family who had just finished theirs, the ladies all in enormous black robes 'that seemed to fall over them in straight chunks, almost square.' They had seen the procession from the residence of the Duke of Connaught in St James's Palace, and Diana had managed to purloin the Kaiser's large black-lined visiting card.

As Patrick prepared for the final academic ordeal, he received a knock on, just missing the Gainsford. Diana's response was hardly comforting, as she suggested that perhaps the failure was 'necessary in the eyes of the good, that your work's perfection may be pure and free from a stain of vain glory, caused by success.' But she was comforting about her own opinion of him: 'Quaint that you should know me as little as to think I should despise and have downs on *failure*. Pity and admiration grow and diminish in my heart as circumstance asks. At present Pity towers above A. She is of course bent a little – such a relief after A's perpetual looking up.' Patrick accepted this, agreeing that her pity was not secretly a contempt, even though she was 'not a soft cushiony person but a sharp arrowy one.'

Now came the spurt at the end of the final lap in the preparation for Greats. Ettie's final letter before the exams read: 'Dearest, I do send you such trillions of throbbing wishes and take such pride in knowing what you'll do in these days. Shall think of you *all the time* with gallons of wish-transference and hope. Go to bed early, and do all the dodges on earth for preserving a cold steel brain and iced concentration. *Bless you.*' The cold steel brain proved itself as sharp as ever, and Patrick worked it to good effect throughout the two three-hour papers each day for five days: he got his First – his Double First – one of the examiners later confiding to him that his was exceptionally good. At any rate it ensured his reputation as a first-class scholar. Ronald Knox also got his First. But the other occupant of 8 Longwall suffered a shock. Edward Horner had aimed high in sitting for Greats, and only got a Third. This was considered a tragedy by his friends. It meant that his ability to secure a profitable position in the law or in finance was greatly reduced. The condition of the Horner estate at Mells was parlous in the extreme, and his parents had seen him as the son who would be able to retrieve it from insolvency. However, of the twenty First Class Honours in Greats awarded by the University in 1910, six had been won by Balliol men.

Others fell by the wayside. George Fletcher and Victor Barrington-Kennett, both former Eton Collegers at Balliol (and the former a Captain of the School), and both to die in the War, only sat for Honour Mods and only got Thirds. The Marquess of Tavistock got a fourth. Meanwhile Julian, since his return after his nervous breakdown, had only aimed for a Pass Degree, which he duly got. Fortunately the results of these examinations were only made known after the viva voces in July, so the enjoyment of the summer dinner of the Annandale, of which Patrick was now the President, was unclouded.

SIX

The Junior Fellow of All Souls

Two bachelors were in constant attendance on Ettie, standing like heraldic supporters on either side of the throne on which she sat. One was Evan Charteris, a parliamentary lawyer, an aesthete, a man of great kindness though of short temper, and the uncle of Patrick's Charteris friends. The other was John Baring, Lord Revelstoke, chairman of Baring Bros, the great merchant bank, presiding over its fortunes from its premises in Bishopsgate. Under the chairmanship of his father Barings had become insolvent in 1890, provoking a major banking crisis, and John Baring had over the years brought it back to profit by means of extreme caution, suited to his extremely cautious temperament. It was in the summer of 1909 that Ettie first put to Patrick the idea that he might be taken on by Barings. As he told Dear, she had reported that John Revelstoke had taken notice of him at a dinner party. He was looking for a young man to become a partner, and had apparently considered Raymond Asquith ('but something had prevented that'), and her son Billy; but she had for long intended Billy to enter the Law, and Julian to enter the Army.

Ettie was unsure whether this would be the right thing for Patrick, pointing out that an acceptance would have to be wholehearted, and could not be regarded as a stepping-stone to politics in the way that being a barrister could be. But for his part he was thrilled by the thought and 'nearly jumped out of the taxi with excitement.' He appreciated the hazards – he might be no earthly good at finance and be cast out a couple of years later – but the glamour of an unlimited salary at an early age for 'an obscure boy without interest' was immense, and he was confident in his power to apply his brain to new things. No immediate decision was necessary because he would only finish at Oxford a year later, but from now on Patrick pondered this idea, weighing in his mind the advantages of possibly earning great sums of money, against possibly achieving a glittering career in public life. Another consideration was that Lady Shaw Stewart's sister Katherine had married Lord Cromer, another Baring peer, and so she would certainly support the banking alternative. Cromer may well have endorsed Lord Revelstoke's offer.

Victory in the Schools in June 1910 impelled the moment of decision about Barings. As with the question of whether to leave Eton in December of 1906, Patrick sought the views of the most important people he knew, in this case notably Arthur Balfour and Richard Haldane, the Secretary of State for War. Both of these were emphatic that it was too good a chance to miss. Haldane, though himself a lawyer, expressed in his expansive way that 'the improbable possibilities of the Bar may be better than the improbable possibilities of Barings, but the probable possibilities of Barings are the best.' Even Cyril Alington conceded it was the right plan, though Hester added 'don't get pompous and horrid will you?' And Eddie Marsh endorsed it, though really believing that Patrick should have remained in academia – 'Oh dear, oh dear, you were my only hope.' Raymond Asquith approved, alleging that it would eliminate a formidable future competitor to him at the Bar.

So Ettie arranged for Patrick to have a quiet word at Taplow with John Revelstoke, which took place on 5 July. The great man naturally said nothing of the possibilities but merely suggested a clerkship at £80 a year, perhaps developing into something like £600. He did however concede that Patrick need not start till the New Year. This would enable him to sit for the All Souls scholarship in October. Confirmation of the offer came in the following month. Ettie was exultant: 'It is glorious news. Bishopsgate is yours if you want it – over Edom shall you cast your shoe.' Patrick expressed his gratitude for the career which she had put in his lap: 'The thanks can only be lived (a) by a life of beautiful dedication in the City (b) if it were possible, by tightening and heightening of the dog-like affection which binds me to your feet.'

The seven-year Prize Fellowships of All Souls had been established in 1881 as a means of attracting a wider spectrum of men into a non-undergraduate college. They were usually confined to two each year, and attracted the most academically brilliant of those who had just graduated at the University. Their limited tenure attracted those who did not intend to remain academics, and no academic work was at this time required, though encouraged. As a result they had included many men who had risen to the most senior positions, especially in the law and the church. These Fellowships were particularly highly regarded by the Liberal ascendancy, and by Balliol. Patrick was uncertain whether to apply, since to apply and fail would in a way be worse than not to apply at all. His main difficulty was that Modern History was an important part of the exam, and he knew very little about it beyond a few hours study when at Eton. The alternative would be to spend a couple of months learning French really well, but Lord Revelstoke had said that he could pick this up 'in house', and encouraged the attempt at All Souls.

So it was back to months of further study, and these began with another reading party at Brancaster, from where he wrote to Diana: 'I have given your love to Saltings, to the Hermitage, to the bathing machine, to the golf course, to the Enchanted Island, to the Rectory (rather faintly) and to Mr Large – to everything except this singularly unromantic edifice and its inmates.' These three other crammers were characteristically dismissed by Patrick for not being within his inner circle of friends. They were intelligent, and were giving 'crisp and humorous views on Impressionism and Art.' But they were 'uninspiring and alien.' There had followed 'a rather shy-making discussion on morality,' in which he had to disguise the fact that he was 'much wickeder than them, really.'

After some time at Carnock in incessant rain, Patrick once again stayed at Rowsley, one among several guests who included George Curzon. To his irritation this precluded moments alone with Diana, though she did drive with him to the station at Sheffield, 'looking like an angel on my inverted suitcase.' She accused him of not working hard enough for All Souls, and he agreed. Yet he wanted it badly. It was during this visit that Marjorie Manners drew her profile of Patrick. According to Eddie Marsh, she found his nose so exceptionally long that, as her pencil went farther and still farther down the paper, she became 'almost frightened'. It was admired by all, and she presented it to Patrick. From this sketch we can well imagine Patrick's exceptional appearance, with his white face, pale freckles, red hair, and ice-blue eyes.

For Patrick the main event was now a second visit to Beaufort Castle for the Northern Meeting. This time the great difference was that Laura had become engaged to Lord Lovat. Patrick, with sentiments similar to those of Eugene Onegin, found her 'vastly improved with betrothal' – efficient, lucid and capable (a sentiment he was also to apply to Laura's sister Diana when she became engaged in 1913 – 'I wish I hadn't underestimated her in bygone years: I was mistaken in my judgements'). He enjoyed it all enormously – the pipers playing at dinner, the informality of dress, the vast house-party, the reeling, the grouse shooting, the stalking, and only regretted that he had never worn a kilt. But there was also a new excitement: he fell in love with a married woman.

Among those assembled for the balls, but in another house-party, were the daughters of the Earl of Verulam, Lady Sybil and Lady Hermione. Sybil was destined to marry Lord Lovat's brother Alastair Fraser, but Hermione was already married to a naval officer, Bernard Buxton. She was seven years older than Patrick, who told Dear that he found her 'a delicious creature with large melting eyes and a fund of wickedness.' She beat him at golf, and in the evenings there were 'more reels, more suppers, and more Lady Hermione.' A chance encounter on the train when leaving Beaufort provided an opportunity for further acquaintance, and a letter to 'Dear Mr Shaw Stewart' soon arrived, asking for recommendations for books to read during her 'prolonged sojourn' in Norfolk. He proposed to visit her there for the day, but she emphasised the distance, and 'likewise you would probably run into the lusty naval officer on the platform here.' But he did go and stay in October, he told Pua, in 'the smallest house I ever was in, with the minimum room for her and two infants. I hope the naval officer won't be after me with a thick stick.' The animated conversation included the pleasant prospect that she should teach him to ride really well, whilst he should teach her Greek.

Brushing these and other social distractions aside, Patrick sat for the All Souls election in late October. When the result was declared, on All Saints Day, he found he had succeeded, in second place to Douglas Radcliffe (one of the unsuccessful candidates being T. E. Lawrence). He was genuinely surprised: as he told Ettie, it seemed incredible that 'a professedly historical prize should be capable of being given to someone who had read history sketchily for some three months, over those who had lived it for four years.' Indeed, he was told that the form of his papers was better than the matter. He was not alone in this, however, for during these years the victors were often those who had graduated in Greats, their ability to define crucial issues lucidly being more impressive than the detailed knowledge of the historians.

He also felt lucky at succeeding in the aspect of the election which involved dining with the Fellows. This was a test that had failed several young men, notably Hilaire Belloc, who had ruined his chances by his over-confident pontificating. Patrick was aware that stories of his drinking and gambling and relentless social life were known to the Fellows, spread, he suspected, by Raymond's lurid description of them, which might well have prejudiced some of them against him. So his triumph is indicative of his charm, which had so seduced his masters at Eton and dons at Balliol and, in this case also, the Warden of All Souls himself, Sir William Anson. Violet Asquith, in congratulating him, wrote, 'There is an absence of variety about your career which the seeker after contrasts, the unexpected, light and shade etc, must deplore.' Cyril Alington suspected he would waste his time there: 'You can't write a book, can you? And in spite of your theory that you have leanings to learning for its own sake, I am inclined to doubt it.'

The provisions of his Fellowship required residence in college for the first three terms, one of which must be continuous, the other two containing 28 nights each. At first Patrick envisaged residing fully for the first term, and then for the other two for the three nights of Fridays to Mondays, whilst working a rather truncated timetable at Barings, a programme that would have shut him out of many parties, especially at weekends. But later in the month he went, at Ettie's suggestion, to see Lord Revelstoke (now referred to as 'The Chief'), who agreed to a retarded start at Barings. Patrick would join the firm on 1 June 1911. 'So that is settled, thank Heaven – my first City coup – and I have two slack terms and two large vacs ahead of me before the gulf yawns,' he told his sister. Meanwhile he settled in, feeling very much the new boy again, very shy and very reverent to the Fellows ('elderly men with distinguished faces and warm moist hands'). As the Junior Fellow (or 'Screw') he had to perform menial offices like making the salad and decanting the port, and was obliged to attend morning chapel regularly. He envisaged learning some French and continuing with the Bar exams. Indeed, this he did so effectively in early November that he was, again to his surprise, awarded the Eldon Scholarship, worth £200 a year for three years, intended to help the most promising of those reading for the Bar. This posed a problem, since he had already accepted for Barings. But the Warden of All Souls, who was one of the Eldon examiners, rather disreputably urged him not to reveal this, and to accept at any rate for the first year. Lord Revelstoke, in private conversation, had told the Warden to let Patrick be aware of the 'vast potentialities' for him at Barings, thus endorsing the presumption that he was being groomed for a directorship.

His last excursion before this allegedly monastic life was to a big party at Taplow, with Mr Balfour, Lord Milner and the Chief all present. (Julian was about to leave for India to join his regiment, the Royal Dragoon Guards, subsequently moving with them to South Africa.) But even during this first term at All Souls, Patrick managed to get away for the occasional night. He went again to stay with Hermione (now 'Mione'), though in a letter to his sister he disparaged her poverty. A night in London began with dinner with Douglas Radcliffe and his family, then to an early dance, then to a late one given by the Duchess of Marlborough. And of course he went to Eton, playing the Field Game in a scratch team against College. When the term ended he went to Knebworth, and thence to Carnock. Lady Alice had wanted the entire Carnock household to spend Christmas at Ardgowan, but Patrick was firm in his intention to be with the Lovats; though in the event found himself alone there with the newly married couple, feeling rather unwanted. The marriages of several of his friends brought small children in their wake. Patrick wrote that by sheer practice he was getting pretty good with them, but 'my heart will never be in it,' whilst Diana confided 'I'm no good at tiny tots.'

The New Year opened with a further round of country house visits. At Panshanger Patrick was able to shine at the shoot ('I was *excellent*') and on the dance floor ('not having danced for months, I took to the floor with childish glee'): in truth, he was only a moderate shot, though an accomplished dancer. At this dance he found Hermione's unmarried sisters, and next day borrowed the Horners' motor to drive over to see her at her father's house at Gorhambury: 'I found myself in the midst of a vigorous Cambridge push and compelled to *play hockey* in my Sunday best. That's what comes of having athletic flirtations.' The athletic Hermione was off to join her husband in Gibraltar for a period of leave from his posting with the Atlantic Fleet. Patrick went to see her off at Victoria Station, though she considered such attention superfluous and deplored 'working oneself into spurious emotion.' She lent him her mare, Lisette, for use in hunting around Oxford, together with a groom and a long letter of practical instructions. He made less use of Lisette than he had imagined in his initial enthusiasm, and had her delivered to Hermione's sister by the end of the term.

But he describes one day's hunting in a letter to Dear:

> We went bravely out with the Drag Hounds (who were trying to hunt a fox, but failing to find one fell back on the red-herring) and were fairly successful. Fairly, because I took two crashing "voluntaries" (one in a ditch and one on my back) and then in achieving a *gigantic* jump broke my left stirrup leather. By the time an intelligent yokel had repaired it for me (three holes shorter, so that I rode knees under chin like a jockey) the field was several counties away so I finished very quietly along the road. I am almost tempted to repeat the performance.

In February he attended Letty Manners' wedding to Hugo Charteris, though in the evening Diana, having suggested he join her at a small family dance, stood him up, and he arrived at Arlington Street 'panting with anticipation at 10.45, drawing on my new white gloves and suddenly running my nose against the banged barred and bolted courtyard door.' This rebuff in no way diminished his longing for her: 'Oh, I am so terribly fond of you, it is bad luck on me, isn't it – you high, far off unsatisfying phantom "child of illusion" – *yes*.' He also attended a fancy-dress ball at the Albert Hall dressed as a revolutionary, with blue blouse, wide trousers, orange socks, two-foot pipe and worsted cap; stayed till 6.0 am; and next day at Oxford rode a horse and ran along the towpath in support of the Balliol Torpid boat.

From All Souls he reported to his sister: 'I continue to live in the greatest idleness, making progress in nothing except expenditure – not even in Spanish. As for my French it goes steadily backwards. I shall just have to wait till I'm planted out in Paris (or Marseilles!). As for the law, it bores me so that I can't open it. London is not infrequent – I'm going there tonight to dine with Ettie (*very* quietly, black tie and waistcoat) and then perhaps to a ball, if I'm asked.' But college life was not without its excitements. At the Shrove Tuesday Feast, so he told Dear:

> The Solicitor General enjoyed his dinner so much that on

coming out of the Common Room he walked into the door instead of through it and got the most priceless black eye. However he returned with it bandaged up, and deceived ten Fellows running with the three card trick (I was one). Lang sang the Mallard Song (national anthem of All Souls) and others sang other things, also we played divers gambling games. All this till 12 o'clock, when we returned to Hall, ate oysters and beer, and the Junior Fellows had to run a race round the Hall over all the chairs. I won, as I shoved Douglas Radcliffe over in the first lap – he broke a chair in his fall, and I afterwards in trying to catch up. But he beat me in cock-fighting (which we had to do afterwards) by two rounds to one. Afterwards all the reverend Fellows set themselves to tug-of-war along the table, cat and mouse, and other boisterous games: a most remarkable sight.

At the end of term Lord Curzon invited Patrick to a smart elderly party at his house at Hackwood, he being the only unmarried guest. He was driven down by the Waldorf Astors, and found, among others, the Russian Ambassador (Count Benckendorf), Sir Edgar Vincent, and Lady Lytton. Also present was Nancy Astor's sister, Phyllis Brooks, over from America. He attended the dance in London given by Ettie for Monica, which had to be arranged very quietly because Willie Desborough's mother had just died. Then it was Carnock and then Belvoir, preparing for the Bar Exam on Constitutional Law. Relying on his usual last minute spurt, Patrick absorbed a cramming book in the morning train from Belvoir and did without breakfast or lunch before entering the examination hall at 2.0 pm. He duly passed the exam, though with only an undistinguished Third, which was all he had aimed for.

For the Easter Vacation Patrick had planned to go to Spain with Edward Horner. But Edward ran out of money, and was unexpectedly firm in refusing to borrow from him. Edward was now working in Freshfields the solicitors, and loathing it; indeed, as Charles Lister wrote to Patrick, 'I can't see him in a solicitor's office unless he was there to borrow money or sell the family estate.'

Edward himself compared his life to that of 'a Whig nobleman who had lost in London at cards,' and went on 'Oh! I do hate not going to Spain, and Roman Law, and the transitory nature of the feeling of love and not being the eldest son of a duke!' Instead, Patrick was asked to join a party going to Portugal and Spain. This was headed by the Duke and Duchess of Wellington and their daughter Eileen Wellesley, and by Mrs Hamlyn and her niece Betty Manners. They were accompanied by Charlie Meade and two other men, and at Lisbon they all expected to be entertained by Mervyn Herbert, who was in the British Legation. The Chief approved of the trip, as helpful to Patrick's Spanish, though there was no chance of learning Spanish in Portugal. They all sailed to Lisbon in a German steamship, and once there saw the sights and went out to Cascais and Bussaco. They went to the bull fight, and afterwards were taken by Mervyn to see the matador in his hotel, who conversed in fluent French and showed them his ceremonial clothes.

The group wanted to linger in Lisbon, so Patrick decided to leave them by going on alone to Seville and rejoining them in Gibraltar. He also intended to see Hermione in Gibraltar. He had received letters from her before he left England, couched in her usual robust style: 'I wonder what's the matter with you. I thought about you all yesterday. *Hope* you haven't broken your stupid neck'; and 'How is my Lisette? Have you ridden bare back? Have you hunted?' The train to Seville was clean, comfortable and punctual, though slow, but he arrived there in the evening of the Thursday of Passion Week:

> The porter and cabby were apparently in the pay of a hostelry called the Cisna y Francia, and proceeded to carry me off thither. Half way we were stopped by men with drawn swords who commanded us to dismount. With extraordinary alacrity my coachman and boy leapt down, seized my baggage and began to *run* with it through small alleys. I asked them why. They said 'Porque el Senor Jesucristo esta muerto' – no carriages allowed in the city after sundown on the Thursday.

Their selection was chock full. They then fell back on a horrible hole next door called the Cuatro Nationes where an odious man demanded 40 pesetas.

Eventually he got the room (really 'a small hole in the roof') at the exorbitant price of 35 pesetas (the equivalent of 30/-). Determined to get out as soon as possible, he tried but failed to catch the train to Gibraltar next day, and sought help from the British Consul. The Consul, greatly impressed by mention of the Duke of Wellington, gave Patrick lunch and got him a seat for the processions. But he had to spend another expensive night in Seville.

Hermione was indeed there in Gibraltar, and so was her husband: 'I've seen her Naval Officer for the first time. I'm bound to say he's terribly attractive. I always fall a victim to husbands! eg Simon (Lovat). A fatal habit of mine, the sure sign of the echt tame cat.' Bernard Buxton also liked Patrick, remarking to Hermione 'Chap's got a fine head,' though probably aware that, when it came to handsome looks, he would clearly outclass Patrick. Patrick put up at the Grand Hotel, and with the Buxtons went out riding on polo ponies along the sands, and went to the races. There was also a ball, at which Patrick danced so much with Hermione that there was 'a slight flutter in garrison circles.'

The ducal party had decided to miss Gibraltar, so Patrick rejoined them in Granada. Here he and Charlie Meade stayed in a good hotel, while the Wellingtons were in a house thirty miles out, on part of the Duke's extensive Spanish estates. But, anxious for Eileen to have a good time, they drove in to Granada every day to be with the two young men. Patrick found the parents 'great dears, both of them,' and Eileen 'nice though spoilt and exacting.' As to Betty Manners, who Patrick thought a rather plain girl, in Lisbon Mervyn Herbert had proposed to her, but been refused. Patrick then returned home by train, stopping in Paris to see Alan Parsons and Bunt Goschen who were ensconced under the strict regime of Jeanne de Hénaut for the purposes of perfecting their French for the Foreign Office exams. Edward Horner was unable to join him there, due to a fall out riding.

Diana had also been in Paris with her mother, and wrote to Patrick from the returning cross-Channel steamer. The eligible Frenchmen had in no way impressed her: 'They aren't worth smiling or spitting at, and they know it, so beg for it. They have the names of kings, and progressing pilgrims, ie, Murat, Bourbon, Orleans, Bon Vouloir, Sanscoeur etc, and they aren't fit to *serve* even the Murgatroyds, Thorneycrofts, or Philpotts.' However, she had 'lunched with Bernstein on opium cakes, in satin and lacquer rooms, hung with undisputably post impressionist.' And she had 'watched for hours Maud Cunard asking the company whether T Beecham's beard, just then so lovingly enclosed in her hand, should remain or be shaved.'

The final weeks of his time at Oxford approached, in which he had to register his twenty-eight nights of residence during the summer term. He restricted himself to one London ball a week. At one of these Pavlova danced, and Patrick and Ettie sat on the floor in front of the front row of seats, after which Patrick and Diana were detailed to sit at the supper table of Prince Arthur of Connaught, and amuse him. But in return for an entire week's abstention from London he was able to go there three times in the following week, in which he attended five balls. A hectic letter to Ettie reads: 'Will you be my partner at the cotillon on Monday? *please*. Tell me quickly at All Souls. I shan't sleep till I know. And will the Derby's ball next night be good, good enough to stay for without a dinner-party?' As he wrote to Katharine Asquith, 'I wish I were better adapted to the cloister life of All Souls: I'm not really, though I have always claimed and pretended to be. I can't work when I'm not driven to it, nor read when I haven't someone unacademic to *relever* my books with.'

He also went to stay again with Hermione in Norfolk, this time in a small house she was renting in Overstrand, near Cromer. The Lusty Naval Officer was not going to be there. She told him, 'It's the comickest house – one rambling passage – in sequence drawing-room, dining-room, my room, bathroom, kitchen, your room.'

And she had a request: 'Can I prevail on you to carve off your hair at the back, quite short, to let me see the shape of your head? Rather a lot to ask – you might make something by selling the locks as pincurls, momentoes etc.' The visit was clearly a success, recorded in verse by Hermione:

> Why! Since you went in outward form
> Where distance hides from view,
> Have all my ways been haunted by
> A pertinacious iew?
> Your wraith upon my footstool sat
> Between me and the fire,
> Your head leant down against my chair
> Your hand crept even nire.
> A north-west wind blew o'er the cliff
> Cold wreaths of mermaids' hair,
> White flying curls, which brought to mind
> Last time when you were thair.
> Drat you!

Writing to Patrick afterwards she tells of mixed views of him among her friends: one said he was awfully nice, another that he was devilish and cold hearted. For herself, 'I have watched you myself take a set-back, and it amused me to see your hackles stand on end one second, then smooth down from the habit of the sage and the persifleur. From this I argue you're the same in heat as the rest, only your tongue is more mendacious and moutarde.' Later in the year Hermione provided a vivid description of Patrick in full conversational flight: 'You've such a perfect delivery, and your voice is unequalled when you're making a point and your chin dives into your collar behind the pugilistic tie, knees straight, heels on the carpet and eyes riveted on toes upturned – it's sensational!.' And also, 'You detonating from your chair, me sitting crushed in mine.'

SEVEN

A Social Figure at Barings

ON TUESDAY 6 JUNE 1911 Patrick put on his white shirt with paper cuffs, his stiff collar, his pinstripe trousers, short black coat and bowler hat, and took the tube to the Bank to arrive at Barings at 8 Bishopsgate at 9.15 am. Baring Brothers was the oldest bank in the City of London, and one of the most pre-eminent British financial institutions. From its original business in trading in commodities and accepting bills, it had risen to the issuing of large loans, notably to foreign governments. The business had grown to extraordinary heights. In time, this had led to an over-commitment in Latin America, specifically in Argentina. Barings agreed to finance the ambitious schemes for the waterworks and drainage system of Buenos Aires, schemes which were riddled with incompetence and corruption. The public failed to support the venture, and Barings was left having to make enormous payments without any certainty of where the money was to come from. Being then a partnership, with unlimited liability, failure would have meant the ruination of the partners. In November 1890 the then Chairman, Lord Revelstoke (father of the present Chairman) had had to go to the Governor of the Bank of England to plead for loans to rescue the stricken bank. Such was the importance of Barings that this provoked a financial crisis that rocked the City of London. The Bank of England decided to save Barings, with the support of City banks, notably Barings' rival Rothschilds. The partners had to pay a price for this, and sell much of their property, but they were not ruined. Barings then formed a limited liability company, Baring Bros and Co Ltd, which became its trading vehicle, and some of the Partners became its Directors.

This shock had a profound effect on Barings, which thereafter pursued a policy of great aversion to risk in their work in forming international syndicates of banks to underwrite bond issues. Twenty years after the crash they had paid off all their debts and made handsome profits: in 1909 the bank declared a profit of £600,000. This policy was manifested in the personality of the present Chairman. John Baring (who inherited his father's title of Lord Revelstoke in 1897) was autocratic and vain, but with good sense and wide knowledge, and above all, cautious. He spoke excellent Spanish, good French and passable German and Italian. A bachelor of fastidious habits, he lived in great luxury with houses in London and Paris, and travelled on the Continent widely in the pursuit of business. He also looked after the investments of several important people, including the royal couple who became King and Queen in 1910. Some of his friends (including Ettie Desborough) were on his Red List for preferential allocations in promising new issues. In 1909 he himself received £100,000 from Barings.

Of the other Managing Directors in 1911, one was Revelstoke's uncle Tom Baring, who had made his career in New York, and another his brother Cecil Baring, an eccentric, a naturalist and a classicist (but not his other brother, the likewise eccentric and literary Maurice Baring). The two sons of his cousin the Earl of Cromer were in the firm, the younger, Windham Baring the Director resident in Buenos Aires, and the elder, Viscount Errington, a diplomat, who had just joined. These family members were supported by four non-family Directors, of whom the most significant were Alfred Mildmay and Gaspard Farrer. Farrer was a man with great experience in American finance, especially in railroads, and a genius with figures and the shaping of balance sheets. In 1911 the directors were not excessively old, Lord Revelstoke himself being forty-eight. But he could detect a problem of succession. He himself had only two infant nephews, and of the wider family, although Lord Ashburton had a thirteen-year-old son, Alexander Baring, only Windham Baring appeared as yet as a potential Chairman. The family must retain control, but excellent new men, loyal to the house and trained and trusted by them, must be found. Hence his hopes for Patrick Shaw Stewart.

Patrick now began his months of apprenticeship, dull work doing clerical jobs in the various departments, with much double-accounting into ledgers and endorsing of bonds and shares, while also being taught the trade. Gaspard Farrer reported that the partners found him 'charming, very modest and gentle, anxious to learn and, needless to say, extraordinarily intelligent.' He applied himself to this with his usual assiduity, the only problem being to arrive on time after dancing till 4.0 am. Already he planned the three weeks holiday that he had secured. This time it would be nearly all in Scotland, with the family at Ardgowan and Carnock, but with several grand house parties also. He ordered a full dress kilt, in the 'old' Stewart tartan, with jacket and an outsize sporran, and a smart suit for grouse-shooting, and borrowed a gun from Edward. Thus equipped, he took the train up north, stopping on the way at Gisburne with Lord Ribblesdale. Among the others there was Tommy Lascelles, who records in his diary that he for the first time had a good talk with Patrick, and improved relations with him. (He also records that Patrick was sleeping in the Oliver Cromwell Room, said to be haunted, especially on the night in question – 3 September – when Cromwell had slept there.)

At Ardgowan he found Hugh Godley and Venetia Stanley, he in melancholic pursuit of her: 'In purely masculine society there's no one I like so much – sympathetic pointful charming appreciative, and with the hypochondriac undercurrent just protecting him from that fatal hearty smoking-room manner that besets so many good men.' At Carnock he got a man to teach him more of the Scottish reels, and thus equipped appeared in his round of parties. First it was with the Duchess of Portland in Invernesshire, then with the Asquiths at Archerfield (where Violet found him 'unflaggingly vital and responsive'), and then to the Duchess of Sutherland at Dunrobin.

Despite recent sales of property, particularly in Staffordshire, the Duke of Sutherland was still the largest landowner in Britain.

His Duchess, Millicent, was a remarkably active and committed woman: strikingly beautiful, an organizer of charities, and a notable hostess, especially in London at Stafford House. However, perhaps busy on more important matters, when organizing this house party of young people for her daughter Rosemary, she failed to assemble young men as escorts for Rosemary and the other girls. Already at Dunrobin, in the absence of several men who had failed to arrive, Patrick was hard put to entertain several girls assembled there, conducting the whole party to the Gillies' Ball and dancing with them one by one. But at the Inverness Ball of the Northern Meeting, to which they all proceeded in the private ducal train, it became farcical. The party for the two nights of dancing now consisted of eight girls, three mothers, one married woman, and four men.

> You should have seen Ettie's face when the composition of the party slowly dawned upon her – *She* of course could have got ten men in two days if she'd been told – and the frigid fury of the Duchess of Portland whose wretched daughter adorned the wall most of both nights. You can imagine I had my difficulties. No doubt it is delightful to have the proportions like that, but it makes one's every action so awfully marked. How could I dance six times with Rosemary and have a good long supper with Ettie when I knew there was a long row of wretched damsels waiting in the far corner for me to select one, less still could I go out of the party.

After this Patrick went to a shooting lodge near Invermoriston in Invernesshire to stay with the Earl and Countess of Plymouth, being met at the pier on Loch Ness by two sumptuous cars, one for himself and one for his bags and presumed servant. This lodge, Ceannacroe, proved to be 'exactly like the Ritz, plumped down in the wilderness.' Here the gender distribution was reversed, there being more men than women, for the purpose of the house party was stalking, not dancing. A sense of rather tragic romance pervaded the party. Tommy Lascelles, who had just failed for the

Foreign Office, was ineffectually pursuing Diana Lister, and Phyllis Windsor-Clive and Sybil Brodrick were sighing for absent lovers. But Lady Plymouth much impressed him, with her pronounced drawl, 'it takes her about 30 seconds between word and word.' Tommy was the hero of the hour in killing a stag, catching a salmon and shooting a grouse all in one day. But Patrick's one day out on the hill was in pouring rain:

> It rained solid the entire day from twelve onwards. At that hour I was squatting on a barren hillside with the damp just beginning to get well established through the seat of my knickers, and a beautiful stag (which I made intermittent ineffectual efforts to see through the stalker's telescope) was squatting opposite half a mile away and refusing to move. "He's still lying yet" was the bulletin each half hour. At last he rose about 3.30 pm. I was then asked if I would mind crawling. I was past minding anything, so we had a very nice crawl for slightly more than an hour through a frozen bog till we were 400 yards off, at which moment the wind changed on us, and off went the stag and all his damned silly hinds to the back of beyond. We then walked eight miles home in persistent rain. So much for the finest sport in the world.

The main restriction for a City clerk, as opposed to a barrister, was that Saturday mornings were counted as normal office hours. And sometimes the clerks had to work late in connection with new issues: for the second issue of the Oregon-Washington loan in early December, Patrick put up at the Liverpool Street Hotel to work round the clock. But occasionally he got away for a full weekend, as for instance in November to stay for a shoot with the Stanleys at Alderley in Cheshire, slinking off on Friday at 4 pm and returning to London at 4 am on the Monday. He also continued to sit for the Bar Exams, studying Criminal Law in the evenings – real work after the nominal work of the day. In October he did a spell in Commercial Credits, and after that was set to understudy the Head Clerk. He was lodging with Edward Horner, but on the look out for a house to rent or buy.

Diana had had her first season: 'Patrick how I loved those three vampire months in London; how far from the Brahms level I sunk, and to what depths of dance-love, dew-drop slavery, and crowned-head worship did I fall. I am afraid our several Baring and world-débuts have tarnished our gold minds, but lawks! it was a primrose path of glorious dalliance.' In September she found herself alone at Belvoir with her father, pitying the moon seen through tobacco dimmed windows 'rising utterly wasted without me to background.' She reflected: 'Sometimes I long to be a man, and hear mad claps from an appreciating multitude. But alas the longing doesn't last long, there is no joy so lazy and delicious as to find one is a woman who *depends*, though the highest she can do must be too subtle for universal praise.' She was planning a party at Belvoir in the New Year, with her parents away. Patrick urged her to 'lay in a good stock of ducals' for it. But if it were to be mid-week, he could not be there, unless to perform 'that most brilliant of all the fever blooded feats of my youth – to come for the evening and leave at 7.0 am sans sleep.'

The social circles in which Patrick moved were uninhibited in making disparaging remarks about Jews, a racial taunt to be added to their outspoken comments about others on the grounds of class. Their anti-semitism was often a question of the robust parlance of the day, just as many English men and women made dismissive remarks about the French, Germans and Spaniards, referred to as Frogs, Krauts, and Dagos. But it was also often vicious in preventing the appointments of Jews who would in all other respects be qualified for positions in commerce or membership of clubs, and Barings certainly saw themselves as a non-Jewish company, in contrast to Rothschilds. In this context, it is interesting to learn of Patrick's intervention in the All Souls' election of new Fellows in 1911. Each Fellow had a vote, as he described in a letter to Viola Tree: 'We elected three miserable specimens, but no one jolly was in; and anyhow, by the strenuous efforts of me and one or two others, the election of a Polish Jew from Balliol, much the strongest candidate really, was prevented.' The rejected candidate was L. S. B. Namier, who was to become the foremost historian of British politics in the eighteenth century. Although All Souls until this time had no overtly Jewish Fellows, other colleges already did. That this blackballing should have succeeded in what was regarded as the most intelligent of the colleges, and promoted by a Prize Fellow who had been appointed for his outward-looking and worldly ambience, is noteworthy – and casts little credit on Patrick. (Three years later, on the election of a new Warden, Patrick in a letter to Raymond Asquith wonders which candidate he will have the greatest pleasure in blackballing).

During the first months of 1912 Bishopsgate was now warily watching the potential for loans to the Balkan countries in the context of the war between Turkey and Italy, as well as to Latin American countries and to China. Patrick was now advising his brother and sisters on their investments, making full use of his insider knowledge. In February he took responsibility for Barings' French Accounts in the absence of the director who normally controlled them. His assiduity and intelligent involvement in the various banking activities that were put before him evidently overrode concern about his habitual unpunctuality. In April he wrote to his sister from a train on a Monday morning: 'O such a row as there's going to be! The nice brisk 8.30 from Yeovil that I got leave to come by not running – and instead a crawler of an 8.41 that has stopped at every station and is over as hour late – and it's past one and we're not in Woking yet.' In March Patrick took the rent of a flat at 44 Piccadilly, just opposite the Princes Arcade, and his sisters came to help him decorate and furnish it.

But now a new figure appeared in Patrick's perennial dalliance with the idea of marriage to an aristocratic girl. This was Vita Sackville West, first met around the New Year of 1912. She asked him to Knole, in Kent, on a Sunday in January. Knole, a vast complex of buildings constructed over several centuries, was the seat of her father Lord Sackville. Her mother was her father's first cousin, and Vita was their only child. Her mother, Victoria, was half Spanish and had for many years lived mainly in Paris with her lover and benefactor, Sir John Murray Scott. Her father consoled himself with Lady Constance Hatch. Vita herself, now nearing her twenty-first birthday, was already remarkable for her tall and manly figure, her quick intelligence and her literary interests and skills as a poetess. Her two closest friends, known from childhood, were Violet Keppel and Rosamund Grosvenor. In February Patrick reported to Tats that he was going to stay at Knole 'which should at least be architectural fun – quite an unexpected success with the West girl,' and he went on: 'She must be a great heiress – and with that divine house half an hour from London – I think I might do worse, don't you?' Pua wrote to point out the advantages of such a union, to which he replied: 'Many of the same considerations (with regard to Knole) had occurred to me, and I did my best not to let the historic grass of the ten-mile park grow under my feet. She's a nice girl, very, one might say: perhaps rather more intellectual than intelligent, but you might say that's a fault on the right side.' Although he learnt from her mother ('a racy old rake with three imperfect languages at her command') that Vita would never inherit Knole because it was entailed to the barony of Sackville, she emphasized that she herself was extremely rich. In March he was 'doing magnificently with V Sackville West'; after Easter he was 'just back from an excellent Knole, but not engaged yet'; in April he was staying with her in Somerset where 'I put in a modicum of courtship'; later in April, at Taplow, 'Vita SW was there and some notable work was done.' As usual he confided all this to Ettie, who was discouraging about it.

Unfortunately for Patrick, Vita's apparent warmth towards him and others, including Edward Horner and aristocrats such as Lord Lascelles and Lord Granby, was tempered by the fact that she had become secretly engaged to Harold Nicolson, now a young diplomat posted to Constantinople. This had the approval of her parents, subject to a year's delay before an announcement. Meanwhile she was not at all sure that she wanted to marry at all. Once again, it was with the mother that Patrick made his hit. It was she who urged him to call on them in London, and invited him to stay at Knole for Easter. She also got Patrick to arrange letters of credit for Vita's visits to Italy in April and again in September. But Vita certainly enjoyed herself with Patrick. In the summer he came several times to Knole. He played tennis, and once again used his ploy of tempting a girl to learn Greek. In August Harold Nicolson was back on leave, and it was noticed that she paid more attention to Patrick than to him. But when she married Harold in the following year, Patrick was relegated to becoming a trustee of her marriage settlement.

In April Patrick was detailed to accompany Rowland Errington to Paris for discussions on the Trans Persian Loan. This related to the proposed construction of a railway across Persia to link Russia (and hence Europe) with India. It was in response to the German financing of a railway to Baghdad, intended to extend to the Persian Gulf. The project was deeply political, the British Government being chronically divided on the question of whether opposition to the Germans was more important than the danger of giving Russia accessibility to India. The French were involved as well as the Russians, but both were prepared to give the lead to the British, as represented by Barings. In 1910 a Societé D'Études was set up, under the blessing of the Foreign Office, with Barings contributing 40% of the £300,000 initially subscribed. By 1912 a point had been reached where the scheme would either be launched or fail. Errington, who had served in the Embassy in St Petersburg, was now the Barings' director on the English Board of the scheme, with Patrick as the Secretary. The Paris discussions took place just before a week's leave that Patrick had secured in order to visit Charles, now serving in the Embassy in Rome. At first it looked as though he would have to forego this visit, since any progress at the meeting would have meant immediate work in attempting to float the scheme. However, after the initial discussions, the French directors insisted that the full meeting could not take place for a further twelve days.

So, abandoning the luxury of the Hotel Lotti, Patrick, travelling second class at his own expense, took the first available evening train south, arriving at Rome two mornings later. Chaperoned and ciceroned by Charles ('my own dear precious and beloved Charles'), he had a magnificent time in Rome. They sat on the Palatine and surveyed the Forum. They visited Hadrian's Villa and the Appian Way. They went to parties, including those at the Embassy, Charles being a great favourite with the family of Sir Rennell Rodd, the Ambassador. After six days they went overnight to Milan for four days, visiting Pavia. Then Patrick travelled back to Paris, arriving in the morning just in time for the meeting of the Trans Persian Board. By dint of careful planning, he had used up only eight days of his precious leave.

Back in London Patrick was busy as the Secretary of the English Board, 'writing haughty letters to applicants for jobs and servile ones to the directors summoning them to meetings.' He also looked forward to being given preference shares. But in the event the project never got off the ground, essentially due to the ambivalence of the British Government. Various compromises were bandied about, such as directing the railway to a Persian port rather than to India. Barings feared they might be left in the lurch, and eventually withdrew from the consortium. This business alternated with periods of boredom for Patrick at Barings through the autumn. But his hard work on the Trans Persian Loan had been recognized, his salary rising to £200 a year. As ever, his social life was constantly effervescent. In June he scribbled a letter to Tats from the office at 5.15 pm. He felt 'half alive and three quarters asleep,' having been out at a ball till 4.30 am. But this evening he was due at a very smart dinner with the Crewes for the Derby's ball. So 'if I post this at 5.25 I will be home by 5.45 and in bed by 5.50 and I needn't be called till 7.45 for dinner at 8.30, so that's all right.'

Then there were the fancy dress parties, the great fashion of the time. In January he had appeared at the big fancy-dress ball at Taplow 'in the full regalia of a pseudo double Earl,' also described as 'my old "Popular Irish Peeress" green indeterminate mediaeval';

in another as Robin Hood; and in another, as a coster in 'a snuff
coloured coat and blue breeks' in an ensemble depicting The Cries
of London'. As to the famous occasion when Diana pulled off her
coup by appearing in a procession of princesses dressed as swans
at a charity ball at the Albert Hall, but unexpectedly in black when
all the others were in white, Patrick was full of praise: 'No one
could have more blindly admired, more fatuously relished, than
me, both the perverse, nebermenschlich idea of getting behind
your young friends, and the particular form which the freak took
– to put you, alone and conspicuous into that colour in which
you are to my eye most supreme and to my heartstrings most
demiurgically irresistible.' Some weeks before he had told her
that she stood alone in his heart, despite his flirtations with other
slightly older girls, and despite her casual treatment of him: 'I am
a little frightened, to tell the truth: I seem to be falling more deeply
in love with you – and so suddenly! – than for a long time – I
doubt if it has been so bad since 1909 (August) and then, how
unhappy I was. As for these other females, I cannot away with
them. God had not ventured on your type before 1892: nor has he
yet succeeded in reproducing it.'

The circle of young men and women, whose friendships had
mostly been forged at Brancaster five years earlier, had given
themselves a name – The Corrupt Coterie – in reference to their
supposed daring in flouting minor social conventions, notably
those of their parents, the allegedly broad-minded Souls. As Diana
put it, 'Our pride was to be unafraid of words, unshocked by
drink, and unashamed of "decadence" and gambling.' This name
had got about and was taken up by the press in deeper criticism
of their conduct, emphasizing the Corrupt. The Coterie essentially
consisted of the young Asquiths (including the not-so-young
Raymond), Horners, Manners (both the Rutland Manners and the
Avon Tyrell Manners), Listers, Charterisses and Grenfells, together
with Viola Tree, Alan Parsons and, of course, Patrick. To the
longstanding intimacy of these had now been added Duff Cooper
and his sister Sybil, as well as Denis Anson, a handsome young

baronet, and George Vernon, a rich young peer. The doings of the Coterie were now beginning to become a staple diet in the gossip columns of the society magazines and the new popular press, and the member of the group who attracted the most attention was, of course, Diana. She was acquiring the sort of attention accorded nowadays to the most famous celebrities or royals. She was also the central figure within the coterie because several of the men within it were obsessed by her, convinced they were deeply in love. To the Oxonians she was Zulieka Dobson personified. Patrick was by no means the only one to write her passionate letters: Duff, George, Edward, as well as Claud Russell and Denis Anson, were doing so also. These she had to sift from a constant pile of letters from slight acquaintances and cranks and her many fans, whom she despised and yet relished.

Meanwhile her mother, the Duchess, an unconventional figure herself, was attracted by the brilliance of the Coterie whilst at the same time determined that none of the louche young men within it should marry Diana. Her opinion of them was later described by Diana as: 'Edward, drunk and dangerous; Patrick, the same and hideous; Vernon, mad; Charles, just a gasp of horror; Alan, a gesture of sickness; Claud, never heard him speak or met his eye; Raymond, missed my character.' The 'modern' girls of the Coterie, whose daring fell short of compromising their virginity, were characterized in the concluding lines of Raymond Asquith's poem 'In Praise of young Women': 'Unbridled yet unloving, loose but limp, Voluptuary, virgin, prude and pimp.'

On 1 January 1913 Patrick became a Managing Director of Barings. At the time there were eight Managing Directors, some of whom (including Patrick) sat in the Partners' Room. His salary was now £500 a year, although his elevation necessitated his resignation from the Eldon Scholarship, from which he had received £200 a year. To Tats he wrote: 'I am the wonder of the Room: so elderly, so sedate, so pretentious, as I jingle my keys and rustle my papers and thumb my securities! Especially when I twirl my glass of sherry with Uncle Tom and Cousin Rowland. Oh yes, it is a beautiful life.' The first document he had to sign was a cheque for £100,000, which gave him 'an exquisite sensation'. But then, in having to sign 500 dividend warrants in twenty minutes, he wished he had taken the partners' advice and abbreviated himself to 'P Stewart'. On another day he wrote 700 signatures – 500 bonds, 100 bills accepted, and 100 letters. But he was now in the swim of things, able to give his view on such projects as the Brazilian Iron Ore Scheme, the Union Pacific Scheme, the Six Power Loan to China, as well as the lingering Trans Persian Loan. He attended dinners with clients, such as with a delegation of Chinese in Lord Revelstoke's house – 'very jolly fellows, mercifully strong in their English.' He was also able to help his family in securing preferential treatment in allocations for new business ventures. The Chinese Loan was launched in May, and Patrick secured £500 for himself, £500 for his brother, and several hundreds for his sisters, while the general public only got 20% of what they asked for. A few months later he reported to Pua 'Buenos Aires was a great success, you'll be glad to hear, and San Paulo are 245.' Meanwhile Rothschild's Brazil Loan had collapsed: 'everyone here wags their heads sympathetically and says "Poor Old Natty" but really they are frightfully pleased.'

When Patrick died his estate was declared for probate at £5,140 gross, very predominantly in investments accumulated when at Barings, both before and during the War. His father's probate in 1908 had been £5,712 gross, but Patrick had received none of that, as it went to his mother for life, and then to his two unmarried sisters. Patrick's own disposition was for his sisters to receive any chattels free of duty, for Dear £500 stock in the South India Railway, and the residue to his brother and two sisters equally.

In the weeks after Christmas Patrick crammed in visits to Panshanger, Belvoir, Cliveden and Taplow, and attended a 'Persian Play' put on in the Great Hall at Knole, in which Vita appeared as a young Caliph, with Rosamund as Zuleika and Violet as a slave girl. He also went to a fancy-dress party for Vita's birthday in March, at which he appeared as a 'Fellow of All Soles,' in a red domino with slippers hung all over it. They went for drives in the car of the absent Harold, 'Green Archie'. Harold, in distant Constantinople, might well have felt rueful about Patrick, especially since Carnock had come into the possession of the Shaw Stewarts from having been the seat of the Nicolson family; indeed, his father, now the Permanent Under-Secretary of State for Foreign Affairs, when enobled was to take the name of Lord Carnock. (Actually, the lease of Carnock came to an end in the summer, Patrick's sisters moving to a house called Ware o Neho, near Lettoch in Ross-Shire.)

In April Patrick made a second visit to Charles in Rome. At first they went on to Naples for a few days, joining the Keppel family there. Alice Keppel, the late King's mistress, displayed her 'glorious energy and gleams of prancing fun,' though Patrick and Charles found her preoccupation with food and money rather shocking. One morning Patrick kept the party waiting, which incurred her wrath – 'a thing that she asserted that King Edward in his prime had never ventured to do.' They were all entertained on the Miller Mundy's yacht, and duly visited Pompei and Pozzuoli. Back in Rome, the great event was the Embassy Ball. This, once again, was to be in fancy dress. Patrick acquired his costume in Naples, that of a humble Sorrento fisherman, but 'luckily they are dressy chaps, these Sorrentine fishermen, the greater part of their costume being exactly like court dress.' However, when he arrived at the party, he found he was the only guest in comic costume, most of the rest being grand Romans in eighteenth-century clothes as worn by their noble ancestors, and plastered with real pearls and jewels. To top it all, Marchesa Casati made her entrée dressed in gold as the Sun Goddess, accompanied by gold-painted attendants and a peacock on a lead. Lady Rodd gave Patrick a quizzical look, but his lithe and close-fitting dress served him well on the dance floor. After this he and Charles went to Pisa, ascending the leaning tower in a high wind, 'each trying to look slightly less afraid than the other.' Charles had by now shed his Socialism for an enlightened Toryism.

Throughout his journey Patrick was keen to buy the latest available edition of the *Daily Mail*. Diana's doings were staple fare in its gossip column. She had fallen ill at Easter when staying at Rottingdean in a cottage in the company of Patrick, Edward, Raymond and Katharine, and Duff Cooper (and his sister Sybil), the inner circle of friends who were to be so close to her during the war years. On the Thursday night her 'hoarse whisper dominated the assembly.' But on Good Friday she was confined to bed, and Patrick wrote a note from downstairs: 'Try and repeat the old familiar story; spend tomorrow conversing with the souls in Hades, and rise glorious on the appropriate morning. I fear Duff may be writing a sonnet in competition with me.' During May Patrick found things very quiet. He had 'a few heavy meals at the expense of heavy matrons, but not many.' An awful thought struck him: 'either there is no true pre-Whitsun season, as the Daily Mail says, or my value must have declined – incredible hypothesis when I am such a parti nowadays.' However at times he felt less frenetic about going to parties: ' I like All Souls more and more in my old age: one needn't talk at meals or shave before dinner or bother about does.'

Still, he continued to rush around energetically. A week in July began with a Saturday-to-Monday at Taplow, then a Tuesday-to-Thursday at the Hague with the Keppels, and then a Saturday-to-Monday at Esher (Lady Helen Vincent). As always, he went frequently to the theatre, for example, in one week in September to plays by Barrie, Tree and Shaw. The principal event for members of the Coterie was a visit to Venice in September. George Vernon had taken a palazzo and among those who came and went were Duff Cooper, Denis Anson, Edward Horner and Charles Lister, as well as several of the girls. Also in Venice, staying with Lady Cunard, were the Prime Minister and his wife, Harry Cust and Ronald Storrs, as well as Diana. Patrick's work prevented him from coming until shortly before Diana was leaving: 'Were we really in Venice together? I never saw you once – not even at the Casatis – my only recollection is your nose powdering at the Vapore – and George's alarm. As for after you were gone, of course it was mere gleanings, and very soon I was gone myself. I don't think Venice is truly decorative without you.' It rained for most of the time he was there, and the dank surroundings and tiresome evening parties with unknown foreigners were not to his taste, pleasure being confined to visits to the Lido for swimming and tennis. Escaping from this, Edward Horner and Denis Anson went climbing in the Dolomites, Denis exhibiting the dare-devilry that cost him his life in the following year (when Patrick was in America) when he drowned in the Thames in an incident which brought discredit on the Coterie.

From here it was to Scotland for the continuation of his five weeks of leave. First to Ardgowan for the grouse shooting, then to Carnock, then on to Ettie at Drummond. He asked himself to stay with the Lovats, but cannot have endeared himself to his host when 'I howled with joy when Simon, the great boy-scout, fell right into a burn in spate which we had to ford – poor man he was dripping for the rest of the day and had to have a bottle of whisky neat for his luncheon.' Thence to Dear at her house at Lettoch; and, after a rush to catch a train, with no time to collect his waiting case, to arrive to stay with Lord and Lady Richard Cavendish at Hooker in Cumbria, 'very jolly, almost the best of all.'

Patrick had now left 44 Piccadilly, where he had twice been robbed, and gone to lodge in luxury in George Vernon's house in Curzon Street, attended by numerous highly-trained footmen. At yet another fancy-dress event, the Picture Ball, he went in a group representing The Birth of Futurism, in which 'my sex (to say the least of it) is indeterminate, as I wear a skirt (white satin with blobs of colours) and carry a symbolic infant in my arms.' Grand weekend visits continued, for instance at Belvoir, in the company of Lord Curzon and the veteran French Ambassador, M Cambon. But in December he was told the firm wanted him to go to America for six months 'to learn the banking methods of that hustling country.'

EIGHT

The New World and the World War

On 24 JANUARY 1914 Patrick set sail for New York on board the Cunard Line RMS *Carmania*. Avoiding conversation with the other passengers in First Class, helped by what he described as his 'plain and rather grumpy face,' he secured a table in solitary grandeur. Typically, he declined the offer to select a tune from the band – 'not feeling sure whether the Liebestod or Yip-i-addy would strike the more congenial note.' He kept off alcohol (food was free but drink was not), lay in bed from 11 pm till noon, smoked a pipe, and settled down to solid reading – Balzac's *Pere Goriot*, Willams' *Life of Pitt*, Conrad's *Chance*, Stephens' *An Agnostic's Apology*, Clare on the money market, as well as passages from *The Odyssey* and poems from *The Oxford Book of English Verse*.

The agents for Barings in New York were Kidder Peabody. Barings and Kidder Peabody had been allies for a long time. Originally, they had supported each other in credits for South America and elsewhere. In 1885 Barings decided to close their own offices in the United States, taking interests in Kidder Peabody, then in Boston, and Baring, Magoun in New York. Both these firms specialized in rescuing and reorganizing railroads which were in financial trouble. In the years of recovery from the Baring crash of 1890 this arrangement served Barings well. In 1910, out of a total of about £15.5 million acceptances by Barings, £8.6 emanated from North America. Three hundred and fifty commercial credits were issued in New York in 1906. One particular success was their participation in the American Telephone and Telegraph Company. In 1909 the ATTC subsidiary, the New York Telephone Company, went on the market, and Barings raised £2 million of the total of £5 million, making handsome profits for its clients (especially, of course, its 'red list,' which included Lady Desborough). Following the demise of Baring, Magoun in 1907, Kidder Peabody opened an office in New York and represented Barings there also.

Clad in his fur coat, snow boots, and Swiss cap (round the chin), Patrick braved the weather (as low as 14 degrees below), moving between Kidder Peabody at 56 Wall Street, and the Racquet Club and his service-flat on 43rd Street, attended by Japanese staff. He was armed with plentiful letters of introduction. Those from Barings were to leading bankers, such as Pierpont Morgan Jnr, producing courtesy calls involving 'a masterly display of inanities on the Money Market.' Those from friends, always personally delivered by him, were to prominent leaders of society, such as Mrs Bridget Guinness, Mrs Whitehouse, Mrs Vanderbilt and Mrs Astor. Mrs Guinness never received visitors from Europe unless they had the reputation of some form of artistic achievement, so Patrick confided to her that he had begun to write a novel, and thought of finishing it on the voyage home, 'which made me fairly safe for the present.'

Unlike many visiting Englishmen, he was good at remembering names, employing his superb memory. But his visual memory was poor, 'so I just have to go about with a fixed idiotic smile which'll do for anyone.' He got used to being greeted by 'I'm vurry pleased to meet you, Mr Stoo'rt' (and to avoid responding by 'Not at all'), and accustomed to such new words as 'highbrow', 'crush', 'bully' and 'Tuxedo'. He found the pervasiveness of classical musical entertainment a strain, but passively attended concerts and the opera, including one at which his hostess wore black, it being in Lent. He stayed with the Pierpont Morgans on Long Island, creating a sensation by oversleeping and missing breakfast. He also went down to Philadelphia for a day to watch the final of the tennis between Britain and America, chaperoned by the artist Neville Lytton. He was enjoying New York tremendously, and Kidder Peabody were being very kind to him, answering his probing questions about the mysteries of international exchange rates and other technicalities, and not asking him to do any work on their behalf.

At Mrs Vanderbilt's he met a Mrs Ethel Cushing: 'tall and thin, with pale red hair, no eyebrows, tiny eyes, an ultra-Rosemaryesque noselessness, and a pearly skin; distinctly plain, but slightly seductive. She asked me to have a "cup of tea" with her; I shall –dog!' Her husband was away in Boston, and her tiny eyes had soon turned his head. Writing to Diana in March at 11.30 pm after an exhausting dinner with one of the Peabody partners, he reported that he was about to change into a beetle-green domino to go to a party with Ethel Cushing – 'I don't mind telling you I'm crazy about her.' Patrick's reputation as *le grand sèducteur* had preceded him across the Atlantic. Letters from Nancy Astor to her sisters secured him invitations but set up signals. Before calling on one of them, Mrs Irene Gibson, he was warned off by two of her sisters: 'Now don't you go breaking up that sweet home on 70th Street,' and 'I hear such things of you, but remember, they are *very happy.*'

It had always been understood that he would spend some months in New York, followed by others in Boston. But in April Barings decided to send him on a trip out West, returning through Canada in the company of Gaspard Farrer. Arming himself with letters of introduction, Patrick went first to Washington. He invited himself to stay with Lord Eustace Percy, an attaché in the Embassy, a serious young man living in some squalor. He saw the sights, and called on Baring's associate bankers. In England he had met Phyllis Brooks, yet another sister of Nancy Astor. She had separated from her husband, and her father, Mr Langhorne, had given her his house near Charlottesville in Virginia, moving to a smaller house nearby. Patrick fished for an invitation to stay with her for a couple of nights. His athletic hostess took him riding and played tennis with him.

Then it was out west, twenty-four hours in the train to St Louis, Missouri, a temperance State, with only ginger beer for comfort, and much discomfort in an upper berth. Pursuing his way, he went to Keokuk in Iowa to inspect the Mississipi Dam, and thence to Kansas City, transferring to the Santa Fe Railroad. He endured the monotony of Arizona – 'endless miles of sand and alkali and sage and scrub, interminably dotted with pale sandstone rocks.' He went down the Grand Canyon – 'nothing but dust and hot draughts, just an inverted mountain with a dirty mill race at the bottom.' After a week's travel from Washington, he reached the West Coast at Los Angeles, encountering the full impact of advertising: 'Los Angeles is a pretty town, with lovely avenues of palm and gum trees, and groves of oranges and grapefruits – it is the most self-advertising town I have ever met in this country, and that's saying a good deal. The "boosters" or town advertisers are a regular profession, and they shout at you from every placard.' He bathed in the surf of the Pacific at a resort called Venice. Thence northwards to San Francisco, Portland, and Seattle (two nights in the train from San Francisco) and so by boat across to Vancouver.

Here he awaited the arrival of Gaspard Farrer. Together they then started back along the Canadian Pacific, usually stopping at hotels for the night, with Gaspard, a man of charm, keen for conversation with Patrick and other fellow travellers. However, this prevented Patrick from chatting up on the train 'a perfectly *divine* young woman, quite unattached, who seemed anxious to make friends: if it had happened before Vancouver *what* fun we should have had: as it was *how* proud and stiff I was!'

> We went through the Rockies, which were in excellent form, travelling by day, and then over the foot-hills and beginnings of the prairies to Calgary, where they have just struck oil and are all as mad as hatters about it: there's really only about a gallon of oil as yet, I believe, but they have samples of oil in bottles in all the shop windows, and lists of oil shares up on slates outside, like "Special Dishes Today". Thus one sees the primitive embryo of the Stock Exchange! Then we changed and went north to Edmonton, which is the gate of the northern wheat country, and depot of all the fur-trade. Not a

bad country, but a filthy hotel, where there was dry-rot: and yet, when we got to Winnipeg, and into a really sumptuous Ritz-like affair, Gaspard had the ingratitude to do nothing but bemoan the improvidence of building such an hotel in such a place, and gloomily repeat that someone told him the management lost 1000 dollars a day on it.

After nine days from Vancouver they reached Montreal, where Gaspard went to Quebec to fish and Patrick went to New York in time to see the English team play polo on Long Island, dancing all night 'in dinner jackets' (probably the first time he had been to a dance other than in white tie and tails).

Finally, on 18 June he reached Boston, but was destined to stay there only for three weeks. Gaspard Farrer thought it best for Patrick to accompany him back home on the *Mauritania*, sailing from New York on 7 July, rather than wait till the end of the month. Patrick was also keen to be back, though he had loved 'this bustling, simple-minded, gaseous, rather incompetent, hospitable nation.' In these last three weeks he squeezed a visit to Newport, Rhode Island, to see Ethel Cushing (she of 'the red hair and asparagus appearance') for tennis and sea-bathing: unsurprisingly he noted that 'Mrs Cushing's husband increasingly lacks geniality.' Also to Quebec, on the grounds of knowing Princess Patricia, the daughter of the Governor-General. On arriving back at Southampton in mid July he could look forward to more years of carefree youth (he was not yet twenty-six) and splendid prospects for settling down in prosperous employment. But it was not to be.

On 28 July Austria declared war on Serbia, triggering a series of declarations of war by the Great Powers. There was panic in the City. From the Continent it was reported that no remittances were available to meet outstanding debts, brokers were flooded with orders to sell, and stock exchanges were closing their doors. On 1 August Patrick wrote to his sister:

It's been a strange week here and gets stranger every day. It seems this morning that war is quite inevitable. Hardly credible, is it? Also, though this is private at present (it won't be when it reaches you) the Bank have authority to suspend the Bank Act: that is, to issue more banknotes against securities, *not against gold*. The result of that if put into operation will inevitably be the suspension of specie payments, and the result of that possibly a general moratorium, or suspension of debts. Not that you and I, as private and extremely small individuals, need worry: some machinery will be invented for daily needs, the banks will keep faith, and they and the Bank are working together. The Bank Rate went from 4 to 8 yesterday, and to 10 today. The Stock Exchange is closed – they couldn't stand the flood of Continental selling orders. "Nothing stands that stood before".

Barings were in a comparatively strong position because they were not much involved in the German or Austrian markets, and had just received big payments from America. But the entire machinery of credit had tumbled to pieces. Three weeks later, on 21 August, he wrote:

The City is outwardly quiet, and the *currency* question is settled – for the time, anyhow; but the *credit* difficulty will have to be settled, and everyone here is cudgeling his brains over it. The main difficulty, in two words, is to prop up those big houses who have debts owing from Germany which will never be paid, and, if they go under, to prevent the whole City coming down like a pack of cards on top of them. This applies (a) to banks; (b) more or less in parallel form to the Stock Exchange. I may seem to be speaking sensationally, and don't repeat this, because the public (mercifully) think all is well now that it's got its notes: but if you saw the length of the faces of those who know, you would realize this is one of the most terrific things London has been up against since finance existed. The remedy will undoubtedly take the form of the Government shouldering the whole thing.

For the five years of war Barings continued merely on holding operations and on a much reduced staff. Most of their younger men left to join the services, and by mid-1915 more than half the male staff had gone, several of them destined to be killed. By 1916 it was mainly women and older men who kept the bank functioning. The issuing business virtually came to an end, and the acceptance business withered though did not cease. But Barings still earned money by acting as the London bankers for the Russian, Italian and Portuguese Governments, and still made substantial profits throughout the war. Meanwhile the leading directors were much in demand on Government committees, and Lord Revelstoke was considered to be the indispensable man in British financial life.

From the British declaration of war on 4 August the great question for Patrick was whether to join the stampede of volunteers for the Services, young men of all classes who believed that the war would be short and sharp, rather in the manner of the Franco-Prussian War of 1870. On the evening of the declaration of war Patrick and Duff and two girls had driven around the West End in an open taxi 'to hear the fools cheering'. But on 12 August he confided to Diana:

> Look now: I am the most unmilitary of men: I hated field days at Eton: I hate the very thought of taking the field now: I do not particularly dislike the Germans; my chief European preoccupation is the ultimate hegemony of the Russians, which it seems to me we are fighting to achieve: and I know full well that though I may be a bad banker I should be a 100 times worse soldier. Again, I frankly recoil from the thought of wounds and death, and I think (with the minimum of arrogance) that others are fitter food for powder than me. These things being so, ought I to go? When I say to myself that I am doing more useful work in the City, do I mean that I am earning a better salary, and that I should be ruining my chances if I went, as well as imperilling my most precious life? Honestly – I don't know.

Lord Haldane himself, now back as Secretary of State for War, told Patrick he would be no good as an officer and was badly needed as a banker. But as the weeks went by the inward and outward pressures to enlist, however reluctantly, grew stronger. Despite the extreme pressure of work at Barings, dealing with all the readjustments, he recognized that his absence would not really inconvenience the other Directors – after all, they had done without him for all the year up to now. He must have been affected by seeing so many of his friends joining up with or without enthusiasm, and by the suspicion that he would seem cowardly not to do so – the potential recipient of a white feather. He must have reflected on what his father would have thought. Diana was keen to be taken on as an auxiliary nurse in France. Raymond Asquith understandably held back, being already over thirty and with a wife and children to support. Ronald Knox, as the Chaplain of Trinity College Oxford, was not to be expected to fight. But of Patrick's other friends, none was more enthusiastic than Julian Grenfell, on his way back from his regiment in South Africa. He was itching for a fight, and the war was all he could have dreamt of as a Regular Army Officer of three years standing.

By mid-September Patrick was thinking of offering his services in some non–combative role, such as that of an interpreter. He consulted General Sir Ian Hamilton, now in charge of Home Forces, and whom he had met more than once at Taplow parties. Hamilton was a man of great intelligence and charm, much favoured by the Liberal Government. He advised Patrick to see Eddie Marsh. Eddie had continued as Churchill's esteemed Private Secretary, moving with him from the Colonial Office to the Board of Trade and now the Admiralty. Patrick was offered a post as interpreter to go to Dunkirk with a contingent of one of the Marine Brigades and the Oxfordshire Yeomanry. He had to spend a week cramming for a French test and, armed with this, he was given a commission as a Sub-Lieutenant in the Royal Naval Volunteer Reserve. To him this seemed a tolerable course, though not an attractive or glamorous one. The Directors of Barings gave him their rather reluctant blessing, the Chief opining 'I don't think I should have done it in your place.' They promised to keep his place warm, and retain him on half-pay. He ordered his uniform from the tailors; Edward Horner and Julian Grenfell (who had just returned) came round to inspect him in it, 'rollicking, just like earliest Balliol.' Julian, in impulsive generosity, gave him his own sword; Tats came to help him pack, and Dear came to see him off. And on 26 September he departed in a taxi for Charing Cross, looking, as he thought 'just like the White Knight', with all his paraphernalia.

The ship he crossed on was carrying transport, including some forty London buses, fresh from the streets and complete with drivers. On his first night in Dunkirk he shared a bed with another officer, a former Balliol man, and next day he presented himself to the military authorities. From them he learnt that the Oxford Yeomanry had already secured their own French interpreters. So it was decided to use Patrick as Embarkation Officer, supervising the passage of men and material in and out of the port. This was an unexciting though necessary job, integrated into the rather incompetent and duplicated logistics of the tail-end of the army. 'Conceive it, I meet all incoming and outgoing boats, hand passengers off and on, see that no one is running away to and from the front without authorization and unload gigantic quantities of jam and soap for our brave fellows.' Patrick was billeted in comfort in the house of a Dunkirk grain merchant, his sword, revolver and wire-cutters, his Wolsey valise and waterproof sheets, all laid aside unused.

But the war was hotting up. The horror was already evident from the September casualties in the British Expeditionary Force. These included the deaths of John Manners and Percy Wyndham, newly married to Diana Lister. And now a military operation was taking place that directly affected Patrick at Dunkirk. The Marine Brigade with which he had crossed to Dunkirk was part of the Royal Naval Division, and units of the RND were now ordered to advance to Antwerp to assist the Belgian Army in defending it.

The Royal Naval Division had been created after the outbreak of war to augment the capability of the Marine Corps in conducting operations on land that affected the strategic requirements of the Royal Navy. There was a surplus of manpower in the Navy, boosted by new recruits, and this new force suited both the needs of both the army, under Kitchener, for more men on the ground, and those of the Navy, under Churchill, in widening their scope of authority. The force was envisaged as comprising some 12,000 men, partly Royal Marines but mostly naval reservists, and a camp was found for them at Sittingbourne near Deal. Although many of the rank and file were upset at not being sent to sea, the RND was attractive to volunteers for commissions, especially from the professions. It was seen as an elite unit, even though it had to be trained by army officers from a basis of complete ignorance of infantry discipline and tactics. The individual battalions were to be named after famous admirals, the four of the 2nd Brigade at this time being respectively the Nelson, Howe, Hood and Anson. Naval ranks were throughout retained. Naval uniforms were initially worn, though soon changing to khaki with naval caps and insignia.

On 3 October the Marine Brigade was sent by train forward to Antwerp and on 5 October two other RND Brigades, the 1st and the 2nd, crossed to Dunkirk and followed in its wake. These three brigades, together with some Army units, came face to face with the German Army outside Antwerp, but had an impossible task. The forts of Antwerp surrendered to the enemy and the Belgian Army fell back across the Scheldt. Most of the British forces were likewise forced to retreat across the Scheldt after three days of fighting, though some of them, including the 1st Brigade, were cut off and crossed the Dutch frontier into internment. The action had at least delayed the German advance, and provided time for the destruction of war material in the city, but it had failed in its main purpose. The remainder of the RND was shipped back to England.

By mid-October Patrick was finding his role as Embarkation Officer at Dunkirk superfluous. The Naval Embarkation Officer, though theoretically co-equal to him, was now a man of greatly superior rank and a rigorous martinet who called the shots. Patrick realized more than ever that his job could be done by an ex-Colonel of seventy. There was no dash about it. It was unworthy of him. After the arrival and departure of the RND, Dunkirk as a port was being run down in favour of Boulogne. There was no opening for him in Intelligence. He had briefly mentioned his dissatisfaction to Churchill when he had come to Dunkirk during the RND operation. And now he appealed again to Eddie Marsh, and in due course was ordered to transfer to the RND at its new depot at Crystal Palace, south of London. Here he was to undergo an eight-week course for training officers.

Patrick endured the shock of military discipline as expressed in petty routines and meticulous drills. He accepted this, as did so many others, and saw the humorous side when the Adjutant did all he could to put the fear of God into the parade: 'It is so funny after all one's academical and financial eminence to stand shivering in a row hoping he won't notice that one of my gloves is unbuttoned.' Patrick's main problem, as always, was to squeeze all the time he could away from the depot. After the last lecture ended at 6.45 he was often able to catch a suburban train to Charing Cross, dine in town, and take the last train back. Diana could sometimes slip out of Guy's Hospital, where she was herself subjected to the strictest discipline, exposed to constant pain and misery, but triumphantly defeating her detractors by her exemplary conduct in the most menial tasks.

After four weeks Patrick was put as an officer into the Depot Battalion, and was able to lodge in Upper Norwood. He found himself in temporary Second in Command of the 'A' Company: 'I may now be seen any day doubling about the parade ground, furtively consulting my *Infantry Training* in my pocket, trying to make 220 men hear my thin reedy tones, or explaining the mechanism of the rifle (a subject I very imperfectly comprehend) to a whole platoon at a time.' He duly acted as Orderly Officer. He expected to be allocated to one of the RND Battalions, now in camp at Blandford, Dorset, being re-formed after the losses at Antwerp. Of these the Hood, the Third Battalion of the Second

Brigade, had special significance. With Churchill's acquiescence, Eddie Marsh had arranged for other young men who were friends of his to be given commissions in the RND. But they had been dispersed rather unhappily in different Battalions. He now got them posted together in the Hood, under the command of Lieutenant Colonel Arnold Quilter, of the Grenadier Guards. Patrick joined it on 22 December.

'A' Company of the Hood was commanded by Lieutenant Commander Bernard Freyberg, a tremendously strong and impressive figure. A New Zealander, who had fought in the Hispano-American war in Cuba, and been his country's swimming champion, he had allegedly joined the RND by personally accosting Winston Churchill in St James's Park on the first day of war, and asking to help. He had also served with distinction at Antwerp. The Sub Lieutenants of the company, now joined by Patrick, were headed by Arthur (Oc) Asquith, the second son of the Prime Minister. Oc had never aspired to the brilliance of his elder brother Raymond, nor to enter the social circles of his sister Violet. He had served in the Sudan Civil Service, and then been involved in trade with South America.

Among the other Sub Lieutenants in Hood, not all of them in 'A' Company, were two friends who had been together at Rugby and Cambridge, Rupert Brooke and Denis Browne. Rupert, the beautiful poet, was already famous, promoted in particular by Eddie Marsh in his book *Georgian Poetry*. He had been elected a Fellow of King's College, Cambridge, and had travelled to the South Seas. Now in the Blandford Camp, he was composing his five sonnets which expressed his excitement at the prospect of the fight to come. Denis Browne was a talented musician and composer. Besides these were the American Johnny Dodge and Frederick ('Cleg') Kelly, a rather older Eton-and-Balliol man. Kelly was an Australian who combined prowess as an oarsman (an Oxford Blue who was thrice winner of the Diamond Sculls at Henley), a musician (had studied piano and composition in Germany and written several works), and a world traveller.

The Blandford Camp in the depth of winter was a bleak and miserable place. A week's leave was granted over the New Year, Patrick staying in London and wining and dining with his influential friends. Then the Hood settled down to training and fatigues, such as making roads in the mud by means of putting down gorse and stones. The men under Patrick's command were former naval stokers, the lowest and toughest element in the composition of ships' crews. They had been drafted into the RND, not volunteered for it, so had 'a sort of standing grievance in the back of their evil old minds that they want to be back in their steel-walled pen, yelping with delight and rolling in the waist, instead of forming fours under the orders of an insolent young landlubber.' They were cunning and coarse-mouthed, but they took their fate as it came, enduring the almost-daily route marches in all weathers that so blistered their feet.

Churchill came to inspect on an appalling day of mud, rain and wind, and the Hood acquitted itself well in plunging through streams and morasses, arriving at a road to find Eddie Marsh and Clementine Churchill clapping their hands and whistling in recognition. Patrick reflected how quickly one becomes assimilated to hardship, but hardship was mitigated by the good spirits of the officers of 'A' Company. These are recorded in the correspondence that now developed between Rupert Brooke and Violet Asquith, Violet's deep love for Rupert bolstered by his close comradeship with her brother Oc. To her Rupert wrote: 'Oc is my one comfort, a great one. His cheerfulness is unfailing. There emerges from the mud, Oc, backed by Denis Browne (playing Petroushka of an evening) and the gnome-like, soulless affable Patrick.' He also wrote, 'The only good news is that Patrick yesterday lost seven pounds at poker.' This encouraged Violet to sound a cautionary note about Patrick, and to distance herself from him so as to emphasise her love for Rupert. From Walmer Castle at Dover, where the Prime Minister, in his capacity as the Prime Warden of Trinity House, now spent his weekends, appropriately close to the combat across the Channel, she wrote:

Do come, preferably without Patrick – I felt a curious – unanalysable distaste when I heard he had been put into your company – and when I tried to diagnose and explain it I found it rooted in an absurd fear – worthy of a baby or a 'tribe' – that his personality and appearance were contagious – and that you might *catch* them?! I saw you – with miles of lilac gum – half-Peccany [sic] – half van-Eyck – saying quick, pat, finite things – getting rich – knowing more and more people, understanding less and less, greeting the unknown at every turn with rather a nasal laugh – *Do* take care won't you?

But now rumours abounded as to the destination of the RND. The Marine Brigade were issued with pith helmets, so various tropical places were freely mentioned, and the Battalion had to practice forming squares, which conjured up visions of fighting tribesmen ('Personally I liked it: it seems to me the only form of modern warfare that gives the poor officers a chance'). On 20 February Colonel Quilter told his officers that their destination was the Dardanelles. Patrick was on sick-leave at the time, suffering from laryngitis and ensconced in the Cavendish Hotel, but he wormed the secret out of Eddie Marsh.

The strategic plan of the Government was now revealed. Turkey had entered the war on the side of the Central Powers, and an attempt to force the passage through the Dardanelles up to Constantinople seemed a quick and simple way of neutralising Turkey and its Empire, as well as assisting Russia. Great was the joy among the officers of the RND. Patrick wrote to his sister: 'It is the Dardanelles, the real plum of this war: all the glory of a European campaign (and greater glory than any since Napoleon's if we take Constantinople and avenge the Byzantine Empire) without the wet, mud, misery and certain death of Flanders. Really I think we are very lucky, and Winston an angel to have got it for us.' And he goes on: 'I am really very pleased and so ought you to be. It is the luckiest thing and the most romantic. Think of fighting in the Chersonese (hope you got the allusion from 'the Isles of Greece' about Miltiades), or alternatively, if it's the Asiatic side they want us on, on the plains of Troy itelf! I am going to take my Herodotus as a guide book.' Oc Asquith, however, refused to romanticize about the campaign, and when Rupert Brooke rhapsodized to his father in Downing Street, Oc was heard to mutter, 'the whole thing is a beastly duty.'

To see them off, the King came down to Blandford to review the departing Brigades of the RND. It was a bright winter day, the brilliant sun sparkling on the frost. Clemmie Churchill and Violet Asquith came cantering by. Then Churchill and the Admiralty Board inspected the parade. Then came the King, taking his inspection slowly, and asking individual questions. The Division then marched past in double columns of fours, followed by three cheers for the King and the National Anthem. After the parade, by special permission, the Officer's Mess of the Hood Battalion entertained the two ladies to lunch, and Patrick, who had just returned from his sick-bed in London, brought with him such luxuries as grapefruit, marrons glacés, foie gras and champagne. Violet could see that Patrick was not well, his face was 'arsenic green'. But she also noted that 'he was much less aggressively on the crest of a wave than I have ever known him – rather gentler and humbler and generally more muted,' and this she found appealing. Charles Lister also appeared. The next day was spent on kit inspection and the distribution of ammunition and iron rations, and on the morning of 28 February the Division marched out in rain to Blandford railway station to be taken to the Avonmouth Docks at Bristol. Violet made a final appearance just before they sailed, and together with Oc and Rupert she had a prescription made up for Patrick's throat, which she delivered to him in his cabin, he 'lying on his bunk amongst cough mixtures and bandages looking I must confess rather septic.'

NINE

Camaraderie on Gallipoli

THE ROYAL NAVAL DIVISION, of around 8,000 officers and men, sailed from Avonmouth on 28 February 1915 in twelve ships. The Hood and Anson Battalions, together with the Staff of their Brigade, were on board the *Grantully Castle*, a small requisitioned Union Castle steamer . The men were extremely crowded, and the officers in cramped quarters. Patrick was fortunate in sharing a cabin with Denis Browne, 'most delightful of companions and most good-natured and unselfish of mankind.' He and Rupert Brooke had 'made me remould all my concepts of Cambridge men.' The voyage was punctuated by irksome, often pointless, parades, and four-hour watches. Inoculation and vaccination was decreed for all and, since the ratings could not be compelled to submit to this, smooth talking by the officers was needed to persuade them.

There were also comic difficulties in the way of Individual Instruction of Platoons: no one who has not tried it knows what it is like to take a "strong" platoon as a semaphore signalling class in the space afforded by about two yards of casing and the deck corresponding thereto, or how irresistibly interesting in such circumstances – to professor and student alike – are the activities of one's next door neighbours. I, for instance, on these occasions was between Johnny Dodge and Rupert Brooke, and my platoon's development must have sadly suffered from the magnetic influence exercised on me by the gently penetrating Americanisms, and tireless oratorical resources, of the one, and the rich fancies of the other garbed in curt and telling prose.

The weather was good and, once in the Mediterranean, the ship sailed close by the North African coast, sometimes in sight of the Atlas Mountains, and often odoriferous. In an intimation of his impending three years of campaigning, Patrick had long hours to spend with nothing else to do but to read. Here he read *Beauchamp's Career*, Oliver's *Alexander Hamilton*, Gibbon's *The New Map of Europe*, and 'some of the *Iliad*.' He also had with him a copy of Herodotus, given him by Eddie Marsh. But there was also plenty of time for conversation and bridge and cocktails. Rupert reported to Eddie Marsh that 'Patrick is the life and soul of the party – the life anyway. Denis is competent, Kelly silly, Johnny inquisitive and simple hearted, and Oc Oc-like.' To Eddie, Patrick wrote: 'It is really a most diverting campaign, and although I suppose we shall all be killed sooner of later, I am (as I said before) almost soppily grateful for being sent on it.' To Diana, on approach to Malta, he wrote: 'Oh it's fun to be a sailor and to be going to fight the Turk – no mud, no cold, very little danger, and infinite glory of avenging the Palaeologs and entering Byzantium.' This historical vindication was confined to a few, most of the men of the RND having more in mind Turkish atrocities in the recent Balkan Wars, and the massacre of the Armenians.

The convoy arrived at Malta on 8 March. On board the *Franconia* had been Charles Lister. On the recommendation of Patrick and others, Charles had at the last minute managed to transfer from his cavalry regiment to join the Staff of the RND as an interpreter. He had served for six months in the Embassy in Constantinople, and his knowledge of Turkish affairs seemed particularly useful. Patrick, together with Oc Asquith and Denis Browne, toured Valetta and dined at the Union Club: here Charles, still in his cavalry jodhpur breeches, made 'a meteoric appearance,' and thence they went to *Tosca* at the opera and (as Charles put it) 'generally razzled – "Jack on Shore" to the manor born.'

From the British naval base of Malta the *Grantully Castle* sailed into the Eastern Mediterranean and on into the Aegean, arriving at Mudros Harbour on the Greek island of Lemnos on 11 March.

Here a great assembly of ships of all sizes, from battleships to the smallest tramp steamers, was gathered for the impending attack on the Dardanelles. It was still hoped that these could be forced by naval bombardment of the Turkish forts on either side of the straits, so as to enable an army to be taken up into the Sea of Marmara to an undefended Constantinople. The plan now was for battleships to attempt to rush the straits, with a fleet of troop-carrying transports ready to follow in their wake.

During the week spent in awaiting this operation parties went ashore, and once Patrick bicycled across to Kastro, the chief town of the island, with Oc and Charles. The spirits of all were high, and for those steeped in a classical education there was an added thrill in seeing places which they had imagined in their studies, and following in the footsteps of heroes. Here at Lemnos Jason had likewise been delayed before sailing the Argo past the 'Clashing Rocks' of the Dardanelles in search of the Golden Fleece: indeed Patrick and his companions could see themselves in heroic guise as Argonauts. Of all military campaigns that which Patrick had studied most closely was the siege of Troy, and with his remarkable memory he was able to recount the famous incidents in detail, embellished with quotations. As Ronald Knox put it, 'he was prepared to greet the plains of Troy as a *habitué*.' Oc Asquith later recalled:

> Patrick's unfailing vitality and good spirits were a godsend to us all. Also he showed the most amazing memory of his classical lore – he remembered every amusing myth about every island in the Aegean. I pointed out Cos to him: he was ready at once with a Latin quotation about legislation in the early days of the Roman Empire, forbidding, on grounds of decency, the wearing by women of translucent draperies woven by the inhabitants of Cos.

The Homeric legend mentions that Philoctetes, the greatest archer in the Trojan war, had been left behind on Lemnos because of a wound from the bite of a snake; and Patrick and Oc were keen

161

to quiz the locals about him, with mixed results. Although made immediately aware that modern Greek was very different from the classical, the primitive peasant life on the rocky landscape seemed hardly to have changed for two or even three millennia.

On 17 March (St Patrick's Day) the RND was ordered to embark for expected action, so farewell letters bore a special immediacy. Patrick wrote an unsentimental letter to Diana: 'I have never seen you one half so glorious as in these times, you were (and by God's grace are) buffier, smuttier, surer of yourself, more central, more indispensible, fairer, wittier, more seductive, than I have ever known you before'; and that 'just in case I should be killed I do want to impress it on you that you have practically the burden of this generation on your shoulders. Be faithful and multiply...'

On 18 March the *Grantully Castle* duly appeared off Suvla Bay, its purpose being to make a feint approach to divert the Turkish army from the access to the straits. The number of Turkish infantry who appeared suggested that the enemy had responded as intended. But on the same day the Anglo-French naval operation, which was intended to clear the Dardanelles for the passage of the transports, failed, three battleships being sunk on a line of undetected mines, and other warships badly damaged. The whole concept of rushing the straits was abandoned. It would now be necessary to land a military force, and this could only be done once the British 29th Division had arrived in the theatre of operation. The forces already present – the RND, the Australian and New Zealand Corps, and the French Corps Expeditionaire de l'Orient – were inadequate for the task. The 29th Division was unable simply to join these forces at Mudros because it had been sent out loaded chaotically. Therefore, after reassembling in Mudros Harbour, the RND sailed on 23 March to regroup in Egypt, arriving at Port Said four days later.

The Hood Battalion pitched camp outside the dock area on the sands at the edge of the town. Officers were to be granted forty-eight hours leave in groups of three. The first batch, comprising Patrick, Rupert and Oc, took the train for Cairo next day, and

Gallipoli, 1915

SAMOTHRACE

Gulf of Saros

Constantinople

Sea of Mamara

Gallipoli

IMBROS

Suvla Bay
Anzac Bay
Gaba Tepe
Krithia

Dardanelles

Achi Baba

LEMNOS

Cape Helles

Sedd el Bahr

Mudros

TENEBROS

stayed in luxury at Shepheard's Hotel for two nights, breakfast in bed. Oc had served in the Sudan Civil Service, spoke Arabic, and had several contacts in Cairo – he was, after all, the Prime Minister's son. He got in touch with Margot Howard de Walden and Mary Herbert, who had set up a military hospital there. Together with Lord Howard de Walden and Aubrey Herbert they all drove out for the customary visit to the Sphinx and the Pyramids and camel ride, Patrick exercising his usual charm on older women: 'How clever Patrick is,' commented Lady Howard de Walden afterwards. During the first night they took a moonlight donkey ride through the old city to the tombs of the Caliphs; and on the next day they toured the bazaar, Patrick bargaining for Ptolomeic coins and Rupert for amber necklaces for his girlfriends back home.

They returned next morning to the camp to find that Charles

had succeeded in being transferred from the Staff to the Battalion. What is more, the four platoons of 'A' Company, commanded by Bernard Freyberg, were to be led respectively by Johnny Dodge, Patrick, Charles and Rupert. A Battalion route march on the day of their return was a testing ordeal, and next morning Patrick, apparently suffering from sunstroke, went sick with a violent headache and diarrhoea. Charles hired a cab and took him to the Casino Palace Hotel, Port Said, and a room facing the sea. He thus missed being on parade when the RND Brigade, under the command of General Archibald Paris, paraded in front of Sir Ian Hamilton, now the Commander-in-Chief of the Mediterranean Expeditionary Force, in their pith helmets and with their trousers cut into shorts. Two days later he found himself joined there by Rupert, who resisted admission to the military hospital in the company of 'tiresome brother officers' on the grounds of being able to share Patrick's room. Here they lay together for a week under mosquito nets, at first completely starved except for arrowroot, then 'with one or two adventures in eggs and the little sham soles of the Mediterranean, which brought about relapse and repentance,' with frequent rushes along the passage to the bathroom, till the diarrhoea finally relapsed. By this time each had grown beards, Rupert's brown and Patrick's auburn. Patrick was conscious of his reticence in exchanging confidences with Rupert ('I suppose I am a bad starter of friendship'), though actually he was 'gloating' over his acquisition of Rupert, especially as he was outside the Eton and Balliol circle to which his friendships had hitherto been so closely confined. But Rupert had reservations about Patrick. He found him 'not a bad fellow-invalid, when chastened by arrowroot: gay and unchanging and superficially (oh, no doubt really, too!) sympathetic.'

Although both still weak, they shaved and left the hotel late on 9 April in order to board the *Grantully Castle*, which sailed early next day. Patrick was on the road to recovery, but Rupert was suffering from a sore on his upper lip. This time the ship carried only the Hood Battalion, so there was plenty of space. There was plenty of time, too, because it was towing a lighter and was steaming at only 4 knots an hour. Near Cos the lighter came loose and had to be recovered, and they took a week to reach Mudros. Patrick and six others (Charles, Rupert, Oc, Denis Browne, Cleg Kelly and Johnny Dodge) secured a dining-room table for themselves, presided over by one of the ship's officers.

> I subsequently happened to hear that this table was known to the others as "the Latin Table"; I do not know what piece of pedantry on whose part was responsible for the title. Certainly some noteworthy conversations were held there; it seemed always somehow to happen that we were left there at dinner among the patient stewards, long after everyone else had gone, experimenting on the rather limited repertory of the ship's vintages, and amusing one another none too silently. I wish I could recapture something of the subject matter: it ranged from the little ways of Byzantine emperors to the correct way of dealing with Turkish prisoners; music, in spite of organized opposition by Philistines such as myself, could not be altogether denied its place.

Of their one night all together in the tent in camp at Port Said, Rupert had written: 'Imagine what an extraordinary, and unprecedented, conglomeration of sound Oc and I and Denis Browne put up with, when you learn that Patrick with his loud titter, Cleg Kelly with his whinny, and Charles with his great neigh, are all in the same tent. The sound of it frightens the Egyptian night...' Music, so displeasing to the tone-deaf Patrick (he doubted whether in battle he would recognize the call for Charge from that to Retire), was provided at the ship's piano by Denis Browne or Clegg Kelly, who played for the customary fancy-dress review – 'Sod's Opera' – on the final night. The usual routine, of semaphore practice, machine-gun drill and Swedish exercises, continued to occupy all ranks during the days. Rupert was still well enough to compose a last fragment of poetry, out on deck at night and watching his friends through the window:

I could but see them – against the lamplight – pass
Like coloured shadows, thinner than filmy glass,
Slight bubbles, fainter than the wave's faint light,
That broke the phosphorous out in the night,
Perishing things and strange ghosts – soon to die
To other ghosts – this one, or that, or I

Mudros Harbour was so congested with ships of the impending armada that the RND was ordered south to Skyros and its large haven, Trebouki Bay, arriving on 17 March. The Hood Battalion was thereupon reduced by some 150 men under Johnny Dodge and two other Lieutenants, in order to provide stokers for the main invasion fleet at Mudros. Here on Skyros were again the ghosts of the past. It was here that the young Achilles, disguised as a girl, had been sent by his mother to prevent him going to the Trojan War, but from whence he was lured to Troy by Ulysses, and later killed. To Ronnie Knox, now serving as a temporary master at Shrewsbury and conducting pedagogic correspondences with old friends and pupils, Patrick wrote:

> This is a pleasant cruise. How can I describe it uncensoriously? First to the island of Hephaestus (or Philoctetes, or Hypsipyle) for a longish stay; then to the Pelusiac mouth to a town famed for its low life, where I escaped a too-sandy camp; then to the island where the fleet-footed Aeacid hid *sub lacrimosae Trojae funera*, and his son enjoyed the advantages of a classical education; and whence the bones of Theseus were taken home.

Now at its most beautiful, Skyros seemed idyllic. Every kind of wildflower seemed to be growing, sage and balsam were profuse, and the place was humming with bees. The sea was blue and there was much pink marble among the rocks. Charles and Patrick took a long walk to the barren southern half of the island, and a solitary shepherd, a 'charming man in blue baggy trousers,' whom they identified as the Homeric Eumaeus, offered them 'milk-cheese and some good damp peasant bread.' They were rowed back to the ship, carrying cheeses and flapping tortoises, by 'a sturdy Greek fisherman and his still sturdier wife,' to be greeted 'with some slight sarcasm' by Rupert, who had stood in for them during their watch.

There followed battalion exercises on the rocky slopes of Skyros, and on 20 March, a Divisional Field Day, Patrick's platoon was placed near the right wing of the Hood Battalion. The advance was mainly up a dried-up river bed, with much scrambling over rough ground. At one point, during a rest break, Patrick, together with Rupert, Charles and Denis, sat in a small grove of olives about a mile inshore, which they all felt to be a place of particular beauty.

But now, just before the terrible battles that were to bring death to tens of thousands, a single death occurred that had a profound effect on Patrick. Rupert had never properly recovered from his illness at Port Said, and it was now clear that he was suffering from something else, his lip swelling badly. The day after the Field Day he lay in bed, and Patrick tried to cheer him up by saying that another feint along the Gallipoli coast was planned, and that Rupert could observe it from the porthole. The next day he was in and out of a coma, and visited by the Brigade Medical Officer who found that he was suffering from severe septicaemea, and arranged for him to be transferred to a French Hospital Ship, where he died.

Since the RND had received orders to embark for action the following day, the funeral had to take place at night, and it was probably at the suggestion of Denis that it was decided to take his body to the olive grove in which he and his three companions had sat three days before. This was in contravention to military regulations, Greece being neutral, and it was a difficult task. Eight Petty Officers struggled for two hours to carry the coffin up the rocky flare-lit path. Patrick was in command of the firing party of four. First came a man carrying a wooden cross, then Patrick with drawn sword (the sword that had been given him by Julian Grenfell), then the coffin followed by a cortege of officers led by General Paris. After the body had been laid in the grave, he gave the orders for three volleys to be fired in the air and presented arms, 'inaccessible to sorrow' when ordering this ceremonial. Charles, Denis, Clegg, Oc and Bernard piled fragments of white marble in a cairn over the grave, leaving Rupert all to himself except for a few shepherds. Clegg Kelly, after being wounded the following month, from his hospital bed in Egypt composed a beautiful elegy for string orchestra, dedicated to the memory of Rupert Brooke.

At a time when in England poets were so highly esteemed (more so, indeed, than musicians), the death of Rupert Brooke affected the entire nation. His poem 'The Soldier,' which so perfectly expressed the frame of mind in which he had volunteered to fight, had recently been quoted in a sermon in St Paul's Cathedral, and published in *The Times*: 'If I should die, think only this of me, That there's some corner of a foreign field That is forever England.' It now became instantly famous. Winston Churchill wrote the valediction in *The Times*, and a legend was born, to stand in comparison with Byron's death at Missolonghi. What is so apposite about Rupert's poem is that, although it refers to a soldier's death in 'a foreign field', it bears no reference to fighting. In describing a young Englishman prepared to give his life for his country, it is equally appropriate for Rupert's death from infection. *1914 and other Poems* was published within two months of his death and went into numerous impressions.

Patrick was deeply affected by Rupert's death, the first of his intimate friends to die, and the first he had seen dying. In his short memoir of the voyage on the *Grantully Castle* he wrote, 'I shouldn't have thought that anyone, in three months, could come to fill so large a space in my life.' To Ettie he wrote from on board ship two days later, 'He had entirely conquered me, and was threatening to dethrone all Eton and Balliol from my affections;' and he returned to the subject of Rupert in a letter to her written in the trenches:

He had wound himself round my heart in the months since Christmas – he was a great charmer both of men and women, and it is awful to think how some people must feel about him. He was a very delicious companion, full of good jokes and perfect at other people's. He held the most violent and truculent opinions, and with the gentlest manner you ever saw. I think he had drawn in his horns and abandoned his insolence (as some others of us have tried to do) for the war, in order to live happily with queer hotch-potchy brother officers.

On the evening of 24 April the transports carrying the Hood Battalion and other units of the RND sailed out from Skyros, and by next morning stood off the Gallipoli coast at the Gulf of Saros near Bulair, at the neck of the peninsula. Their immediate task was to threaten a landing to divert Turkish forces from the real attack that day by the 29th Division at Cape Helles and the Australian and New Zealand Corps at Gaba Tepe, later to be known as Anzac Cove. To add to the reality of this Patrick's company commander, Bernard Freyberg, with great daring volunteered to be landed alone on the shore at night to light flares to simulate invasion. The tactic worked perfectly, fooling the German General Liman von Sanders, who directed the Turkish forces, some of whom remained in the area for two days more, when they could more profitably have been deployed to where the real landings were. Freyberg was an amazingly strong swimmer (he had swum the English Channel), and was extremely fortunate to be picked up, cramped and nearly dead with cold, after two hours in the sea.

For the next three days the Hood Battalion remained in reserve on board ship close to the Gallipoli shore, watching the action at Anzac Cove and the five other landing points further down the coast near Cape Helles, and the pounding of the hills and woods by the big guns of the fleet, puffs of earth marking where the shells landed. The landings had been far more difficult than expected, and severe casualties had been suffered. On one of the beaches the SS River Clyde could be seen run aground where hundreds of men had been slaughtered by enemy machine-gun fire as they had clambered down on to the ground. Some units of the RND had been involved in the invasion, but only in the organization of working parties and beach control. Not to bring the reserves into the battle during this crucial period was a major error, as it gave time for the Turkish forces to regroup and strengthen their defences at strong points a little inland. Not till the night of 29 April was the Hood Battalion ordered to disembark. The selected place was at W Beach at the tip of Cape Helles, which had been stormed by the Lancashire Regiment three days previously.

The Hood landed under a full moon, transferring to lighters and barges and then wading, bivouacing on the grass and heather above the beach, huddled together against the cold, the officers' spirits fortified by rum. Next day they marched about a mile and a half north and began to dig in under fire. They then returned to their bivouac area, and the following day was spent in preparing support trenches. On the night of 1 May the Turks carried out a major night attack, but were repulsed, and next morning a counter-attack was ordered, with the Hood Battalion comprising part of the front. They advanced into a dried-up ravine called the Achi Baba Gully and to an exposed ridge, and attempted to dig in. But within twenty minutes they were forced to withdraw, the position being untenable. Five officers and seventy-five men had been killed or wounded, mostly by enemy shrapnel. One of those hit was Charles Lister, hit in the rump, and now evacuated. The next couple of days were spent in fatigues and working parties.

The ground ahead of them led up towards the summit of a hill known to the British as Achi Baba. Although only some 700 feet high, it dominated the tip of the peninsula. Though subject to bombardment by British naval guns, the Turkish defences were strong, devised by Liman von Sanders and deployed by Colonel Mustapha Kemal (Atatürk, later founder of modern Turkey). They were placed in small but well-designed machine-gun emplacements hidden in thick undergrowth, scrub and clumps of trees, unidentifiable to artillery. They could also move their men around by use of the gullies, invisible from the ships. In front of Achi Baba was the village of Krithia. An attempt to capture it on 28 April had already failed and so a second battle for it was planned. This would have been better done by night, but unfortunately the Corps Commander, Major-General Aylmer Hunter Weston, decided to mount the attack by day. Hunter Weston, a bluff thick-headed character, who referred to the probability of casualties as 'blooding the pups', as much as any other exemplifies Siegfried Sassoon's chilling lines about the 'cheery old' General who 'did for them both with his plan of attack.'

At 11 am on 6 May the attack began, with the Hood Battalion at a point near the centre. For the first 300 yards no opposition was encountered, but from then on they were constantly under fire. By means of short rushes they got to a building called the White House some 1,000 yards forward, and the leading platoons a further 300-400 yards, still under full enemy fire from hidden positions: so hidden, indeed, that Patrick never saw a single live Turk throughout the day, merely listening to the incessant 'ping, ping, pong, chuck, chuck, plop, plop, fzzz, woof, woof, and all the approved noises from revolver to big gun.' For several hours Patrick and Denis found themselves in the most forward positions of the whole Brigade, having to lie absolutely still ('to pretend to be a daisy') till dusk and then crawl away. Contact had been lost both with the French forces to the right and the British forces to the left.

The attack continued next day, but the Hood was held in reserve, in support of the French. Krithia had still not been captured, and the advance had come to a standstill. The Hood had lost its Commanding Officer, Colonel Quilter, and the Battalion was now reduced to ten officers and 343 men, having begun the campaign (before the transference of the stokers) as a force of around 900. Bernard Freyberg had a stomach wound, Denis Browne a neck wound, and Oc Asquith was shot through the knee. Patrick was very lucky not to be wounded in this engagement. But next morning a rifle was fired in error by one of his own men from within three yards, hitting him in the chest. This would assuredly have killed him had it not been stopped by a steel mirror from Aspreys that he kept in his breast pocket (penetrating his tunic, three sheets of Bromo, and his Platoon Roll Book on its way). 'Almost as good an advertisement for Aspreys as Oc's wound was for the government,' he felt.

Patrick now had time to reflect on his first week of fighting. To Ettie (in a blood-stained letter) he wrote 'it is very exciting, and a thing a man should not have missed; but now I've seen it and been there and done the dashing, I begin to wonder whether this is any place for a civilized man, and to remember about hot baths and strawberries and my morning *Times*.' He is surprised at his absence of tiredness, even though for 'three nights running (with a fight in between) I had practically no sleep.' A week later he wrote to Diana that his method as an officer of avoiding being picked off by snipers is 'to lie flat on my stomach, carry a rifle, and look exactly like a stoker: an illusion now assisted by my fortnight's auburn beard.' Also 'I have discovered why one is braver than would naturally be expected: there is only a contingency of pain to be faced, not a certainty as at the dentist. If only one man in five who went to the dentist got hurt one would be far braver and so in action I was throughout firmly convinced that the Turkish bullets were destined for my next door neighbours (who indeed were picked off *three times* in one day).'

Patrick found himself in close quarters with nature – its beauties, such as 'the most divine poppies and vetches making the whole place red and blue' and 'the startling beauty of blue jays and cranes,' but also its insects, the peninsula being 'marvellously rich in various species of ants, spiders, and beetles, with which, in our troglodytic life, one becomes curiously familiar. I am constantly reminded of the invocation of Achilles in the *Iliad* which mentions the Selloi, a peculiar tribe of dervishes sacred to Zeus, who crouch on the ground and never wash their feet.' He reported on his first profitable encounter with the French. As he led a party of ratings down to bathe in the Dardanelles he passed a group of French artillerymen, and bartered four pots of jam for four loaves of bread. On the strength of this he was made Mess President. His letters to his sisters specify his simple wants. Shortbread and cakes are most acceptable; tinned butter can be excellent. Socks, bootlaces and plenty of notepaper, with pencils and matches: 'Oh, and I want a *really good* air cushion, that must be tested by *sitting* on it – the fattest shopwalker for a good stretch, as they nearly all leak if you put them under the hip-bone.'

But in horrible contrast to nature were the scenes of battle. To Dear he wrote that the worst part of the war was the dead bodies of man and beast: 'There was another heap of dead in front of the trench, and at dawn a lark got up from there and started singing – a queer contrast. Rupert Brooke could have written a poem on that, rather his subject.' To Diana he wrote of 'the squeal of men hit near you and the jelly like appearance of their wounds, and far worse, the smell of the very dead and the curious way the hot sun puffs them out to three times their size and *blackens* them . . . but mine is a strongish stomach, as Balliol Quad, and the Savoy, and Bob Chanler's house in E19th Street can witness.'

In contrast to the practice in Flanders, where every third week was spent a long way back from the front, the troops at Gallipoli were only occasionally carried back to the islands for recuperation, and their rest camps were in trenches near the beach only a mile or so behind the firing line. These were constantly under desultory Turkish shellfire. Towards the end of May the Hood Battalion received reinforcements. In these weeks the nature of the battle changed. From a fluid pattern it developed into trench warfare. The RND, now all under a single commander, covered about 1,000 yards across the Achi Baba Nullah. To its right, stretching to the Dardanelles, was the French Army; to its left was the British 42nd Division, then the 29th Division, and the Indian Brigade covering the Gallipoli coast.

A third major battle to capture Krithia was planned for 4 June. The 2nd Brigade, comprising the Howe, Hood and Anson Battalions would lead the RND attack. Despite the experience of 6 May, it was also to be in daylight, but now it had to be a constricted frontal advance, without the possibility of outflanking movements, because by now the line on both sides had become entrenched. Also, although the attack was preceded by a bombardment by the guns of the ships, their accuracy was diminished by having to fire when under way, for fear of enemy torpedoes and artillery. A bombardment of the Turkish lines began at 0800 hours, intensified at 10.30, and stopped at 11.20. The troops were then instructed to cheer and show their bayonets: this was intended to draw the Turkish reserves forward and be caught in the bombardment when it resumed ten minutes later. It provoked a violent response from the Turks. At midday the troops climbed out of the trenches and ran forward, only to be mown down in great numbers by the Turkish machine-guns on front and flanks. Only half the troops got across the first 50 yards to some dead ground. Nevertheless the RND First Line did succeed in penetrating the front Turkish trenches, which had mostly been evacuated, and a few of the Hood got as far as the third trench. However here they were impossibly exposed, the Howe having made little progress and the French not advanced at all. Ordered to retreat to their own lines, the survivors had to step over the bodies of their dead or wounded comrades who had fallen in the initial rush.

The whole battle had been an absolute disaster. Of the 70 officers and 1,900 men of the 2nd Brigade, 61 officers and 1,319 men had been casualties, of which twelve officers and some 300 men were of the Hood Battalion. What is more, on Gallipoli all those who could walk and were unwounded were considered fit, unlike those in Flanders who were considered too weak and exhausted to fight. In Patrick's own company that day, of the four officers, three, including Denis Browne, were killed, and the fourth wounded. Freyberg was wounded, and Edward Nelson took command of what remained of the Hood.

But Patrick had been saved from the carnage and probable death by being ordered at the last moment to Brigade Headquarters to act as interpreter for the co-ordination of the French Artillery barrage, an appointment which, as he wrote, 'shows the advantages of a sound commercial education.' Three days later, in a resumption of the battle, he was seen running among the French Colonial troops, waving his cane and shouting '*Avancez! Avancez!*' The Senegalese came out of their trenches, advanced 17 yards, and then bolted back into them 'like so many gigantic rabbits, after which nothing would persuade them to show themselves again.' No further attempt was made to break through to capture Krithia or secure Achi Baba, and for all the remaining months of the campaign the Cape Helles front was merely a holding operation while initiatives were made elsewhere: 'That damned old Achi-baba (or 'Archibald'' as we waggishly call it) still frowns at us with an impregnable frown.'

After the disaster of 4 June, the Hood Battalion, strengthened by drafts from the Collingwood, was sent for recuperation to the base camp on Imbros, the nearest island some fifteen miles out, or, as Patrick put it to Ronald Knox, 'the island whither Miltiades escaped the Phenisians.' Patrick was now promoted to Lieutenant (the equivalent to a military Captain), and was the sixth most senior officer in the Hood. Oc Asquith, on the grounds of being his senior, in having joined up a few days before Patrick, got a double-promotion to Lieutenant Commander, and was put in command of 'D' Company, with Patrick his second-in-Command. After two months subject to continuous shellfire on Gallipoli, Imbros was heaven. Instead of trenches, there were tents. Instead of wretched huddles of men, there was conventional drill. Charles Lister was back. Patrick left the camp whenever he could, and visited the chief town, or else went over the central ridge to Panagia, 'where there was delicious coffee and beer and eggs and mullets and marvellous mulberries that dropped into your mouth and covered you all over with blood-red stains that turned blue-black, and you could forget for a day that you were a damned soldier.' In July he returned again to Imbros on one week's leave (waiving a claim for Alexandria), with the added intention of having his teeth seen to. He installed himself at Panagia, trudging back and forth to camp to see the dentist. But after only three days he was recalled, on the grounds that the composite Battalion was to move up to the front line. He had to get up and leave his billet in the village at three in the morning, only to find, when he got back to the peninsula, that the order had been countermanded.

It was here on Imbros that Patrick wrote the poem which has gained him lasting renown, and is printed at the front of this book. Although he does not allude to it anywhere, it was found written in his pencilled handwriting, and with corrections, on a blank page at the end of his miniature edition of A. E. Housman's *The Shropshire Lad*. It is rigidly in the style of this collection of Housman's short poems about doomed youth, simple, lyrical, and direct. From the text it was assumedly written at the pier on Imbros while waiting for the trawler to take him back to Helles. It provides the perfect epitaph for Patrick. The poem begins with an opening stanza that expresses a fatalism about death after seeing so many friends killed, an ambiguity about the urge to live. It then breaks into a cry from the heart at the thought of the hell of Gallipoli, and the feeling of being sent there capriciously, just as the Homeric heroes had been in their dispute about Helen of Troy. This evokes the spirit of Achilles, like Patrick a reluctant but resolute warrior, sent towards death by cruel fates.

The final evocation is what arrests the reader of this poem. Achilles, when finally persuaded to join the Achaeans in their desperate attempt to save their ships from destruction, protested that he had no armour, having lent it to Patroclus, since killed by Hector. But the goddess told him the need was so urgent that he must immediately show himself to the enemy as he was, and she swathed him in a blazing light. In *The Iliad* Homer compares the flames of Achilles to a battle area seen from a nearby island which, as it happens, was exactly what Gallipoli would have looked like at night from Panagia on Imbros (I use Rieu's translation):

Athene cast her tasselled aegis round his sturdy shoulders; and the great goddess also shed a golden mist around his head and caused his body to emit a blaze of light. Thus, from some far-away beleaguered island, where all day long the men have fought a desperate battle from their city walls, the smoke goes up to heaven; but no sooner has the sun gone down than the light from the line of beacons blazes up and shoots into the sky to warn the neighbouring islanders and bring them to the rescue in their ships. Such was the blaze that made its way to heaven from Achilles' head.

It would be nice to think that Patrick was inspired by this particular image to write his poem. But his last verse is a correction from an inferior text which suggests that this was not so, and that 'flame capped' was an afterthought. The uncorrected last verse is of three lines, to which I have added a supposed fourth line:

> I will go back this morning
>   From Imbros to the fight;
> Stand by me, son of Peleus
>   [?And shout with all thy might]

Likewise the mention of the 'trench' would not have been in the first version. The Greeks had built a trench to protect their ships and their bridgehead in front of Troy, just as had the Allied Army on Gallipoli. Achilles stood *by* the trench, on the defensive side of it, as would have been normal in the days of swords and spears, thus exhibiting himself fully. Patrick has to transpose this image to one of standing *in* the trench, protected from modern bullets and shrapnel, though Achilles would have seemed much less remarkable there, especially with his head below the parapet. But he correctly mentions the great shout of Achilles, 'as piercing as a trumpet call', which threw the Trojans into chaos. This was a technique that still applied in modern trench warfare, and had been adopted by the RND on 4 June, albeit unsuccessfully.

After the War Ettie showed Patrick's poem to an anonymous acquaintance, whose appreciation of it cannot be bettered:

It cuts the heart strings, one feels the reality of life, that this is not mere poetry but the bitter intolerable truth. The verses stand apart: the dry stark matter of factness at the beginning, and the sudden passionate out-cry, which makes the wistful questioning so poignant, and kindles the white hot blaze of the close. It is as when the throb of a stringed instrument rises above the orchestra's veiling concord of sounds, and seems to lay bare the nerve of the music, its inner meaning. Strange how the old epic and old myth still hold such power to hearten souls as heroic but far more complex than Achilles' own.

The poem stands in contrast to the poem – 'Into Battle' – written by Julian Grenfell only a few months before, which exults in the thrill felt by the fighting man in close contact with nature and danger. The difference stems from their quite different approach to the War. Julian had written from the Front 'I *adore* War. It is like a big picnic without the objectlessness of a picnic.' Patrick had from the start recognized the futility of the War, and loathed being caught up in it. Ettie in later years must have reflected on the distinction between these two famous poems by the two men she had so loved. Patrick's certainly has more in common with other War poets, such as Wilfrid Owen, Siegfried Sassoon or Edward Thomas, who expressed the horror of trench warfare and rejected the cavalier frame of mind in which so many had at first entered it.

Julian Grenfell had been wounded in Flanders on 13 May, and died of his head-wound on 26 May. In a long letter to Ettie of 22 June, Patrick recounted many incidents in his relationship with Julian, whom he had seen so constantly at Eton and Balliol, though losing touch with him from the summer of 1910. In it he revealingly admits that his acceptance within the inner group of fast-living rich young men was dependent on earning their approval by condoning their excesses and patching up their quarrels, sometimes at the cost of demeaning himself and subduing the more reflective side of his nature. Describing the digs he shared with Julian and others in 1909, he writes of 'some excruciating moments for one prone, like me, to feel other people's floaters'; and 'I believe I acquired some merit for all-round loyalty and reconciliation: I really worked hard, you know, solely to avoid social agonies for myself.'

His condolences for Ettie are naturally profound: 'my heart is torn for you. You write with your own courage: but my phlegm is melted at the thought of the years that are lost, and I cannot dwell on it or speak of it without new despair and new rage at this iron nightmare in which we live.' Since his departure in February,

Ettie's letters to Patrick continued in their tone of warm affection, but with the added poignancy of fear for his safety. In April she had written, after learning of Rupert Brooke's death: 'Dearest Patsy, I cannot at all tell you how anxious I have felt about *you*. I cannot at all tell you all the things I think and should like to say'; and 'more and more through all these months does one feel that the one clear gain is happiness and that not one hour of that was ever in vain.' And in June, after Julian's death ('He seems very near to us now – happy and strenuous – I like to think all his horses are winged'), she concludes: 'It is my birthday today, and I am writing to you for a treat. Goodbye beloved, and do go on writing to me . . . In whatever circumstances and in whatever planes you and I will keep near each other.'

Back on the peninsula Patrick endured the stifling summer. The classical history of the Dardanelles was never far from his mind. To Edward Horner he wrote: 'It is really delightful to me to bathe every day, when not in the trenches or standing by, in the Hellespont, looking straight over to Troy, to see the sun set over Samothrace, to be fighting for the command of Aegospotami, and to restate Miltiades's problem of the lines of Bulair.' To Diana, on the first anniversary of the War, he wrote:

> Shall we ever have fun again? I suppose yes! Some of us, when the Russians have made their grand stand on the Urals and a few bearded survivors of the RND have been carried in litters to the top of Achi Baba. Gott straff the heat, the flies, the tepid drinks, my smelly lousy grousing men, and the damnable inaction wearily alternating with the yet more unspeakably damnable action. Not so much the Turks, who are really very nice, not the scenery which is admirable – but the poppies and bright birds are gone, and our end of the peninsula, which was a dream when we landed, is now simply a dusty fly-blown maze of dug-outs and latrines.

Charles Lister described the dugout he shared with Patrick, Patrick being such a fine officer and '*gai comme un pinson*'. It was only some two feet deep, a protection against shrapnel but little use against the high explosive shells which rained down from time to time from the Asiatic shore. One of these succeeded in 'riddling Patrick's best khaki tunic (luckily he was not in it, but it was hanging on a tree) and covering his sleeping bag with soot.' On another occasion a shell which landed in the officers' kitchen had plastered his bed with innumerable dried apricots which had been in the process of cooking. Despite this chronic uncertainty he usually slept well, having sheets, pillow case, pyjamas and mosquito-net. But the rest on Imbros had not much improved the state of the Battalion, which was in poor shape, the filth and the flies, the continuous shelling, the integration of new drafts, all taking their toll: dysentery was rife, jaundice common.

On 16 July the Battalion was moved up to the front line in the wake of yet another attack that had gained some ground. In the captured trenches Turkish bodies lay everywhere, the weather was sweltering, the flies universal, the stench overwhelming, and many men physically sick. Some of the rotting corpses in the area were of members of the Hood who had fallen on 4 June: 'It's a grim thought that Denis may be disturbing ones repose.' It was necessary to dig more communications trenches, even though within two hundred yards of the enemy. For four nights this was undertaken in darkness under the vigorous leadership of Bernard Freyberg, the Acting Battalion Commander. In an area designated for Asquith's company, and known as the 'Asquith Triangle,' Patrick and Cleg Kelly distinguished themselves particularly. Although six men of the company were killed or wounded, including their petty officer, these two remained above ground during the entire nocturnal operation. Charles Lister reported that the trench would be called Shaw Stewart Street (all the trenches had names, some of them English places – Chelmsford Street, Clapham Junction, some after regiments – Lancashire Street, Fusilier Bluff, some after individuals – Frith Walk, Clunes Sap). Once again, Patrick had been lucky, and by the end of July was one of a much diminished number who had been on Gallipoli for over three months and not been hit.

Charles shortly after got hit once again, this time only slightly: 'he will do himself an injury one of these days,' Patrick told Diana. His prediction was correct. Charles returned soon afterwards, but on 25 August he was hit in a trench by a shell through the pelvis, his bladder damaged. He was taken to a hospital ship but died of his gangrenous wounds three days later.

This was the most immediate blow Patrick had yet suffered, greater even than the death of Rupert Brooke. Charles had been his closest male friend for ten years, and the only school-friend who had been with him on Gallipoli. He was the Patroclus to Patrick's Achilles. It had been Patrick who persuaded him to come out with the RND and join the Hood. On 9 September he wrote to Ettie. 'Charles is dead. If there was anything that could add to the weight of misery I am carrying, that was it. It seems our generation at Balliol is doomed. If I live through this war I shall be almost without friends. Charles was the nearest to a perfect character I have known: he was utterly unselfish and devoted.' To Ronnie Knox he wrote more dispassionately but more descriptively about Charles as an infantry officer. He never groused, he ignored danger, he was constantly reckless 'walking between the lines with his arms waving under hot fire from *both* sides,' and the men, both the veteran stokers and the new recruits, adored him.

Charles was constantly asked for by the Intelligence as a Turkish expert but 'the trenches were his only joy.' Had he accepted he might well have had experiences comparable to those of Aubrey Herbert, another (rather older) Balliol man, who was attached as an Intelligence Officer to the ANZAC forces, and who achieved many astonishing interchanges with the cultivated Turkish officers, and memorably supervised a truce on Whit Sunday to bury the dead. Charles was a lovable man whose early espousal of Socialist ideals had come from the heart. On Gallipoli his boyish enthusiasm proved infectious to all ranks, and although he never absorbed the public-school ethos, in him we can see the image of the schoolboy who (as in Newbolt's poem) rallies the ranks when 'the sands of the desert are sodden red.' In contrast Patrick, though equally brave in battle, led his men by example and by discipline. In common with most of the officers, he was unable to treat them as friends: in a letter to Tats at this time he wrote: 'I was never much good with the smellier orders! who are always grumbling and all pig-headed as mules.'

Even before Charles' death, the realization of the loss of so many of his friends sunk in to Patrick, bringing moods of deep gloom. But the loss intensified his longing for Ettie, for a hurredly-written letter begins: 'I just want to tell you I am always thinking of you and always longing to see you and tell you how much I love you and how I want nothing so much on earth, if I live through, as to try always to make up to you by my love for one hundredth part of what you have lost, or rather, of what you have given.' (Here he was referring to her double-loss, because her younger son Billy had also been killed, on 29 July, in the Second Battle of Ypres). To Tats he wrote on 25 August: 'My dear I am so very depressed, I can think of nothing but Billy dead and what Ettie must be feeling'; and he lists those who have died – Denny Anson, John Manners, Percy Wyndham, Twiggy Anderson, Hoj Fletcher, Volley Heath, Julian and Billy Grenfell, Douglas Radcliffe, Rupert Brooke and Denis Browne. Edward Horner had been wounded. 'This generation of mine is suffering in their twenties what most men get in their seventies – the gradual thinning of their contemporaries.' However, after going through a list of things needed in her next parcel ('toothpowder and bromo and pencils and notebook and a toothbrush now and then'), he goes on, 'Sorry to be depressing. I am very happy really . . .'

In late July the junior liaison officer of the British to the French Forces alongside them was wounded, and the Corps headquarters asked the Brigade for Patrick's release as a temporary replacement: he had been picked out by Sir Ian Hamilton himself. The Commodore of the Hood at first refused this release (which was, of course, a compliment to Patrick) but was overruled. Though sorry to leave his unit, he did not object. His life on Gallipoli was now transformed. Though still in the battle zone he was based at Corps

Headquarters, and made regular visits to the French, sometimes on horseback – taking a toss or two on the way. He found the French headquarters differed greatly from its British equivalent. The latter had plenty of service, but the food was plain and poor, whereas the French 'with far less fuss, make their mess exactly like a Paris restaurant.' He was also summoned to GHQ on Imbros, where the great difference to life on the peninsula was to be in a tent rather than a trench. It was not always so comfortable even there, however. In September he wrote to Tats about a night spent there when the wind blew ceaselessly – 'talk about the trenches – I never knew such discomfort before – a cold flapping tent with draughts instead of my nice warm dugout – I woke up every half hour with new nightmares and worse neuralgia, and before dawn had a handkerchief and two socks tied round my head.' The transit to Imbros could also be unpleasantly rough. On one occasion Patrick, nearly sick himself, saw a Turkish prisoner 'rendering up all he had over the stern,' clutched firmly by the seat of his trousers by a stern British sergeant-major. And later in the year he feared for his life in a particularly dangerous crossing, in which the trawler was unable to land on Imbros, and Patrick was on it for twenty-four hours and was sea-sick for the first time.

On 6 August the last attempt at the conquest of Gallipoli took place with an advance from Anzac Bay and a landing on Suvla Bay, five miles to the north of it, in support. The forces on Cape Helles staged an offensive in support, which Patrick witnessed together with a French Staff officer. But the complicated operation failed, particularly in its aim to capture Sari Bair, the central feature above Anzac Bay, which would have isolated the Turkish forces on Achi Baba. So the only question now was whether to stick it out on Gallipoli or to evacuate. The RND continued through the autumn to alternate between spells in the firing line, spells in reserve trenches, and rest on the beaches or at base camp. But it had lost its backbone of battle-hardened men with the transference of the stokers, and was now only a holding-unit: sickness was far more serious than enemy action. Patrick knew that his brother Basil was at Suvla and was determined to see him. They corresponded, and in early September he succeeded in getting there – on the date of their father's birthday. The two brothers enjoyed a good lunch and inspected the front 'from a safe distance'.

On one of Patrick's visits to Imbros he had a long talk with Compton MacKenzie, an Intelligence officer who had made his name with his novel *Sinister Street*, famous for its descriptions of Oxford in the early years of the century. When waiting at the landing pier for the departure of the trawler going back to Gallipoli late in the evening, the two of them sat on a couple of barrels under the lee of the low sandstone cliff in a gusting wind, and for a time forgot about the war in the joy of talking about Oxford and Magdalen and Balliol and Cyril Bailey and Rupert Brooke and books. But the seeming endlessness of the war, and the apprehension about the Suvla initiative, brought with it a realization that the end of an epoch had come, and that Oxford would never be the same again. Then 'the long talk with Patrick draws to an end. Waving lanterns are seen coming down the slope from the camp. The bags are flung into the cutter, the passengers for the "Imogen" follow the bags. We push off into the gusty murk of the harbour. I wave farewell to Patrick, who reminds me in that moment, of the Pied Piper of Hamelin, as he stands there in the flickering lantern-light.'

The Pied Piper allusion was inspired not just by Patrick's tall thin silhouette and long nose, but by his beard: 'He did not look much like a Fellow of All Souls in his RND uniform and long pointed red beard.' Charles Lister had earlier referred to Patrick as looking like 'a holy man in his bright red beard, which might have been died with henna' [actually, it was auburn]. In contrast to the Army units, in which shaving was demanded except when at the front, the RND kept to the naval tradition that beards were acceptable, and Patrick's, with its colour, was surely the most remarkable of all.

In September Patrick's colleague Major de Putron, the senior British Liaison Officer to the French force at Helles, was hit by a shell: 'he was outside his hut at the time and I was (prudently) inside.' Patrick had impressed both the French and the British and stood in for him. Until October he was based at the British Corps Headquarters, but thereafter at the French. The difference was great. Quite apart from the cuisine, the French had taken far more trouble to make their dugouts more habitable, and their trenches were infinitely superior to the British, with stone and clay instead of sandbags. They had carpenters' shops with steam-saws, and plenty of firewood – all prepared to last through the winter, in contrast to the British whose preparation seemed to be confined to the provision of footballs. Patrick's billet was now a little wooden cubicle with a bullet-and-rain-proof tin roof. With the cooler weather the activity of the flies and fleas was dropping and that of the mice and rats was not yet serious. Yet all the time they were subjected to desultory shells fired by the Turks from the Asiatic shore, fortunately limited by their shortage of ammunition. This common threat to everyone on Cape Helles – British and French, front-line and support-lines, combat forces and Staff alike – acted as a booster to morale and encouraged a closer camaraderie.

These comparative comforts provided, as Patrick told Raymond Asquith, 'an unparalleled opportunity for becoming Better Read.' To Ettie he wrote:

> I have read *Lord Ormont* and *Redgauntlet* and *Lavengro* and Finlay's *Greece under the Romans*, and *Madamoiselle de Maupin*, and Hewlett's *Open Country*, and some of Herodutus, and some Lucretius, and re-read *The Egoist;* and I am reading Bosanquet's *Theory of the State*, and Macaulay's *History*, and *Love and Mrs Lewisham*; and I have also read some Gibbon, and *Guy and Pauline*. I sustained my opinion of *The Egoist* (which is an exalted one) very completely in re-reading. I have now lent it to a Frenchman who thinks he knows English well.

The French had likewise their views about what to read. Of *Madamoiselle de Maupin* 'a French officer said "*C'est pas un des livres qu'il faut lire ici"*, and I said *"Why?"*, and he, enigmatically *"Parce que".'* Patrick also reported that he had got Arthur Balfour's *Theism and Humanism*, in which the former Premier steered a middle line between the inherent contradictions of religion and science. To Dear he wrote, and knew she would be pleased to know, that he had enjoyed *Redgauntlet* and was now a confirmed admirer of Walter Scott.

In response to a request from Patrick, Ronald Knox sent him a summary of the history of the Dardanelles, the Hellespont of classical times, with accompanying maps. These provided several illuminating instances of operations by combined military and naval forces, though none of them had been of such long duration as the present. With the Homeric description of the siege of Troy ever in his mind, Patrick must presumably have reflected that the Greek encirclement had gone on for twenty years without achieving its aim, and success had only been gained by a ruse.

In May Churchill had resigned as a result of the Naval failure in the Dardanelles, but Asquith held on as an ailing Prime Minister. Patrick was in receipt of letters hinting at Asquith's philandering with the young women of his circle – particularly Venetia Stanley and Laura Lovat – but this by no means diminished his respect. Ignoring the real problem of Asquith's private life – his excessive drinking – and his lack of political direction in time of war, Patrick merely wrote tolerantly to his sister: 'Isn't he a funny old gentleman? I daresay he directs our destinies all the better for his little relaxations, and I (speaking fearlessly from a skirtless land) blame him the less for envying him the more.' Perhaps Patrick would have been less tolerant had he known that Asquith never once wrote to Raymond on the Western Front and only rarely to Oc on Gallipoli.

Attention now shifted to a new military front. Bulgaria had entered the war on the side of the Central Powers and was about to invade Serbia, which was supported by the Allies. A joint Franco-British force of two brigades was sent to Salonika by the agreement of the government of Greece. The Greek Government was pro-western, motivated by fear of Bulgaria and Turkey, whereas the King and his court (he was, after all, a German prince, and his Queen was a sister of the Kaiser) were sullenly pro-Central. But by the time the Brigade got there, Serbia had been largely overrun. Liaison had to be made with this force, and Patrick put in a bid to go there, but was baulked in this by de Putron, who went instead. But Sir Ian Hamilton once again stepped in. He was being relieved of his command because of the strategic stalemate. But in one of his last acts before handing over to General Sir Charles Monro on 16 October, Hamilton confirmed Patrick as the senior liaison officer and appointed him a GSO III on the Staff, with a theoretical pay increase (to £400). Patrick wrote contentedly to Raymond that his functions were 'of the most gentlemanly: I seldom speak to anyone under the rank of a colonel, and do not disguise my preference for Major-Generals. A pleasant life, if smacking slightly of eternity . . .'

Patrick in his turn now had a junior colleague assigned to him. Viscount Duncannon was a Member of the House of Commons and well-connected to French financial circles. As the son and heir to the Earl of Bessborough he had impeccable credentials, and Patrick could enjoy explaining to the French officers, '*Oui, il est fils d'un Earl, puis par consequent il est Viscount, ce que nous appelons titre de courtoise, mais il n'est pas pair.*' But Patrick found him 'a very dull dog', and was not at all put out when Duncannon withdrew with a stomach complaint and did not reappear. With his staff of seven signallers, in charge of a landline telephone, Patrick was fully confident in alone maintaining the liaison with the French officers, with whom he got on so well. As an instance of the jocular relationship he enjoyed with them, his letter to Dear in thanks for a cake she had sent him deserves its own mention:

> I never told you properly the noble history of your last cake, one of the glorified currant loaf kind with a crust (which keeps them fresh as new mown hay). General Birdwood was doing temporary Commander-in-Chief in between Sir Ian and Sir Charles Monro, and invited himself to tea with

the French General. The latter was in despair at not having anything sufficiently "serious" to offer the English general for tea – knowing that we tend to make a meal of it – and I stepped into the breach with the offer of my "plum cake" (an adopted French word pronounced "ploom kak") which had then just arrived. It made a noble show in the middle of the table and had the greatest success. "Is this from France?" asked General Birdwood between two mouthfuls. "No, it is the gift of Capitaine Stewart," said General Brulard. "From Scotland, sir," said I, amid loud cheers. So the cake had a really worthy fate.

As with everyone else on Gallipoli Patrick's harsh existence was alleviated by the intermittent arrival of parcels and letters. Parcels, sent by his sisters or Dear, mostly contained food or clothing, often in response to his requests, backed by cheques. The food was usually shared with others who messed with him, and jam was the most usual barter in return for French wine. The hazards here were the beach-robbers. When Charles had returned from his convalescence on Imbros in July, he brought with him fresh fruit, vegetables, wine and other luxuries, but all got lost on the beach due to the incompetence of his soldier servant: 'I think we should make him an officer,' was Charles' typically lighthearted comment on this discouraging news.

Mail was scrupulously delivered once disembarked, but took two or three weeks in transit. In April, having not heard from Diana since his departure, he had been 'inclined to condemn the coterie en masse.' But in a letter written in June she roundly asserted that she had sent him two, and Charles another, and that the fault must lie in 'those luckless mailbags', rumoured to being lost at sea. He then had to wait impatiently for her next – 'you are convicted of a *lacuna* or *hiatus* of at least forty-five days.' But he also heard about her from reading the social news in *The Observer*, followed by a letter from Katherine Asquith. Early in July Diana and Duff had gone to Brighton in the company of Raymond and Katherine and Venetia Stanley and Edwin Montagu (a Cabinet Minister, and shortly to be her husband). Duff was still a civilian, working in the Foreign Office. After dinner the two of them had gone for a tipsy late night stroll along the esplanade, where she had fallen down some steps and broken her leg. The fact that she was with Duff had not been given out, nor mentioned by those in the know and kept from the Duchess, so Patrick was spared feelings of jealousy, though he writes: 'No one will tell me *how* it happened – K mysteriously hints at Brighton fun and odium on her (which I can well believe) Raymond points gloomily to Denny's anniversary – but no wealth of detail. Tell me about it, Darling I am so sorry.'

Actually Diana was having a wonderful time, lying in bed in a nursing home, her pain dulled by morphia, and being visited by everyone. Edward Horner, now recovering from being wounded in Flanders, and losing a kidney, wrote that Diana had confided to Katherine that Edward and Patrick were now 'her only two marriage alternatives.' Edward added that he had himself given up any hope of marrying her as 'I am penniless and gradually becoming a melancholy maniac,' but that 'I dare say she will actually marry you. It's too awful to think of not liking either of you if you pulled it off!' Such suggestions must have been encouraging for Patrick, ignorant, though suspicious, of Diana's increasing dependence on Duff. Edward's general sense of hopelessness is also expressed in this letter to Patrick: 'With her, Diana, or a substitute, money, a seat in Parliament or partnership in a thriving firm, a title, a Lieutenancy, the Military Cross, interesting staff appointment on the "general" side, plenty of exercise, no skin trouble or asthma, I should be happy. Without *any* of these how can I be?'

The experience of living for months in imminent danger and proximity with death by no means led Patrick towards the consolations of religion. The great majority of British soldiers in the Great War paid lip service to religion, and many were true believers, though there certainly was never any revival of religious fervency as a result of the horrors seen and felt in the front lines. Others might pray in the trenches, but Patrick retained his stoic fatalism and scepticism, as also had Charles Lister. The Bible and the Prayer Book were not among the books in his knapsack. But his heart went out to the woman who meant more to him than anyone else – Ettie – and he recognized that her faith was helping to pull her through. In September he wrote: 'do remember those who love you, and remember me, who have no faith and no hope in this world, and little except you. I cannot do without you.' In October she wrote that she had nearly succumbed from sorrow – ('for a time the waters went over my head, I don't know what it was – the second blow on the same wound') – but 'through all the breaking anguish, one's body torn to bits, there has been no instant of doubt or misgiving about them. You and I don't think the same, but you don't mind my way Patsy? It doesn't irritate you? I have believed all my life, but now I know.'

Patrick was now able to secure a short leave to visit Athens. This was done by taking the regular boat which plied between Imbros and Athens with the official mail under the charge of the King's Messenger, for onward transit to Italy by another boat and thence by train. The leave was for twenty-four hours at Athens, plus the journey back with the returning King's Messenger. He arranged for Oc Asquith to go with him. The weather was fine, and on arrival they headed for a hotel with baths, only to be told that the baths were unavailable because a conduit had burst. Patrick's indignation was so colossal and so forcefully expressed (presumably in French, and with bluff military directness) that they gave way, and, alone of all the others in the hotel, they had baths morning and evening on both days, the ultimate luxury after months in trench or camp. Though the champagne tasted like orange-juice, they wined and dined in comfort. They saw the Acropolis and its museum, of course, and later Patrick went to a night club, relieving nine months of enforced chastity, rediscovering, as Diana put it, 'the aromatic balm and *le parfum douce et savoneuse des femmes.*' Oc, suffering from some form of jaundice, went to bed.

Next day it was to the museum and then to Eleusis. Here they had a curious encounter, because the other visitors there were a group of Germans – with a dachshund – out for a Sunday excursion.

The Germans eyed them coldly, realizing at once who they were, for their attempt to look like Swiss civilians was only nominal. Although their khaki tunics had been deprived of their buttons, their trousers were unmistakable, and the only real disguise was that Patrick (at any rate) wore a bowler hat that he had picked up from the stranded SS *River Clyde*. The incoming King's Messenger was delayed in arrival at Athens, so they could have stayed longer. But the British Minister to Greece was summoned to Mudros to confer with Lord Kitchener, who had come out to resolve whether to stay or to leave Gallipoli, and Oc was anxious to be back with the Hood. So they set off on the official yacht, and when off Sunium were transferred to a small cruiser which bore them at great speed to Lemnos.

The outcome of Kitchener's visit was to agree to a withdrawal from Gallipoli. One crucial consideration was that with Bulgaria's entry it would be possible for big German artillery to be brought to the area, able to destroy the fragile bridgeheads. The decision to withdraw from Suvla and Anzac was made in mid-December. Elaborate precautions were taken to disguise the withdrawal from the Turkish forces, by means of keeping the trenches manned, retaining the encampments, and evacuating progressively under cover of night. The deception worked perfectly, and was completed on 20 December. The decision about the Helles front was not made for another week. On Christmas day Patrick wrote to Tats, 'I wish they'd evacuate us, I confess.' Christmas lunch at French HQ was a splendid affair, and comprised Homard Mayonaisse; Tripes á la Mode de Caen; Faux Filet Jardiniére; Salade; Tarte aux Pèches; Fromage; Gaufrettes; Confiture; Café – Rhum.

The French now insisted that their force would leave anyway, and the gap that this created was filled by the brief return of units of the 29th Division to the front. Once the decision to evacuate the British forces was made, the operation took place with all the skill that had been shown at Suvla and Anzac. It might be supposed impossible to fool Liman von Sanders and his Turkish staff twice, but this is in fact what happened. Still believing that the full defensive force was still there, and that the British planned to create a mini Gibraltar on Helles, the Turks staged a bombardment of extreme intensity on 7 January. But the Turkish infantry, whose morale was now very low, failed to follow up and the attack failed. The Greeks had captured Troy by means of a deception, and now the British were leaving the Hellespont by another. It was a withdrawal and could be treated, if not as a victory, at least as a military success, in the manner of Dunkirk. Had the British been massacred when embarking, or forced to surrender, the impact on opinion among the Muslim populations of the British Empire would have been severe.

On the afternoon of 8 January Patrick paced up and down with the French artillery commander, whose men had already gone but whose guns remained. From time to time they lit bonfires to burn anything useful, maps and papers particularly, but also personal effects. Patrick's khaki suit and bowler hat had to go, and also his twenty books, though the thought of an intellectual Turk wanting to read them seemed remote. He retained his landline telephone to the last moment.

All day we have been looking at the weather in terror in case the wind should rise, but, thank the Lord, it is still only a gentle breeze. It takes one back to that other night, in April, when we waited on the ship and listened to the terrific bombardment at the landing – now it is just the opposite. I am waiting on shore and it is quiet as the grave, except when the batteries from Asia send us an occasional shot. If they had any idea of what we are up to they would simply make hay of the beaches, and it's rather satisfactory to feel we are cheating them, and they will wake up in the morning and find us gone. But, on the whole, it's nothing to be proud of for the British Army or the French either – nine months here, and pretty heavy losses, and now nothing for it but to clear out. I wonder what next?

TEN

Loneliness in Macedonia

PATRICK was evacuated to Lemnos. The Royal Naval Division had been under Army Command for the purposes of the Gallipoli Campaign, but was now returned to the direction of the Admiralty, under the command of Vice Admiral de Robeck. It was given the task of providing garrisons for the islands of Lemnos, Imbros and Tenedos, as well as sending a Brigade to the Anglo-French force in Salonika. However, the future of the Division was now a matter of debate between the Admiralty and the War Office. It was argued that it should be disbanded completely, or else handed bodily over to the Army, severing all links with the Admiralty. Both alternatives were strenuously opposed by General Paris, its Commander, and by most of the men, whose *esprit de corps* had been welded on Gallipoli. The division had received large reinforcements and was now far larger than the force that had set out for the Dardenelles.

After nearly three months of discussion, the decision was made. The RND would continue. For administrative purposes it would still be the responsibility of the Admiralty, and would retain its naval ranks and insignia. But it would be transferred to the Army for all operational purposes, including all questions relating to commissions and promotions, coming under the terms of the Army Act. It would also be available for use in any theatre of war, not merely to those associated with Naval operations, as had applied at Antwerp and Gallipoli. The personal intervention of Arthur (Oc) Asquith and Bernard Freyberg with the Prime Minister and his entourage was probably crucial in tipping the balance in favour of the continuation of the RND, despite the fall from power of its originator, Winston Churchill.

Meanwhile, from the moment of evacuation on 8 January 1916, the vexed question of home leave dominated the minds of those who had been on Gallipoli. It was expected that home leave would be allocated to those who had served there longest. General Paris made a false move when he initially decreed that only a number of officers should be granted this privilege, other ranks merely being granted leave on Malta. The officers refused to accept unless the home leave draft was composed of all ranks. It was not until the end of February that a contingent of five hundred men (thirty-eight of them from the Hood battalion, and including Asquith and Freyberg) sailed home for ten days' leave. But Patrick had not needed to wait for this. Immediately on arrival on Lemnos he had appealed to General Paris that his was a special case, pleading urgent business affairs. As he had not yet rejoined the RND but was still a displaced liaison officer attached to the Army, and thus not claiming a place which would otherwise go to one of the officers being considered for leave, this was granted, the length of his leave to be determined by the Admiralty, but set at three weeks.

To get home he had to go first to Cairo, which he reached in mid-January. Here he was told, unofficially, that he would very probably be required to go again as a liaison officer to the French, this time at Salonica, but that it might take some time before the order was definite: he should keep in touch with the War Office about this when back home. His successful relationship with the French on Gallipoli had been recognized with an award, that of Chevalier of the Legion of Honour, and (as was now the normal practice) he was permitted to wear the decoration on his British uniform. On arrival in England later in the month, Patrick duly reported both to the Admiralty and the War Office. But, as the period of his leave approached its end, he had heard nothing. So he adroitly sought and got permission from the Admiralty to defer his return to the RND until he knew for certain whether or not he would be needed by the Army, and to remain at home in the meantime. He also approached Sir Ian Hamilton, now licking his wounds in London, but, as he expected, was told that nothing could be done until the War Office had themselves received a definite request from Salonica. As a result Patrick enjoyed a protracted leave of over six weeks, since it was not until 12th March, when at Mells, that he received the telegram confirming his appointment, with orders to sail three days later. He was to be appointed a Captain in the Army, with the option of returning to the RND later if he wished.

Patrick put up at the Ritz. We have glimpses of him at Barings in Bishopsgate, at an All Souls Dinner, and as a guest of the Prime Minister in Walmer Castle at the end of February. For this he had to beg Diana, who would be there, to get him asked. It was she, rather than Asquith, that he wanted to see, and his letter asking this displays some desperation.

> Darling, I am in such a state, and have been nearly all day – so rare with me: I have got into that frame of mind in which one throws off telegrams and trunk calls in reaction to every wave of emotion, and God knows where it will stop: Listen again. I do want very much to come to Walmer – I see you so hideously little in London: and I am almost bound to go away next week. I wouldn't mind asking Margot straight out – only you would do it so much better. And really my dearest I have rather important things to say to you or hear from you – no?

She was certainly elusive, and he suspected her of not receiving him when he called at Arlington Street: she was 'still in bed', or she was 'out.' But not always, as this scribbled note from Guy's Hospital affirms: 'Drop into Arlington Street after lunch or lunch there . . . or drive with me tonight from 9-10 light dinner at Cheshire Cheese or somewhere. Keep this dark. Desperate haste against all rules, writing in the sink, D.' A later letter from him refers to intimate moments in Bedroom Number 10 at Walmer Castle and on the back stairs of the Cavendish Hotel, the establishment in Jermyn Street frequented by Lord Ribblesdale and owned by the famous Rosa Lewis who tolerated much raffish behaviour by her aristocratic clients.

His foremost plan was to establish a weekend at Mells before he left, and this was achieved just in time. Raymond was on the Staff in France, and Edward had been posted to Egypt, but Katharine agreed to have Patrick, Diana and Duff to stay in the Manor House. It was a weekend to remember. Patrick took charge of the drink, bringing 1 ½ dozen bottles of Perrier Jouet champagne as well as claret and cognac. In the three meals 10 of the champagne were drunk by the four of them. The summons from the War Office came just after he arrived on the Saturday afternoon, so he became the centre of affection in what became a glorious send-off party, helpful in his unspoken rivalry with Duff. After dinner on the Saturday, Duff records, they first read aloud from the Bible, then went to the bedroom shared by Katharine and Diana and gave themselves morphia injections, and then all lay on the bed reciting or reading poetry in turns till about three o'clock. But the Sunday was the climax for Patrick. His letter to Diana from the troop-ship a week later vividly describes it:

> . . . the middle-aged constitutional with Duffy before luncheon: then the wise choice of champagne for luncheon and the praiseworthy return of Duffy to his oldest love for the afternoon, and our sweet sober walk to inspect the true inwardness of Edward as a landowner (noteworthy among other things for the charm of the lodgekeeper, the match-provider). Then the very touching and very laughable expedition of Katharine and me to Dr Helps, so perfectly thought out, so utterly frustrated in fact: us and our little bottle of non-soluble pills! Then, ah then, dinner and the flowing Boy and my (possibly infelicitous) suggestion of the King's Peg. Looking back, I feel confident you will not deny that it was a good drink: but neither can I deny that it was an unfortunate nostrum for K. Then the precipitate withdrawal to the bed-sitter, the very cold reception, the reading of Jezebel (which Duffy cannot remember) and the melancholy retreat to

Duff's room and picquet. I remember clearly saying to myself: Well, rather a manqué evening, and the end of me for this leave, I suppose – and yet, philosophically speaking, it has been a good deal of fun. And then, philosophy and picquet overturned together by your radiant entry, and the rapturous shepherding to my hearthrug, and those delirious minutes when the conversation (apart from poor K's troubles) seems to my memory to have wound itself rather inconclusively round the 10.27 train. Jour de ma vie – so I said to myself. But already it has had its rival – a swift strong sudden rival, a fraction, not a day, a puma-like instant striking suddenly out of the night after dinner at Venetia's, in my last dizzy seconds of departure, from the darkness of Westminster to the blue blinding arclights of Paddington. A serious rival. 100 years hence I shall simplify it by counting the two as one day: but at present it is still perplexing. Oh darling, very perplexing. Was it accident or design or sheer benevolence that made you engrave yourself so fatally on my very last hours? Whichever it was, it is done. Twice you have sent me to war with a kiss. This time it surpassed all things. I am drunk with you darling, quite drunk and silly. Your gold chain is round my neck and the chain of yourself round my heart. O love, o life, how can I leave you? I am miserable, but I am terribly happy.

But if Patrick expected to receive responsive love-letters of this intensity from Diana, he was disappointed. She had by now secretly given her heart to Duff, and Patrick was not aware of it. 'The way she deceives those boys is astounding,' wrote Duff. Equally deceived was Edward Horner, soon to be back in England, whose passionate letters to Diana exceeded even those of Patrick in frequency and intensity, though much inferior in quality. He had the advantage over Patrick of seeing much more of her since 1913, and their effervescent flirtation is recorded in his almost daily scribbled letters, of which the constant theme is that if she married him he would become a reformed character, diligent, sober and steady.

Diana's letters to Patrick in the early summer of 1916 are as amusing as ever, but not declaratory of love. One of them describes barbed remarks made about her by Margot and reported to her. The first was: 'What a pity Diana, so pretty and decorative, should let her brain rot.' And the second (to Duff): 'I'm fond of Diana and I know you are: she is witty and amuses Henry – but she always reminds me of what I most dislike in appearance – *German Greek*.' Both these shafts found their mark, as Diana recognized the element of truth in them. Another letter was written at night from a deserted Gare de Lyon, where she and her mother were awaiting a night train with Letty on board. They had to reach the station by the Metro 'in a crowd so big that I saw a man being killed and others sinking without being able to impress anyone with the fact. Mother lost 2 good jewels and I a gold purse. Men cursed us and called us 'ces anglaises' with as much spittle as ever was spat out at "L'autricienne" .' The Duchess's proposed hospital at Boulogne was being handed over to the Army, and Diana had been pestered by a smooth French liaison officer, the Marquis de Castellane, 'with every time-withered opening of "Fate having made us meet", and reincarnation gambits.' Patrick must have needed to feel philosophical when he read this cool reference to their own relationship: 'I don't hear from you often – the last you seemed on the discontented side – hope it was a phase, as you are a calm thought to me.'

Instead the rapturous letters he did receive were not from Diana but from Ettie. Unlike those between Patrick and Diana, with their allusions to kisses and more, the love expressed in Ettie's letters comes from her emotional reliance on him as the companion of her two dead sons:

> It was beyond telling to see you, you were perfect, there is no other word. I had felt a kind of terror, and yet above all and through it all, it was you I wanted to see. Your face and your eyes as you spoke of them told me all – and of Julian's poem. Because to you love for him would never indent what you thought there. How I lean on your utter honesty – as much as

your gentleness. I value so inexpressibly all points where we think the least alike. They are precious in a two-fold sense, because I feel there the hard edge of reality in both our souls, and because there is a kind of over-mastering at-oneness that simply sweeps over any possible pang of division. It helped me to see you beyond any power to tell – grief has a curse of solitariness in its train, and with you, there it was, you just knew and helped me to put suffering in its secondary and true place – because in your eyes was the trust that you felt, and the boys feel, that I will not fail you – and the almost gladness that what was given had been so infinitely precious. I do feel that too sometimes, to the depth of being, though the deep waters almost obliterate at moments, the glory does shine clear, so that the first thought of them is always a passion of joy, even though the drowning pain comes after. There is so little left of anything you loved in me, a ghost's husk moving mechanically, but the great love for you and the belief in you burns undimmed. No one could feel more proud.

On 15 March Patrick sailed from Devonport on the *RMS Ionian*, bound for Alexandria, 'covered with red tabs' and 'looked on with holy awe by all the junior subs on board.' The awe was all the greater because he certainly wasn't going to fraternize: 'By the grace of heaven I have had hardly any slight acquaintances on board, and have avoided with almost complete success making friends with anyone.' Alone, he steeped himself in reading, as on his voyage to New York. Indeed, as he wrote to Sybil Hart Davis, the war had brought him boundless leisure, in contrast to 'Baring Bros, tennis, dining, dancing and love, which have usually taken most of the time between 8 am and 3.30 am, and left only a little surplus to bestow on sleep.' For the record, his reading matter included '*Homer and History* by Walter Leaf, *The Geographical Aspect of Balkan Problems* by some female don (very dry), Macaulay's *History* (progress made), finished Flaubert's *Education Sentimentale* (a triumph), Thais again, *La-bas* by Huysmans (mostly about devil worship), A. E. W. Mason's *Mystery at the*

Villa Rose in Spanish, Edgar Vincent's *Modern Greek*, Henry James' *Washington Square*, some Lucretius, and a lot of Eddie's *new* Georgian Poets.' He was able to seize twenty-four hours in Cairo and, although he missed seeing Basil, he saw Lettie and spent the evening with Edward Horner (now briefly on the Staff) 'who I'm sorry to say seemed rather mopsey and unusually broke.'

The situation in Salonica when Patrick arrived there was one of unusual political and military complexity. Since the outbreak of the war Serbia had been threatened by Austrian-German forces to the north, and had successfully fought them back. But in September 1915 Bulgaria had declared for the Central Powers, encouraged by the apparent failure of the Allied campaign in the Dardanelles, and calculating that participation in a defeat of Serbia would win back losses it had been forced to accept as a result of the Second Balkan War in 1913. In response the Allies forced the Greek Government to admit an Anglo-French force to land in Salonica with the aim of advancing to the aid of landlocked Serbia. This had been very reluctantly agreed by Greece, which was split between the King and the Army, who were pro-German, and the Democrats headed by Venizelos, who supported the British and the French. But hardly had it been agreed than Venizelos was dismissed by the King, with the result that the Greek military and civil authorities were both obstructive to this Anglo-French Army of the Orient. And anyway the force had arrived too late to save Serbia, which had been swiftly overrun by the Bulgarians from the east and the Austrians and Germans from the north. After engagements near the Serbo-Greek frontier, it had been obliged to retreat to an enclave around Salonica, and to create a defensive fortified zone known as the Birdcage.

From this insecure military position, the Allied Generals faced a country of formidably harsh geography and explosive ethnic mix. Macedonia was inhabited, in different degrees, by Greeks, Turks, Bulgars, Serbs and Albanians of fluctuating identification and loyalty. It had never since classical times been occupied by a single ethnic group, indeed Salonica itself had for centuries been predominantly Jewish. With the establishment of independent countries in the Balkans its boundaries had been constantly disputed. It comprised a central plain surrounded by mountains, from which flowed three principal rivers: the Vistritsa from the west, the Varda from the north, and the Struma to the east. Three principal roads spread out from Salonica: one to the west to Lake Ostrovo and on to the Serbian border and the town of Monastir; one north to Lake Doiran and the Serbian border, with Strumitsa beyond; and the third across the Struma branching to Bulgaria in the north and Turkey in the east. Other than these there were few roads. There were also three railways. One went west, branching south to Athens, and north to Monastir. One went north into Serbia, joining the European system. And one went first north, then east, close to the Bulgarian border. The Bulgarians and the Germans had halted at the border, so as not to provoke the neutral Greeks, but the threat of an advance was ever-present.

The merchants of Salonica enjoyed a windfall of trade from the Allied soldiery in the city: almost miraculous, indeed, since no tourists had been seen in Salonica before. The drab hotels, eating-places and markets, had never had it so good, since no price-control was imposed. A Pathe cinema, an Allies Bar, Au Rendezvous de Poilus, and Tommy's Square Meal, all suddenly appeared. The girls were there, of course, in the café-chantant and elsewhere, those from Marseilles taking full advantage of the rich clients by charging 50 francs *pour le petit moment* as against their standard charge at home of *cent sous la nuit*. But in the maze of winding streets, low houses, and latticed windows, the population was watching the occupiers closely, and every military move was immediately reported to the Germanophile court at Athens, even after the expulsion of the foreign consulates.

For his first fortnight Patrick was stationed in Salonica, shuffling between the British and French Headquarters by tram. He had not been expected. The weather was good, the war seemed far away, and all comforts were provided. Or rather, British Army comforts of the sort that he found trying, for the mess to which he was allocated was in a hut and served with stodgy food. Patrick considered taking his meals in a hotel but, realizing what bad blood this would cause, resorted to the device of going to a sumptuous tea-shop and sating himself with eclairs and beer before each meal, then toying with his food at the mess. He visited the lines of the Birdcage, where 'rows of happy Tommies were putting the last touches to trenches already finished off almost beyond human perfection.' He secured a car to try to visit Alexander's birthplace, but was frustrated by three punctures. He thought of writing a novel, but didn't feel inspired. He secured a teacher to learn modern Greek. But already he felt himself to be superfluous among several other liaison officers. In Kitchener parlance, he was not 'pulling his weight', and to Ettie he confided that he was seriously considering applying to return to duty with the RND.

Then came the not-unexpected order to go up country to the forces operating outside the Birdcage. Patrick's immediate superior was David Scott, who had been Captain of the School at Eton in 1905. In the hills north of Salonica, around Likovan, British and French units were operating in a fluid proximity to each other, and local liaison was very necessary, Patrick travelling on horseback between the respective headquarters. Here Patrick's mood changed. To Ettie:

> I must correct (provisionally) the impression of gloom and discontent I gave you in my last letter. Almost immediately after writing it, I left Salonica, and the country has (as they say) cleared the cobwebs out of my brain. The old perpetual *fête-champêtre*, less the dug-out and the enemy; all the other familiar facts, the army bread, the army cook, the too penetrating earth, the too familiar insects, the gentle drip down the *nuque* [nape of the neck] due to the substitute for a tent: plus terrifying Macedonian snakes of gigantic proportions, and a spaciousness really amazing to a Gallipoli veteran, for whom a waddle of 200 yards was the last word in military locomotion. Now it is interminable rides in every direction in (mostly) lovely spring weather with a thought too much

sun and a great number of storks, magpies, and tortoises: really rather jolly, as I have a fairly sound though horribly lazy piebald horse.

Patrick continued in this mood despite discomforts such as torrential rain and eating in messes which had no cooks. He had to deal with the local population, a miserable lot, who spoke variously Serb, Bulgar, Turkish, Kutzo-Vlach, and Judaeo-Spanish, and developed a contempt for the modern Greeks, several of whom were obstructing the Allied army and often had to be interrogated. But his doubts about his acceptance of his posting were still nagging him, despite the moments of excitement and the uncertainty of how the campaign would develop. He learnt that Raymond had, at his own request, left his staff posting in France and rejoined the Grenadier Guards at the front.

To Diana he wrote in strict confidence: 'I should be an extraordinary fool to "return to duty": and yet, you know, I contemplate nothing else. Perhaps it is Raysie's deplorable but stirring example: perhaps the reflexion that if I became a Guardsman (the RND being hopelessly marooned and having no claim on me) though doomed to ineluctable slaughter I should at least be fattened for the market in London: and I rather mistrust, you know, letting you out of my sight for another year.' Before May was out Patrick had written to Bernard Freyberg asking what chances there were of rejoining the RND. The reply came that they would be very pleased to have him back, but that the War Office was now tending to fill senior positions with their own men. The Hood had now been enlarged to two battalions, one commanded by himself and the other by Oc Asquith, with Cleg Kelly as second in command.

The Commander-in-Chief of the Allied Armies in Macedonia was the charismatic French General Sarrail. But General Milne, now commanding the British Salonica Army within it, had authority to consult the War Office about any plans which he deemed to be inadvisable. Sarrail planned a spring offensive, which went off to a bad start. Any direct advance into Bulgaria would have been up the Struma, but would depend on reaching the Bulgarian frontier through the Rupel gorge. On 26 May the Bulgarians crossed the border and seized this gorge and the forts which commanded it, unopposed by, and probably connived at by, the Greek Army garrison. This blocked the line of advance. The Allies retaliated by blockading Salonica and cutting the Greek Army units off from their base, and imposing martial law there.

Patrick was present when the French batteries attempted unsuccessfully to capture the Rupel forts from the Bulgarians. Diana still ruled his lonely hours. By mid-May he still hadn't heard anything from her in response to his love-letter on departure: had she got it? He could imagine the time she was having, and a letter from Raymond told him how 'Duff and I and Diana motored down to Brighton and spent a very enjoyable twenty-four hours there, eating and drinking and playing electric bowls on the pier.' She was there in his dreams: 'Last night, just two months before I went away, I dreamed you married me. It only went as far as the ceremony and was very respectful, but amusing, rather like a royal wedding. I remember Her Grace was very benign, her only anxiety being because she thought I was only 22. Also there was a moment's uncertainty during which I was almost married to K by mistake, and you to Raysie.' But after briefly visiting Salonica for a debriefing after the failure at Rupal, he reported a more earthly encounter to Diana:

> This time, coming back to it after a month away among the little red ants, full of rustic vigour and simplicity, I not only found the town charming and luxurious but experienced a noticeable impulse towards the first woman I saw. Even now, looking back on it, I think she was above the ordinary: a Serb, quite black and thin, mixture of Bridget C and Lady Granby. Anyhow, for 48 hours I seldom left her. It was rather funny because she could speak nothing but Serb and a little Greek, and my Greek which is painfully struggling with problems like 'Your eggs are too dear' and 'Have you any antiques?' was a little immature to be plunged suddenly into

endearments and domesticities. However we understood each other in essentials, and it was quite agreeable.

In Salonica he took the opportunity of raising the question of his future posting with the Chief Liaison Officer. He did not help his case by name-dropping, referring to Colonel Pollen, the Military Secretary in Egypt, as 'Peter.' 'Now then,' he was told, 'I don't advise you to start pulling any strings.' All the same, he wrote to 'Peter' soon afterwards, receiving no reply (until much later, when he said that he could do nothing, since the Salonica Army had full authority about postings).

From Salonica he went to Likovan on the Seres road, to be attached to the French 17th Colonial Division, the same as he had been with on Gallipoli, commanded by General Gerome. This greatly improved his morale, not merely from the pleasure of French cuisine, but because he had established such a close rapport with them – 'the agreeableness, consideration, independence and fun.' 'Instead of ferocity, insolence, and class hatred, urbanity and almost absurd consideration: instead of suspicious supervision, aerial liberty.' And instead of bully-beef, all the art of a resourceful chef. He enjoyed the company of some young French aristocrats, such as Jean de Vilmorin, 'handsome and mercurial'. He had grown a moustache (no beard on this posting) and was learning demotic Greek.

His comforts had been improved with the arrival of Private Parlett as his soldier-servant, a veteran who had served in the South African War with the 10th Hussars. Parlett arrived on horseback leading a horse for Patrick, a 'great coarse brute, specially acquired for the original chief liaison officer, (who weighed eighteen stone), with no apparent mouth.' Parlett did not share Patrick's appreciation of French cuisine: 'I can't eat that French food, sir, I've 'ad nothing but a bit of bread today.' When Patrick told him severely that French cooking was renowned throughout Europe, he replied, 'Maybe, but that there grease they puts into it!' The General, by contrast, greatly appreciated titbits of English food, in the shape of the strawberry and rhubarb jams that his sisters and

Dear sent Patrick, which went well with the 'yaourts' that were purchased locally.

The Allies held great expectations that the Rumanians would declare for them and invade Bulgaria from the north. The French sought to encourage them by an offensive in Macedonia, but the British were unwilling to do so until Rumanian aggression became a reality. When General Sarrial planned an offensive up the Vardar valley, General Milne, after consultation with the War Office, declined to participate, other than by providing flanking support. In consequence it was agreed that British and French forces would regroup, the British effectively taking over the eastern sector of the front, that between Lake Butkovo and the sea. Patrick was involved in the implementation of this. It involved long days on horseback going around to farms and settlements in the hills overlooking the Struma Valley, liaising between the units of the two armies, and interrogating locals. The French 17th Division was to be transferred to a position to the north, overlooking Lake Dojran. On the way to the Division's new base at Kukush, they had spent a night in a Turkish cemetery, reeking with the smell of badly buried soldiers from Balkan Wars, and thick with flies, wasps, and mosquitos. But the next halt was at Kurkut, where Patrick found himself in more romantic surroundings, as described in a letter to Katherine:

> For the past week my unit was encamped on the banks of a river (the ancient Echedorus) which, though greatly reduced, tinkled agreeably over the stones and furnished, if you lay down in the deepest part and splashed, a very nearly adequate tub. I pitched my tent within about two feet of it under (I think) a tamarisk tree: but as the tent (French, and lent) was far too small and infinitely too hot to get into, I took the – for me – heroic step of sleeping outside it with only my mosquito net between me and the moon. When one retired to bed (of necessity about 9.45 pm) the surroundings, what with the tinkling Echedorus (as above), the fireflies doing their stunt, and the silvery-voiced toad doing his, were almost intolerably

romantic when one considered that one not only had to lie down alone (the camp bed would see to that in any case) but that the nearest eligible partner for a little moonlight ramble was at least 2000 miles away. Very distressing.

In Kukush, a town ruined in the Balkan Wars, he was billeted in a former convent. It was subject to enemy artillery fire and air raids, and Patrick was taken up in a French reconnaissance plane. The French Army now had two Divisions in this sector: the 17th around Lake Dojran, and the 51st to the east, straddling the railway line (which led on to Seres) and close against the Bulgarian frontier and the chain of hills which lay along it, the Belasica Plani. In July Patrick was sent for three weeks to the 51st Division. Although he found the cuisine inferior, and the staff were in dilapidated village houses rather than in tents, time in the mess was enlivened because the General commanding it was an enthusiast for culture in general and antiquity in particular. 'He used to ask me terribly difficult questions at meals suddenly, and as everyone else was much too frightened to talk there was a tense silence while I evolved my reply (which had to be in classical French: such expressions as 'tout de même' and 'sauf' were not tolerated, let alone such appalling barrack-room slang as my French is getting filled with).' The Fourteenth of July was celebrated with warm champagne and cigarettes and a sing-song.

In mid-July Patrick, accompanied by Private Parlett, set out on a three day ride to the British units to the east of the French, fortunately departing on the day after a violent thunderstorm which cooled the air somewhat. The first all-day ride was 28 kilometers to the nearest British battalion, a lovely journey, winding through the mountain passes and coming to a coll looking down on the flat plain of the Struma. The second day was in the plain, to the brigade headquarters and back, 12 kilometers each way. The path followed beside Lake Butkovo, on which were cranes and egrets and diving duck: bathing was forbidden. In the valley the heat became intolerable, and at night the mosquitos were terrible. Patrick was protected by a net, but Parlett was bitten so much that his face reminded Patrick of a plum pudding. On the return journey their dry dusty and dangerous ride, more suitable for mules than horses, took them through hostile villages occupied by Turks, and at one of these they were fired on. A few days later Parlett had to pass through the village again and, in face of hostility here and in other villages, shot dead a Turk: when he told Patrick, 'the Captain smiled'.

At the insistence of General Gerome, Patrick returned to the French 17th Colonial at the end of July. The Bulgarians had launched a major offensive on the two flanks of the Allied Army: in the west, against the Serb forces around Ostrovo, and in the east, from Rupal into the Struma valley. In response the French were instructed to attack in the centre, the 17th Colonial having as its immediate objective the railway station at Dojran and a nearby hill. This kept Patrick really busy for the first time since his arrival: up at crack of dawn, attempting to make telephone calls along an improvised system that often malfunctioned, writing instructions at a table without even primitive appliances, being driven about on dusty roads in a Ford to and from the British forces which stood in reserve. As an example of his responsibilities, on 18 August he sent this note to the General Staff of the British 12th Corps:

> Herewith attached evening report and orders for aviation
> I also attach a report from OC French armoured train
> on certain Cypriots employed by the British Army near
> COGUNC and elsewhere, which he appears to suspect of
> cutting his wire
> Capt PEYONNET now tells me that the 21st is the *earliest possible* date for their next phase and that even that is not very probable
> With regard to Major ANDERSON'S personal letter to me
> of today, the numbers of the battalions will be found in
> the Order of Battle which I have already sent you, but the
> French invariably refer to them by the name of the battalion
> commander, which I shall also do unless you wish otherwise
> The 56th Regt relieves the 51st tonight. The 2nd battalion

(CORONNAT) will be on the left in liaison with 26th Divn, the 3rd (CHANDELL) on the right and the 1st (BRISON) in reserve. I am told that the 54th Regt has lost over 600 men (confidential)

From the hills he enjoyed a panoramic view of the artillery and infantry action, which attained its objective, despite enemy superiority in the air. General Gerome and his staff moved forward to Kilinder, at first occupying the former house of a Turkish Pasha. But what with enemy artillery bombardment and rats and reptiles abounding, it was not a comfortable billet, and they moved to a tented camp nearby. A big grass fire broke out on 1 September, enabling the Bulgarians to bombard it at night as well as by day, and on 8 September it was shelled heavily. Seven of the Staff were killed, and Parlett was wounded by shrapnel in the head. He had to shoot the two severely-wounded horses. He was able to collect two replacement horses from Salonica a fortnight later, though by now feeling more dead than alive. General Gerome, flushed with success, nominated several officers and men for the Croix de Guerre (Silver Star), among them Patrick, (dark green ribbon with narrow red stripes).

In his letters from Macedonia, as from the Dardanelles, Patrick makes only brief references to political events at home, such as remarks generally supportive of Asquith and Kitchener and pessimism about the endlessness of the war, though he did write to his sister urging moderation towards the Germans in any peace settlement, 'After all we've got to live with them when it's all over.' He also eschewed strategic observations, for example writing in August 'What the idea is, what we think we are doing, or what the enemy and Rumania intend to do about it, is all Greek to me'; or that the French actions were 'so confusing from the strategic and political as to be sometimes rather irritating.' But at the end of August the Venizelos supporters in Salonica staged a revolution which rendered the Royalists impotent, to the great advantage of the Allies, who had to tread carefully to prevent a civil war. Patrick's view was: 'As for Greece, my one anxiety now is that we may waste time and energy persuading or bullying them into coming in; if they do, they add nothing to our strength, and they constitute another beastly obligation at the end. Whereas, if they remain in our bad books, we can use chunks of their territory to placate the Good Boys afterwards.' He was scornful of the Greeks who so swiftly changed sides.

Ettie had decided to write a memoir on Julian and Billy, and Patrick had sent her his contribution back in April. In his accompanying letter he wrote that he felt it 'annalistic and impersonal': some things could not be said, such as that the Sutton Courtney memories were 'the quintessence of Balliol purged of that dreary backgound of disapproving grammar-school louts.' 'I seem never to have said what glorious beings they were, how curly and how big and strong and shining, and how shaded between the Greek demi-god and the (young and undebauched) Roman emperor – Julian cracking his whip in the quad, or punching a ball, or rowing: Billy running (like a great steam engine), or lying on the grass, or volleying at tennis, or reading very far back in an armchair: these are really the things I want to remember. Oh, and Julian at Sutton, in his green silk bathing-drawers, that is almost the best.'

When he received the book in September he found it deeply moving, particularly the quality of the letters of the two brothers. Emotion overcame him in the description of Julian's last words before he died in hospital, gazing at a shaft of sunlight. Patrick was at this moment eating a rather unappetising piece of plum-duff, prepared by his soldier-servant: 'At the same time I was reading near the end of the book, and when I got to where Julian said "Phoebus Apollo" I suddenly found myself crying like a baby, catching my breath, with a slice of plum-duff in one hand, a bit in my mouth, the tears streaming down my face, and my nose muzzled in my other sleeve.'

Pages from a Family Journal had this effect on other men, portraying as it did the two heroic figures set in the bosom of a devoted family, as described in a journal by Ettie and with many extracts of their own letters. Patrick expressed disapproval of the contribution by Philip Sassoon, but, when pressed by Ettie, had to admit this was mainly because Julian so loathed Philip. There were many references to Patrick as a friend. But, of course, Ettie had edited it to produce the effect she wanted, and Patrick would have been deeply hurt if she had included disparaging remarks about him, such as those of Julian, who had written to her from South Africa in a particularly sour mood, jealous of her continued affection for Patrick:

> About Patrick I don't know. But I look back with growing animosity on his memory. I hated him when he was so wallopy. I hated him in the mornings. I didn't like him much when he was drunk. I liked him very much sometimes when he was a long way off, and I liked being told the things he said. But I didn't like the way he walked, even when he was walking away. I didn't like his hands or his feet or his streaky hair, or his love of money, or his dislike of dogs. Animals always edged away from him, and the more intelligent they were, the further they edged. I think there is something rather obscene about him, like the electric eel at the Zoo.

Meanwhile Eddie Marsh had written a memoir of Rupert Brooke. Although only published in 1918, a draft had been privately circulated. Ettie strongly disapproved of it, revealing herself once again to be prudish. She told Patrick it was wrong to expose the trivialities of Rupert's life and to destroy the image of the soulful poet. 'There are jokes it is cruel to re-warm in after-print, like heating a year-old omelette, and he serves up countless of these plats du jour.' EM's 'own fatal mush pervades the book,' and 'makes one really dislike the subject.' The impression to an outsider is one of 'deadly vulgarity': 'Could E be persuaded to leave out the ejaculations, the vocatives, the hysteria, the fausse râguerie (as about lewdness, nakedness, Polynesians, no trousers, parrots) in 9 out of 10 of the jokes. It would leave a small book but a bearable one.' Previously she had been on the side of nonsuppression, 'but how could one know it would be like this?'

In April came news that Ego Charteris (now Lord Elcho) was missing in a skirmish with Turkish forces in Sinai. It was not until July that confirmation of his death was received. Patrick defined him in a letter to Diana:

Some things about Ego were impossible to exaggerate – his unworldiness, his seeing jokes against himself, his apparent helpnessness and real philosophy. He was tremendously attractive to me. I do profoundly worship unselfishness, and Ego was as much God's fool, with less exuberant folly, as Charles. I have not pressed the comparison with Charles to Letty, because she might perhaps not think it flattering, but to me it is very striking. They were both not of this world, both regarded as flats by the baser sort, both apparently clumsy but really exquisite, fools to the world and philosophers before God, scholars, observers, and unrivalled seers of jokes against themselves. They were both exaggerated, but in what rare direction, and what a refreshing contrast to the sordid exaggerations of most of mankind. Where they differed, Charles had the better brain, and he had enthusiasms, driving power and competitive ability: Ego had physical attraction and athletic prowess, and repose. But in the main they were very parallel: and they formed, for me, a little sect apart from the hustling, intriguing, lusting, coveting, money-loving herd of us. Someone may say, it's all very well to be unworldly for eldest sons whose future is more or less assured without competing: but I don't think that's fair: and just think of most of the other eldest sons we know.

But for Patrick more terrible news was on its way. Raymond was killed in France on 14 September. Only two weeks beforehand, in expectation of a major attack and premonition of his death, he had written to Patrick that he was 'flying right into it, so if this letter turns out to be my last you must remember to say that I was calm and cheery to the end,' followed by a cynical description of a man falling from a balloon. Once again, Patrick expressed his innermost feelings not to the widow, but to Diana, in a letter in which his sorrow and misery is bound around with personal despair. His letter is punctuated with expressions of inability to write on about Raymond. There was no one like him. 'How incandescent was his mind; what an instrument his gem-like speech,' and 'how gentle, humane, and merciless was his unsleeping irony.' Raymond had influenced him, he was his 'master mind'. Only in French conversation and in riding had the competitive Patrick been able to outshine him. His lack of drive was due to his being 'in smooth water between his young academic triumphs and his political (more than legal, I think) future: he was just on the threshold of that.' His death was in contrast to that of Julian, and Ettie's exaltation of it: 'the regulation military "glory", which was not unfitting to thoughts of Julian, is a mockery to Raymond.' Patrick wrote to his sister: 'Decidedly it's queer – when people like Julian died, you felt that at least they had enjoyed the war, and were gloriously at home in it: but Raymond! That graceful, elegant cynic, who spent his time before the war pulling Guardsmen's legs, to be killed in action with the Grenadiers, it is so utterly incongruous, and he so completely devoid of any shred of support from glamour.'

Diana had rushed to the side of Katharine, doubly distressed for her own widowed sister Letty, Ego's widow. It was clear that Raymond's death would place Katharine, with her two small children, in financial straits. Raymond had died at 37, not yet making big money at the bar. Patrick wrote to her to say that, once back in England, he would do what he could to help her 'in technicalities about a lease, an investment or an insurance.' But Diana had a wider vision, believing that Patrick and Katharine should marry; and, since Katharine never did remarry, it is possible to imagine that this would have happened had Patrick survived.

Three further friends were added to the sacrificial pyre. Foss Prior and George Vernon were both killed on the Western Front. And Bron Lucas who, despite an amputated leg, had volunteered for the Royal Flying Corps, took a reconnaissance flight over

German lines, never to be seen again. In his view, all the men Patrick had really cared for were now dead, whilst casual acquaintances seemed merely to incur comfortable wounds. To Duff he wrote that it seemed as if the fates had some particular grudge against the coterie: 'I suppose the Greeks would have said we were too proud, which we certainly were.' But mercifully his brother Basil was all right, and had indeed just got married. Also just married was Nancy Cunard who, Patrick told Tats, 'must have £5000 a year besides the best figure in England, and I don't mind telling you *now* that I was within speaking distance of marrying her myself in 1915,' but who had not replied to his recent letters. Edward Horner was still recuperating from his wound, and Eddie Marsh sent Patrick an account of an evening spent with him. They had been at the opera, where the music had appealed so much to Edward that he burst into tears at the finale. They then tried to rejoin Diana, and eventually found her at Duff's. Then chemin de fer. 'I'd never seen *real* gambling before. Edward made me sit by him as a mascot. He was at the top of his form, in uproarious spirits and very amusing, but infinitely touching and pathetic behind it. When I went away he came into the hall and kissed me, which he had never done before.'

At the end of September the French 17st Division was transferred to the left flank of the Allied Army around Lake Ostrovo in preparation for an attack, in conjunction with the Serb Army, with its aim the liberation of Monastir. But Patrick was retained in the central sector for much of October, liaising with other French units, based in villages such as Hirshova and Yanesh. There were enemy air raids and artillery fire. But otherwise things were quiet. He shot partridges with a dangerous shotgun and useless cartridges. He felt more optimistic about the success of the Macedonian campaign. He shared a room with Jean de Vilmorin, and appreciated that in the company of completely indifferent Frenchmen he was helped in overcoming his loneliness and sorrow over the deaths of so many of his friends. He had come through the sweltering summer in good health, which he attributed to his healthy upbringing by Dear and 'a constitution supremely adapted to coping in treacherous climates strengthened by overeating at Eton and overdrinking at Oxford.' His desire to return to the Hood now seems to have been ambivalent since, in response to letter from Oc Asquith asking him to do so, he replied in late September that he had decided to wait and see how developments in Macedonia were developing.

But in early November he was summoned to Salonica and told his liaison with the French on the Dojran front was no longer needed. He immediately repeated his well worn application to rejoin his unit. But this was refused because the Chief of Staff, General Gillman, wanted him as a Staff officer on Military Operations, an appointment which, he was told, would be 'so good for his career.' The refusal was confirmed in writing: 'Officers must recognize that it is essential for them to be employed in the manner which is most advantageous to the Army in general and hence that it is not possible, except in rare occasions, for individuals' wishes to be entertained.' He was told there was no way he would be permitted to go to France, but if he insisted he could be sent to one of the infantry regiments in Macedonia. That was the last thing he wanted: 'Being killed in France, after a nice leave in London, and in the Hood with my old friends and my old status, is one thing: being killed chillily on the Struma after being pitchforked into God knows what Welsh Fusiliers or East Lancs regiment is quite another.' So he accepted the Staff job, inwardly determined to get leave home in the near future, from where he could work his way back to the RND by pulling all possible strings.

The fact is that throughout his life Patrick was socially confined to a clique. He was not what would nowadays be called a 'people person', not a ready mixer. He did his best to avoid talking to fellow travellers on ships or trains. He was dismissive to fools and bores. He found it awkward to converse with those who might be called 'middle class'. He made clear his belief in the social superiority of Eton and the intellectual superiority of Balliol, which caused resentment. He was not alone in this, of course, but others from the same stable as he, contemporaries in College at

Eton, notably Charles Lister and Ronald Knox, found it easier to mix with a wider world. As a Naval officer, Patrick went out to Gallipoli in the company of a group of remarkable brother-officers with whom he bonded unreservedly, surrendering himself to the charm of Rupert Brooke. And then as an officer on liaison with the French, he empathized superbly and enjoyed their spirited company. But these apart, he found it difficult to live among more ordinary British officers, whether in Macedonia or Flanders, so the thought of joining a line regiment filled him with horror. Like most of the officers, he found it difficult to relate in personal terms with the other ranks under his command.

Diana continued in the forefront of his mind, his long letters to her craving for her love, he a lonely soldier from afar. He had felt a chill when in a letter about Raymond she had written of the help she derived from '*you all*' – 'that "you all" of yours, that elaborately emphasised plural.' Writing on 21 December, and not having heard from her since hers of 14 October, he wrote, in a moment of truth:

> I thought how long it is since I'd been with you, and how short a time last time, and how seldom and how little since the war or since America – three years in fact: and for how short a time, in all probability, next time. And then it seemed to me that I was to blame for mismanaging the war from the point of view of absence and distance; and it seemed to me it was utterly preposterous to expect you, back in London, where there are people – and lots – who love you, to think of me as I think constantly of you, in this womanless (even, you may say, personless) wilderness. It is so evident that you, moving up to the zenith of your divine youth and loveliness and supremacy, cannot have had, and cannot be having, your best years sterilized as mine have been: and thus that not only must there be reams of other people in your life – which I (try to) love to think of – but that I must be the shadow of a dream – which I can hardly bear. More, it seems to me I ought to rejoice in it, that you should not be crippled by war-

geography as I have been and am, and the less you think of me, the less crippled. Thus it seems to work out that I ought to be glad that you should not think much of me nor miss me overmuch: but this conclusion was so grim and unstoppable that I finally fell asleep.

He found himself installed in a magnificent though hideous house built for Prince Andrew of Greece, from which a Turk had been summarily evicted. With him there were the Senior Padre, the Legal Claims Officer, the anti-gas expert, and 'little Amery'. This was Leo Amery, the hyper-active Member of Parliament now assigned to Intelligence and about to be summoned back to London and appointed as an Assistant Secretary of the Imperial War Cabinet. A fellow member of All Souls (they dined together on All Saints Day to celebrate), it was he who had recommended Patrick for this Staff job. So he settled down 'to sticking pins into a map from 8.30 to 1, 2 to 7, and 9.15 to 11. God help me. Do pity me. I am ashamed and annoyed: annoyed, childishly, most of all at not getting home when I had made sure of it. Anyway, you may certainly feel I am SAFE here.' To Tats he compares his work rather more favourably to work at Barings: 'The same drafting for the MGGS on "How I propose to take Sofia" as one would do for John Revelstoke on "How I propose to issue an Argentinian Loan for £100,000,000"! and one's draft being cut to ribbons and rewritten in illegible pencil by the great man.' What was also like old Baring days was being ticked off for arriving late in the office. But, when all was said, being a subordinate Staff Officer in a large formation was the easiest thing in the world.

Meanwhile poor Parlett had been in a French field hospital with malaria, bronchitis and typhoid. He resisted evacuation to Malta in order to remain with Patrick, whom he rejoined in Salonica. He accompanied Patrick on a short mission to Athens at the beginning of December, both in the regulation civilian clothes, and they were there when the Royal Navy fired on the Palace in response to a local Greek attack on some Allied troops. On 8 December Patrick was briefly sent to Monastir, which had just been recaptured after months of very fierce fighting, the Serbs losing some 27,000 men and the French some 13,000, in their advance from the land around Lake Ostrovo. From a distance the white buildings and minarets of Monastir, set in a fertile plain, looked most attractive; but once inside its walls, the filth and misery were overwhelming, and most of the inhabitants had fled. It was also symbolic, as being the only corner of Serbia recaptured from the Bulgarians and their German allies. Patrick described his own experience to Diana:

> I spent a week in Monastir the other day. The chief difficulty was getting there: I tried to go by Ford car, but (encouraged by a Serb captain) I drove straight into a lake which at one point had invaded the road, and my chauffeur, my servant, and I, had to take off practically all our clothes, tuck up our shirts under our arms, and shove first 1000 yards forward and then (as it got deeper) turn the car by manual labour and shove about 300 yards back again, an indecent spectacle loudly cheered by the Italian army. The car having failed, I had to go that night by the French 'trolley,' a small open truck propelled by a sort of motor that runs along the railway. It started at one in the morning and took about 10 hours. It was one of the coldest things I ever did: but it was fun waking up in the dawn at Ostrovo and seeing the sun hit Kaimakchalan through the mist: all the country from there to the Monastir plain is lovely, and the greatest change from Salonica. The Frenchman, Leblois, now commanding the Army up there, was an old friend of mine and was very nice to me. I stayed there four days, and did about half the things I wanted to. Monastir is a jolly-looking town in a lovely situation.

In some notes of his own Private Parlett gives a more graphic description of Monastir, with the remaining inhabitants starving; women and children begging for food; the continual shelling by the enemy; the wounded and dying all around; air battles; and watching 'the French 17th Colonial (all Blacks)' in action, frost-bitten, and 'losing a lot of men.' And 'Captain and me captured

7 Turkish spies next day and they were shot next morning in the
street and left there as a warning to others.' It seems that Patrick's
duties on this visit were concerned with espionage.

Patrick exchanged affectionate farewell messages with General
Gerome, who he met again at Monastir. To the General: 'It is rare
for a stranger to feel so much at home in the army to which he
is accredited, and though everyone was very kind to me, it was
you especially who from the start put me at my ease and made
my posting a continual pleasure.' To Patrick: 'I have passed your
sentiments on to, I will not say your comrades, but your friends,
in the Divisional Staff. You know what friendship we all hold you
in, and how much we would like to have you among us again.
Everyone sends their warmest good wishes.' Courtesies such as
these were not uncommon in the French Army, but there can be no
doubt that Patrick had achieved a special relationship, and been a
very successful liaison officer. He had also enjoyed himself, despite
moods of depression and boredom.

His new Staff posting was the envy of most British officers and,
had he remained in Salonica, his duties would have varied and
expanded into work far more interesting than sticking pins into
maps. The Macedonian campaign was complex and fluid and
had been further complicated by the arrival of Greek, Italian and
Russian units to join the French, the British and the Serbs. Patrick
might well have become an indispensable member of the Staff,
receiving promotion to field rank, and remaining there till the end
of the war. It is true that many other staff officers, on whatever
front, felt they should be fighting, as Raymond had. But Raymond
had not been in the trenches before his staff appointment, whereas
Patrick had been in the thick of it on Gallipoli. Besides, Patrick's
ambition was not merely to be fighting anywhere, but to rejoin his
old regiment and specifically the Hood. Since nearly all his brother-
officers of early 1915 had now been killed, with only Freyberg,
Asquith and Kelly remaining, this pursuit of a former camaraderie
appears illusory.

The principal reason for his determination to come back from the Middle East is surely because he was homesick; or rather, lovesick. His home and his sisters were in Scotland, but it was not that he was pining for. It was for London and his remaining circle of friends, mainly the girls, and principally Diana. As he put it to Katherine, he would 'willingly assume the most murderous and uncomfortable degree of combatancy in exchange of being within weekend reach of London.' He felt he was never made for exile, which had been his lot for nearly three years, and was haunted by memories of the brilliant society in which he had so shone. He was not alone in this, for Edward Horner, who had been posted to the Staff in Egypt after having been wounded in France, likewise manipulated his return to his regiment on the Western Front.

Anyway, this was solved in the New Year when he was granted two week's home leave. Carrying military dispatches, he left on 3 January on an empty French mail boat, the *Duc d'Aumale,* arriving by sea to Taranto and onward by train through Rome, Nice and Paris, reaching London a week later. Also on the ship, also heading for Paris, was the Duc de Mouchy, a French officer who had become a great friend in Salonica.

ELEVEN

Destiny on the Western Front

PATRICK *a*rrived back in England on 19 January 1917 and went immediately to Belvoir for the night to see Diana. This was not an entirely welcome visit. Diana feared he was going propose to her, and wired to Duff, 'Pray God with me to face this great ordeal and to let me triumph.' Her brother John Granby now disliked Patrick. However, all went well, and she succeeded in keeping Patrick at bay. Next day he went for a Saturday-to-Monday at Panshanger, to Ettie's great and unexpected joy. She was in the process of having four such weekend parties, as the house was about to be let, and this was the third: she asked him to the fourth also, on the subsequent weekend. At these he was plunged into the great world he had missed for so long. Among the great men there were H. H. Asquith (recently resigned as Prime Minister), Arthur Balfour, Lord D'Abernon, Sir Louis Mallet, Sir Ian Hamilton, Field Marshal French, Lord Revelstoke, and Lord Hugh Cecil, and Patrick's presence presumably brought the Macedonian Campaign into their conversation. Among the great ladies were Consuelo Duchess of Marlborough, Lady D'Abernon, and Margot Asquith. The Desboroughs kept up a brave face and a determined brightness, but the shadow of their sons' deaths lay over the festivities. Patrick went, of course, to Barings at Bishopsgate, and continued to do so regularly throughout this leave, and put up at the Ritz.

In early February he went north to his sisters at Kessock for three nights, and thence to Ardgowan, now an auxiliary military hospital, for a wider family reunion, including Basil and his new bride, though mourning the death of Sir Hugh's nephew Neil, killed in action as a Lieutenant in the 1st Rifle Brigade. After coming south he visited All Souls and Eton, and stayed at Taplow. Many dinners, evenings of gambling (usually poker) sessions at the Cavendish Hotel, and several Saturdays-to-Mondays, ensued. Duff and Edward were his most constant gambling companions, Edward constantly asking to borrow money from him to honour his debts at the gaming table. In her memoirs Cynthia Asquith recalls sitting next to Patrick at a large dinner at the Ritz at which he confided that he was in love with four women (one of them Diana), but in her view 'I believe him to be incapable of specialising.'

In March he made a further flying visit to his family in Scotland, though, as he wrote to Katherine when in the train between Perth and Inverness, 'London is the candle and I fly into it and back to it.' Also from the train he wrote to Diana, referring to their last meeting 'in those little rooms with wheels': 'you were Diana, suprafeminine, mysterious, entirely unpossessed even in the manifest concession of a fraction.' Thus stimulated, he continued: 'If you have ever seen a cock rise from his almost hourly but not ungrateful task, take two or three stately steps, erect his comb, flap his wings, and crow shrilly: that would be me if you divided the cock's harem – which probably runs to a score – by 20, left him with one infinitely desirable hen who happened to be a bit of a freak, and compelled the poor old bird to read "yearly" for "hourly" and to interpret his task as best he might.' As always Patrick's wing-flapping didn't last long, when dejection took over after a later encounter in which he complained of her surliness. He knew she was surrounded by admirers, younger men and older men, some charming, some, such as Lord Wimborne, the Lord-Lieutenant of Ireland, extremely rich and powerful. A final encounter took place at Beaufort Castle, when Patrick was not the only house guest to enter her room late at night, preceded by a morning spent by her reading Meredith's *The Egoist* aloud in bed, with her two admirers, Patrick and Duff, eying each other suspiciously.

Meanwhile he deployed his energies to returning to the RND, now in Flanders. The influence of great men whom he had expected to assist him in this had evaporated with the resignation of Asquith and the appointment of Lloyd George as Prime Minister. Above all Eddie Marsh was no longer in a position to help him, though he did attempt to enlist the help of Edwin Montagu, who had remained in the Cabinet. Immediately after his arrival he put in his application to the Admiralty. The next stage was to get the War Office to give permission to wait for an answer, as he had done a year earlier. While waiting, he got a dentist to write that the state of his teeth needed further attention. But then came a letter from the War Office saying that Salonica was refusing to release him, and it looked as if his ploy had failed. This refusal was doubtless all the firmer because of annoyance that he had used his leave to secure something that had previously been denied him.

But a second ploy was then played, at his own suggestion. This was that, although perfectly fit for general service, he had allegedly suffered, when in the Mediterranean, from dysentery and jaundice, and that to return there would be dangerous to his health. In early March a Medical Board agreed to this rather spurious conclusion. Salonica could not now claim him, and all that remained was for the War Office to endorse the medical ruling, and for Bernard Freyberg to request him for the Hood Battalion, and then the Admiralty to agree to the resumption of his naval ranking. This took time, but was achieved in mid-April, after three months of leave. In a letter to Patrick General Gillman accepted the medical decision with good grace, and wished him well.

He was sent first to a fortnight's 'refresher course' at a Base Depot near Calais. This was a rude shock to a former Staff Officer, involving 'humiliating exercises in the company of immature grocers from 8 am to 4 pm,' marching about and forming fours, sloping arms, and listening to indifferent lecturing, just as he had at the Crystal Palace. 'The change from being endlessly pampered as Staff to being endlessly bullied and humiliated as a poor silly regimental, well though I knew it and thoroughly as I had foreseen it, is constantly catching me by surprise and producing some new effect of grim comedy.' But he was prepared to tolerate it, and recognized that the comforts of a bed and tent to himself, and a respectable mess, were in themselves luxuries in comparison with what was to come. Meanwhile he found he was close by the Sutherland Hospital, set up by Millicent Duchess of Sutherland and personally supervised by her. At the outbreak of War she had taken an ambulance service to Belgium, been captured by the Germans, escaped through Holland, transferred her ambulances to France, opened a temporary hospital near Dunkirk, and finally had established her tented hospital on the dunes outside Calais. To do this she had badgered the French and British authorities, and the hospital was supported entirely by voluntary contributions.

Although exhausted after the day's training, Patrick was able to get permission to dine at the Sutherland Hospital in the evening, which he did seven times, by means of a mile's walk to a tram service, usually having to be back in camp by 9.0 pm. Once he joined a picnic lunch on the dunes, in the company of the Duchess's children, Rosemary and her brother Alastair, who was on short leave from the front. To Ettie he also wrote, 'How I love Rosemary when I see her! It is strange that it has never attacked me badly when I *don't* see her.' Rosemary's older brother, now the Duke, also appeared, together with his wife, 'a beautiful creature', thought Patrick. Also working in the hospital was Diana Lister (now the widow of Percy Wyndham). The Duchess referred to her 'hutful of toilers' in 'the only life till victory's won', which Patrick thought savoured so much of the older generation of the Souls. Patrick's familiarity with duchesses (Rutland, Sutherland, Marlborough, Wellington, Portland) was a source of amusement among his friends, and Bernard Freyberg remarked that he collected Duchesses as he himself collected Major-Generals.

The Royal Naval Division had arrived in France in May 1916, moving to the Abbeville area. Although preserved as a distinct Division, it had been unable to attract the manpower originally intended for it. Conscription had not yet been introduced, and so it was necessary to attract volunteers both for officers and other ranks. From neither the Army nor the Navy were sufficient men forthcoming. So the infantry was to be composed of two Royal Marine Battalions, six RNVR Battalions, and four Army Battalions. These, now designated as the 63rd (RN) Division, were formed into three Brigades and the second of these, the 189th Brigade, comprised the Hood, the Hawke, the Drake and the Nelson. The Hood was commanded by Bernard Freyberg, with the Rank of a Commander RN, and his Second in Command, as a Lieutenant Commander, was Oc Osquith. There followed a month of intensive training, and detachment to various courses, while all had to become accustomed to Army practices not required on Gallipoli, though Cleg Kelly from the start succeeded in retaining permission for the officers to wear beards. Kelly established himself as an eccentric, a keeper of cats and conductor of the Battalion band. In this capacity his ambition was to perform Tchaikovsky's 1812 Overture to the background roar of artillery. The ensuing months were spent in and out of the line, but not on the offensive, training and absorbing the realities of trench warfare. By October the RND was holding a section of the line on the River Ancre in the basin of the River Somme.

On 3 November 1916 the Hood and other Battalions were paraded and told by the General that they were about to attack one of the most formidable redoubts on the whole of the Western Front. Five previous attempts had failed, but 'We must have that ridge at all costs.' On 13 November they went over the top. In three days the Hood covered itself with glory, capturing the fortified village of Beaucourt. Freyberg, wounded three times, received the Victoria Cross. The losses had been heavy, and nearly all the officers were wounded and many killed, among them Cleg Kelly. A few days before the assault, Oc Asquith had been closely missed by a heavy mortar bomb, and declared unfit for service due to damage to his ear-drums. He returned to the Battalion in February, but was wounded once again, in an action on the same sector, in which the Hood suffered a quarter of their numbers killed or wounded, and for which he was awarded the DSO. The Royal Naval Division then spent the winter recouping and recovering.

The next major action in which the Hood was involved before Patrick rejoined it was the battle for Gavrelle, a small town to the east of Arras, as part of the attack on Vimy Ridge. The 189th Brigade, with Bernard Freyberg now its Brigadier, was to be on the right of this attack, with the Nelson and Drake in front, and the Hood, now commanded by Asquith, in close support. On 22 April 1917 the attack began at dawn. Within an hour the ruined town had been entered, and there ensued vicious hand-to-hand fighting among the ruins throughout the day. The position was precarious, especially because of a windmill that overlooked the town, around which the Germans had constructed a strong-point. Next day the Germans counter-attacked, but were beaten off, and during the following days the new line was consolidated, a small but significant victory. But the Hood had suffered severely: 7 officers killed, 5 wounded; other ranks, 27 killed, 134 wounded. 'My dear Patsy,' Asquith scribbled in a note on 25 April, 'Come as soon as you can. I lost 3 Company Co.s the day before yesterday. Love, yrs Oc.' It was to the battle-hardened Hood, licking its wounds, that Patrick returned on 9 May, as Senior Company Commander, escorting a fresh draft to replenish the recent losses. Apart from Asquith, none of the officers had been with him on Gallipoli.

Patrick found himself acting as Second in Command in the Battalion, in the absence on leave of Mark Egerton. The Hood was enjoying a short rest, working at night behind the line. From there it was taken further back into a camp with comfortable tin huts, still with night work. It was then rotated in inter-Brigade reliefs, with spells in rest camps, then in support trenches, then on the front line, which was quiet at the time, though always subject to random shelling. At one point Patrick initially found himself occupying a German dug-out, deep and spacious, though claustrophobic, and in which he avoided sleeping by bivouacking outside, possessing his own bed. To Dear he wrote that he was glad to come back to the Battalion after the course, and that he also liked 'being quit of that old Mediterranean which got in the end to bore me so much.'

He had expected the comforts and discomforts of regimental life, but had not appreciated the routines imposed on the Western Front in 1917, so different from the boundless leisure enjoyed between the bouts of fighting on Gallipoli in 1915. 'It would be hard to beat the modern Company Commander in France for galvanized activity, out of the line as well as in it. Most comical it is to see me struggling with my drill as a man struggles with a half-forgotten nightmare, and more comical still to hear me instructing men in musketry, bombing, bayonet-fighting (just three inches, my lad, and put it well into his groin), and other subjects of which, little as they know them, the most miserable scallywag among them knows twice as much as me.' He felt he was not a natural leader of men, as he told Diana:

> Once more I have discovered a rather doleful though perhaps creditable truth about myself as compared to others (I really knew it before). It is that I believe that almost everyone except me is slightly but distinctly upheld, through the horrors of regimental life, by being a little tyrant over 50 or 150 or 600 men and perhaps 2 or 20 officers. They *do* enjoy it, you know, more or less furtively. They lecture men and scold them and nurse them and become benevolent little despots. Now I on the other hand never cease to suffer acutely from ordering men about (I don't so much mind ordering half-baked officers). I dislike them all pretty heartily to start with (because they nearly all smell) but feel the least I can do is to leave them alone – but that is what I'm never for one moment allowed to do.

He also felt doubts about his capacity as a lover. He felt he had made a mess of his amorous pursuits on his latest leave, as also on his leave of a year previously. To Ettie: 'O dear, do you think I have an incurably bad touch, or incurably bad heart, or indelibly rotten theories? I always seem to make either myself or someone else unhappy.' When he was with her, he was in the habit of confiding about his successes and failures. These she was more than content to hear, realizing that they would pass away and that his filial love for her would remain constant. She was asked by him to report on 'his standing with D'. Ettie, who had just returned from a quiet retreat on the second anniversary of Julian's death, replied sympathetically: 'I *cannot bear* to think of you not happy in any kind of way.'

Of course, it was Diana who, more than the others, brought him unhappiness, as letters to her written from France reveal. He refers to their recent encounter at Beaufort Castle. He had been pressing her and she had resisted, but 'you might have conducted the incident to everyone's satisfaction if you had (say) begun with a little maidenly resentment and consternation, and gradually merged that in forgiveness (rather conditioned, if you liked, on departure for France) and sweetness, all the time keeping your foot on the brake the moment it became expedient: I really can't believe you couldn't feel sure of being capable of that.' She had compared his aggressive approach to that of the predatory Lord Wimborne. To this accusation he indignantly replied, 'These words I have no hesitation in describing as arrogant, pompous, question-begging, brutally wounding, and in every way unworthy of you. What moral law are you enunciating, you incredible prig?' In a second letter Patrick reveals something of his sexual experience:

Cast a glance back, you who know me indifferent well, over my rather intricate sexual career. You will find fully twice as many notable failures, misfires, eludements, downright rebuffs, as transient successes. I am really 'umble, you know: I am diffident, and honestly surprised when I am favoured: I may sometimes have strutted a little to you for example, when I thought it might be profitable, but I am not fatuous. Think again of the proud women I have been up against, so many and so unreasonable, and for Christ's sake don't begin to regard yourself as the Scourge of God appointed for me – that would be the last straw.

She had heard about an affair of his before he left, so he felt obliged to step into the confessional:

> During the last part of my leave, as you may have observed,
> I flirted violently with --- loved her suitably, and enjoyed it
> immensely. Till the last few days I was under the impression
> that she reciprocated almost the same shade of affection
> that I offered, and congratulated myself on so fortunate a
> coincidence of two young people's mentalities. But at the end
> I suspected – which you now confirm – that the balance had
> tilted a little. But, my dear, you know the difference between
> my temporary and my permanent affections, between the
> lesser and the greater: you know also that in the last analysis
> there is only one in the latter class.

Duff, his real rival for Diana's heart, also had his many affairs.
But he had established himself with her in a way that Patrick had
not. In part this was because he had been in London all the time,
constantly with her and providing continuity when all others had
gone. But it was also surely because he was able to express himself
better in his love-letters to her. Besides the passionate desires
poured forth by both suitors, Duff introduced the use of poetry that
appealed greatly to her. He wrote her sonnets. He was constantly
quoting words and phrases from Shakespeare through to Kipling.
Poetry was one of the arrows in his Cupid's quiver. When finally
in the trenches, he memorized reams of poetry. Patrick was also a
poet, and is remembered for his famous poem that appears at the
front of this memoir. But he didn't practice it so frequently as did
Duff, and never in his letters to Diana. As a soldier he had plenty
of time to compose, in the way that several great War poets had,
but he didn't get round to it. Nor, for that matter, did he write the
book which he at times said he intended to do.

When the Hood was in the front line in June it had the task
of consolidating the position at Gavrelle. It was ordered to dig a
front-line connecting trench (a chord trench) at night, a dangerous
task. Patrick was put in charge of a digging party from 'D'
Company, and a scheme for speeding this up by using explosives

proved impracticable. But when he received reports that the digging had not proceeded as fast as expected, Brigadier General Philips wrote Asquith a severe reprimand, blaming him and the Company Commander concerned. In his reply Asquith wrote: 'I am prepared to account for the activity of my Company Commander Capt Shaw Stewart, and of these men and of myself, and if your order is persisted I shall request that I may be allowed to do so to the Divisional Commander as I am clearly of the opinion that an injustice is being done to all concerned.' The General backed down.

After this Patrick was sent on a three day visit to an Artillery Brigade, where the Battery Commander proved to have been with his brother Basil at Suvla, and fell on his neck in friendly welcome. There followed more weeks of training, including weapon training at which Patrick became bewildered and cross. He found himself being mocked for his ignorance in the tiresome mechanics of modern war: 'I wish I had lived in the flint-arrow period; I could have instructed a company much better in them.' This induced Oc Asquith to send him on a Lewis gun course at Le Touquet. Here he was not confined to barracks by 9 pm, and so was able to dine, at Paris Plage or Etaples, on soles and strawberries, washed down with moderately good champagne: he could also bathe in the sea. He had a pearl of a soldier-servant, named Thomas. Then back with the Battalion, in and out of the line, writing of a quarrel in the trench with his second-in-command, complaining of his smelly socks, only to discover that the smell came from 'a recently deceased gentleman'. At the end of July Oc Asquith went on leave and Mark Egerton was away for a few days with an Artillery Brigade, leaving Patrick in temporary command of the Battalion in the front line. Round on an inspection came the Brigadier, Freyberg's successor, who disliked Patrick, suspicious of Oc addressing him as 'Patsy'. This, to the Brigadier, was an over-familiarity with connotations of 'pansy'. He found four men unshaven and sent Patrick 'a snorter of a letter'.

In August Patrick was granted leave to go to Paris for five days, a permission granted in part for his need for dental treatment: ('my teeth are getting feebler and feebler as I get older and older,' he wrote to Dear, 'I shall be 29 in a few days, isn't it an age?'). He suggested to Freyberg, as also to Conrad Russell, that they might go together, but had to go alone. On reaching Etaples on the leave train, and breakfasting in the YMCA ('I always have a terrible conscientious scruple about going in there, but I believe they don't mind really') he decided to deviate to Calais to see Rosemary. Entertained there for lunch, tea and dinner, he sought tips on Paris. Rosemary provided the important information that only at the Hotel Lotti could one get a hot bath. Alastair gave him the names of the leading *maisons de tolerance*. And the Duchess gave him a letter of introduction. Thus equipped, he took the night train to Paris, reached the Lotti, and had his long hot bath and a sumptuous lunch. He then sallied forth in search of friends. This was an optimistic idea, since everyone who could be was away for the month, in the country or at the sea, from Aix to Deauville. At the Quai d'Orsay de Vilmorin was away. But then he thought of Mouchy, and by great luck found his mother in, who said that her son was arriving from Deauville that evening, *en convalescence* from Macedonia after malaria.

Patrick modulated his account of this visit to Mouchy to his three principal correspondents. To his sister he wrote: 'So I went to dinner with them, and Mouchy at once took me under his wing and set about showing me life, beginning at 10.0 pm (which is late in Paris nowadays) and continued without intermission the next three days, except insofar as he had to pursue a little love affair (but he apologized most politely for leaving me even for that). He made me come and stay at his house which was very comfortable, and even went so far as to gratify my passion for real tennis by playing with me every evening and letting me win.' To Diana he confided: 'His great feat was to intervene personally for me to halve the price (at Alastair's "most expensive") of the most perfect woman, in a purely mercenary way, I have ever embraced, and to find a sort of vacant palace for me to embrace her in.' To Ettie he described the only unsatisfactory part of Mouchy's hospitality:

> His only mistake (an easy one to fall into) was to invite a charming woman of his acquaintance to dine with us one night and "bring a friend". She – as they always do – accepted with alacrity and brought a *monster*, whom I had to deal with for an hour and a half while Mouchy got ahead with his own affairs. The monster was horrified and incensed at my insular chastity: the joke of it was that she had planted herself firmly on the only (and very obvious) sofa in Mouchy's *garçonnière*, on which I had to sit primly beside her, while he and his friend were overtaxing the capabilities of the two rather decorous chairs which constituted all the furniture in the next room.

For the rest, Patrick was able to make his name with Baring's Parisian affiliates. M Turettini of the Banque de France complimented him on his French, better than that of Lord Revelstoke, he said, though having a slight 'Jura accent'. Gossip seems to have smoothed this courtesy call: ' *"Et Gilbert Russell, qu'est ce qu'il est devenu?"*. I said he married the other day the daughter of old Nelke of the *Bourse*. *"Ah-h pourquoi? Est-ce qu'elle était sa maitresse avant de devenir sa femme?"*. Difficult to answer.' The Duchess's contact, Mrs Leishman, materialized and gave him lunch in the company of the charming creole, Princesse Natty de Faucigny-Lucinge. British officers, such as Keith Menzies and Maurice Hely-Hutchinson (a former Eton Colleger), turned up for meals when Mouchy was 'off duty'. He also duly went to the dentist, who 'pushed and pulled me about, filled my mouth with gold, and charged me 200 fr, damn him.' Altogether it was a 'ever such a Paris', reverberating in his mind as, on the fifth day, he made his lonely journey back, stopping at Amiens for lunch and visiting the cathedral, a city to be revisited together with Asquith a few weeks later.

There followed some weeks of the usual company rotation of 7 days in reserve, 4 in support, 4 in the front line. On the front, raids and reconaissances were carried out on an almost daily basis; in support and reserve, the usual round of training and reorganization. But on 10 September the Hood was entrained for the rear area. Here they underwent intensive training, including simulation of advance and breakthrough. They were being prepared for being thrown into the Third Battle of Ypres, which had been raging since July, its main objective being the capture of the ridge around the village of Passchendaele. On 3 October they were moved forward to the battle area, with the task of improving the trenches and communications in the sodden, bomb-blasted ground, constructing roads and placing duck-boards. Warned that they would be going into action on 26 October, Asquith conducted an acerbic interchange with General Philips, complaining that such work would not properly prepare his men for the impending battle, but was overruled. Actually, the Hood was for this operation transferred to the 188th Brigade, coming under the orders of General Prentice.

By an amazing piece of good fortune, Patrick was spared this battle, just as he had been spared the Hood's catastrophic battles of 4 June 1915, 13 November 1916, and 3 February and 22 April 1917. On 29 September he was sent on a five-week Company Commanders' Course at the Army School of Instruction at the Chateau d'Hardelot, near Boulogne. Asquith had intended to send Patrick's Second in Command, but was ordered to send a real Company Commander, and as Patrick was deemed the most in need of instruction, the lot fell to him. Patrick had accepted this posting 'with suitable reluctance'. (Asquith had also put Patrick's name forward as a candidate for the Staff, but the Brigadier's antipathy to him made this unlikely). Another source of amazement was that the Chateau d'Hardelot was where the Duchess of Rutland had intended to establish her hospital. On the ground floor were 'Marquis of Granby Ward' and 'Violet Ward' (altered by some wit to 'Violent Ward'); and upstairs 'Marjorie Ward' and 'Diana Ward' (as if, he thought, she had married a Mr Ward). Patrick, assigned to a nearby hut, heard there was a good supply of blankets in the chateau, only to be told by the storekeeper, 'Sorry, sir, but these are the private property of the Duchess of Rutland, and she cannot allow them to go outside the chateau.' The chateau was set in a wooded valley close by the sea.

Patrick endured this highly-disciplined and comprehensive course, reporting merely on social events. He visited the Sutherland Hospital and there met the Prince of Wales, who made a good impression on him: 'perfectly sweet, very good looking, bright and chatty and completely human. Altogether a great fillip to my loyalty.' As to his fellow officers on the course, he found them 'very much like modern representatives of their class.' He got on best with the batch of Americans and Canadians who were there. These 'two nations have in their wisdom seen fit to amalgamate the upper and middle classes in one, an arrangement by which, if you miss the former, you should also (which is more important in the Army) miss the latter.' Edward Horner was much in his mind. His cavalry regiment was stationed close by at Etaples, though they were unable to meet; there had been a fire at Mells Park; when on leave, he had been involved in a car crash with Diana. Diana fed Patrick brilliant accounts of her summer, with visits to Blenheim, Knole and Vice Regal Lodge in Dublin. She and Ettie had been together at Mells for a week, and both sent Patrick an account of their interchanges there. Ettie's reservations about Diana seem to have faded, or at least she wanted Patrick to think so. She wrote enthusiastically: 'I *loved* Diana, she was so perfectly charming, do you know I have never been four days in the same house with her before. I saw her a great deal and had lots of talks with her. She was looking most lovely.' But Diana's report on Ettie was qualified: 'My admiration for her grew till at times it obliterated everything dark in the world, as also any self appreciation I have ever mustered, any expression or any chance of manifesting itself to her, so the situation is not yet purely satisfactory.'

The action of the 188th Brigade at Passchendaele began at dawn on 26 October. The Anson were on the right, the 1st Royal Marines on the left. Through these then advanced the Howe and the 2nd RMs. Behind them was the Hood, now in the former front line, waiting to act in the face of the expected German counter-attack. But the front battalions got bogged down under heavy shelling in the frightful morasse, and enemy pill-boxes blocked them. Asquith himself went ahead and helped to consolidate the small gains. Next day, the Hood relieved the Howe. But the impetus had been lost, the gains once again of only some hundreds of yards. On 30 October the 190th Brigade took over and made some very small gains and suffered large casualties in the same sector. And then over the next four days it was the turn of the 189th Brigade to push forward, the Hood now transferred to it in reserve. The success of this final effort, in which the original aims were achieved, is in part attributable to the influence of Asquith, who persuaded the Brigadier to authorize night attacks, in which the pill-boxes could be surrounded and eliminated one by one. On 6 November the Hood was bussed out of the battle area. Only two officers had been killed, though several wounded, in these ten days of fighting.

Here, at a camp west of Cassel and only some ten miles from the coast, Patrick rejoined the weary Hood, fresh from his course. A few days later Asquith went on extended leave, and Patrick was once more in temporary command of the Battalion. In typical style he wrote to his sister: 'Oc Asquith has gone on leave and left me in command, by Jove! No nonsense from the junior officers, I can tell you. My first action was to put myself in for immediate promotion to Lieutenant Commander, sound, don't you think? My second, to place a man who has just arrived from spending three years in England, more or less, and who is senior, not only to all my company commanders, but to myself, handsomely – to place him, I say, *second in command of a company*.' His promotion to Lieutenant Commander (the Naval equivalent of Major) was confirmed shortly afterwards. He received a poignant note from Diana: 'My darling, This is no letter but because I have thought of you all today and longed for your return, and prayed, after my fashion, for your safety and happiness. I felt compelled to write and assure you of my steadfast unfaltering love. Your "Bright

Star". This is not prompted by loneliness, desolation, lack-love – as it might read – if anything from *embarrass*, but in truth it is unstimulated by anything but devotion.'

At the end of November Patrick was granted ten days home leave, overlapping with Asquith's (the battalion being in rest camp). A deep sense of forboding was felt by all, especially because on 22 November Edward Horner had been killed in the new battle for Cambrai, and Diana found Patrick's reappearance 'macabre'. She felt it hard to keep up appearances when this latest leave was so 'weighted with the dread of war and blackened by the deaths of his dearest friends.' Patrick and Duff were now the only two men alive of the original coterie. The beleaguered survivors of the group, though all still in their twenties, felt an age away from the eighteen-year-olds they met at parties, ingenuous youths groomed for war, in such contrast to the liberated circle in which they had passed their careless years.

Patrick went to Scotland to his sisters and, just before returning to France, to the Herbert's house at Pixton in Somerset for a weekend at which Venetia Stanley, Goony Churchill, Diana and Duff were also present – Duff who had just been commissioned in the Grenadier Guards, but not yet sent to France. Five guns shot fifty pheasants, 'not a bad change from the winter campaign,' Patrick told his sister. On the last evening of his leave Diana was ill and could not see him, and a letter expresses his regrets that he did not see more of her. They had been alone together only for an evening at Taunton and two lunches in London. However affectionate her feelings for Patrick, Duff had by now established himself as her favourite suitor. Before Patrick's death she told Duff that she would marry him if only he had money, though she never said this to Patrick, who certainly had financial expectations.

Ettie's farewell was more touching. As she told a friend after his death: 'I said to him "Hasn't this time somehow been even happier and more than ever?" and he said, with such a dear *childish* look of trust and affection, "You see, to me it never could be more".' Seen off by Bernard Freyberg at Charing Cross, he wrote her a letter from the train. She had suggested that he would be scribbling farewell letters to his girl friends, but, 'I did buy the notepaper, but it was to write to you to tell you how infinitely I adore you and how perfect and essential you have been to me this leave. What should I do without you? You are Julian and Billy, Edward and Charles to me, and then you are yourself.' In response he received a last letter from her, dated 17 December: 'Patrick darlingest, How I loved your adorable letter from the train, and how above all I loved you. And blessed you for holding on in trust through all the frozen time – never, never fretting . . . How I shall miss you, how I love you.'

A comfortable journey in the Staff Train ('by virtue of being a Major by Jove!') and a smooth crossing, in the company of a former Balliol don, got Patrick to Boulogne. Here he learnt that the Hood was no longer at the nearby rest-camp, nor on the front at Ypres, but had been moved to quite another sector. In the battle for Cambrai the Germans had counter attacked, creating a vulnerable salient for the Allies around Flesquières, southwest of Cambrai. The Hood had been called in to support this, on a line that ran along a feature known as Welsh Ridge. It took three days in smelly troop trains, unheated and unlighted, for Patrick to find them. He found the Battalion in tents in rigorous cold on a grassy plateau. Trench digging was once again the order of the day, and Patrick strolled up to the front line: 'after that, not so good, as I lost my way back to the horses, and, having found it, lost the horses, which had been shelled and shifted – hence an hour's trudging, shouting, cursing.'

On 16 December Asquith's expected promotion (assured to him before he had gone on leave) to the command of the 189th Brigade was implemented, and Patrick once again was in temporary command of the Hood, pending the arrival of Asquith's successor, Mark Egerton. His now almost daily bulletin to Diana describes something of his first two days:

> Yesterday after the chilly awakening I wrote of, had still some
> bad moments in store, notably, Church Parade at 11 am for

which I thoughtfully issued an order that great-coats might be worn; then, proceeding through the icy blast to put on my own – the one you know too well – I found it caked with mud and with the blood of my faithful uncomplaining horse. So, mindful of Hector's rule that 'it is impossible to make prayer to Zeus, lord of the clouds, all bespattered with mud and filth', I attended without, and nearly died of cold, besides having to sing two hymns without the band. The rest of the day was a frozen ride round my scattered troops, but the end was a distinct improvement, as I inherited Oc's half-shed, and succeeded by putting on first, silk pyjamas, then flannel pyjamas, and then a fur lining, and putting everything else on top, in not waking more than twice in the night feeling cold. But I still wonder if it is not a simpler plan to refrain from undressing at all.

Today I rode again towards the front, a martyr to duty, having evolved a new system of *leading* my horse the first mile, thus becoming almost entirely thawed before making myself immobile. It really is an excellent plan. I inspected a vast amount of "work" (digging in fact) and had an amusing first interview with Oc as Brigadier, in the course of which I took a very fair luncheon off him and made nearly all my points.

There has been a two day port famine in the battalion, a serious thing in this weather, fortunately terminated this evening, with the result that now (11 pm) with a stiff whisky and a sparklet, a good dose of ports, and a generous rum punch inside me, I can practically defy the elements.

Alcohol and fur are the twin secrets of winter campaigning.

Three days later, on 20 December, a most distressing incident occurred: Oc was badly wounded. As Brigadier he had arrived at Patrick's battalion HQ and announced that he was going to inspect the line. Patrick was in bed at the time, having been up at dawn, and offered to accompany him. But Oc waved him back and went on alone with his runner. On reaching the support line, when standing in the snow on a parapet, relying on a thin mist, Oc was shot by a sniper through the bone just above the ankle. It was clearly a serious wound and agonizing till the morphia was injected, a wound which was to cost Oc his left leg below the knee. Patrick was with him at the dressing station, watching the ministrations of the heroic Surgeon McCracken. Beside his concern for his splendid comrade in arms, Patrick realized that he had lost his mentor, indeed his patron, one who had been with him from the beginning of the war and represented the tenuous link with the original Hood Battalion of 1914. Also his friend, one with whom he could unbend in the laughter of shared experience. For his part Oc now considered Patrick to be 'the only officer left in whose combination of gallantry intelligence and gumption one could put complete trust.'

It was a premonition for the fate that awaited Patrick ten days later. Till 30 December all was quiet at the front except for enemy aircraft activity. During this lull he had been able to share a Christmas meal with his brother Basil, now a Lieutenant Colonel in the Artillery. But at 7.0 am that day the Germans launched a terrific bombardment along the line of the whole Division, pounding the Hood's position and cutting all the fragile communication lines. At 7.30 their infantry advanced, camouflaged in white (the 'storm troops') and lay in no-man's land too close to be subjected to British artillery. From here they came on and entered some of the Battalion's trenches, with vicious hand-to-hand fighting. The battle raged all day, with machine-guns, bombs, rifle grenades and trench mortars all wreaking their havoc, and continued on the following day in a grizzly stalemate.

But Patrick was not there to see the conclusion, for he was killed at the outset. At the moment the German barrage began, he was going round the line. He was accompanied by a gunner liaising with the artillery. The gunner beseeched him to send up an SOS rocket, but Patrick refused and maintained it was only a minor raid on another part of the line. Suddenly he was hit by shrapnel, the lobe of his ear cut off and his face splattered with blood. But he refused to go back to battalion HQ to be dressed, and insisted on continuing his round along the communications trench. Very soon afterwards a shell burst on the parapet and a fragment hit him upwards through the mouth and killed him almost instantaneously. The ghost of Achilles had failed to save him this time.

When Patrick's death was announced Duff Cooper went immediately to Panshanger where he found Ettie sitting alone in her room, almost in the dark. A tearful exchange of empathetic sentiment ensued. Ettie took some weeks to recover and resume her normal life. Diana's response was to rise above it and refuse to mourn, a course she had adopted when so many others had been killed. But later she wrote movingly of 'his instantaneous death – and an end to his brave heart and his mind teeming with methodical designs for a life of fine aims, fortune, fulfillment. His memory will last as long as we who knew him live to remember.' Patrick's two unmarried sisters were devastated.

In reviewing the lives of those killed in the Great War the question inevitably arises as to what would have happened to them if they had lived to old age – their careers, their families, their appearances, when age would have wearied them, and perhaps the years condemned. With high-flyers like Patrick the question is challenging. Laying aside the element of chance, it is probable that he would have risen to some very prominent position – but in what? Since 1913 he had been a Managing Director of Barings, and would immediately have returned to full-time work with them. It was axiomatic that the Chairman would always be a member of the Baring family, a successor to the formidable Lord Revelstoke. But in the late 1920's there was no obvious younger Baring able to take his place, and so the device was adopted of bringing in a Canadian, Edward Peacock, who effectively ran the firm under a nominal Baring Chairman. It is perfectly possible that Patrick, with his zest and energy and receptiveness to new ideas and prospects, might have been chosen for this role. Peacock retired in 1954, as Patrick, by now in his sixties, might likewise have done, doubtless as Sir Patrick, with a string of other directorships, probably having been a Member of the Board of the Bank of England at some stage.

Alternatively, Patrick might well have used Barings, and the accumulation of a certain amount of capital, as a springboard to enter politics, even though he had shunned that arena when young. Or he could have been called to the bar and later taken silk. Or he might have combined the two, as a potential Attorney or Solicitor General. It is pointless to speculate further, but his ambition would surely have taken him as far as circumstances would have allowed. His success as a banker and then as a warrior had already proved that, although he shone socially in a clique, he had mastered the art of persuasion within a professional spectrum. As someone with a brilliant analytical brain linked to exceptional clarity of expression, he could have enjoyed success in the style of John Maynard Keynes in finance or Lord Simon in law and politics.

Meanwhile, cured of his obsession with Diana by her marriage to Duff, he would surely have settled down with some admirable wife, from a choice made wider with the slaughter of so many of his contemporaries. He would have wanted a house in Scotland, and maybe a sporting estate. Children and grandchildren would have been born to him. If he had lived to seventy-five (few of his generation would have survived beyond that age) he would have died in 1963, a respected member of the so-called Establishment. Two old ladies, Katherine Asquith and Laura Lovat, would for long have kept fresh the memories of his youth with the Horners and the Listers, though he would never have shared the consolations they found in Catholicism under the guidance of Ronald Knox and Maurice Baring. Ettie would have remained an important figure in his life. His two sisters, neither of whom married, would have remained closely within his family orbit.

Of Patrick's friends who survived the War, the most prominent was Duff Cooper. His fiery political career brought him into the Cabinet of Neville Chamberlain, then resignation from that, then back into it in the wartime government of Winston Churchill. This he combined with a distinguished literary output and a rather raffish life style. Next to him one would cite Sir Alan Lascelles, the Private Secretary to two kings (Edward VIII and George VI). Ronald Knox, spared the slaughter as being a priest, became an influential Catholic writer, a translator of the bible and director of the Oxford Chaplaincy. Several others known to Patrick, though not in his immediate circle, became famous: at Eton, Julian Huxley, the biologist, and Hugh Dalton, the politician; at Balliol Alexander Cadogan, the diplomat, and Harold Nicolson, the writer. Patrick's military colleague who rose to greatest prominence was Bernard Freyberg, New Zealand's national hero. Oc Asquith, weakened by his wound, married Betty Manners, who inherited Clovelly. Though six years younger than Patrick, and not really known to him, Harold MacMillan, who had been tutored privately by Ronald Knox, attained the Premiership as a product of Eton and Balliol and a severely wounded soldier: Achilles had not been so far from him either, as, lying in the shell-hole awaiting rescue, he had consoled himself by reading Aeschylus.

As to those others who did not survive, one cannot but have visions: of Edward Horner, charming as ever, settling down at Mells and living long enough to see the estate returned to profitablity; of Julian Grenfell rising in rank in the Army, but increasingly leading the life of a country sporting gentleman, temperamentally pugilistic to the last; of Raymond Asquith, smoothly sitting in the Commons then the Lords, but forbearing to engage in the cockpit of political struggle. Rupert Brooke would surely have become a national treasure, though his poetry would seem out of date; Foss Prior would perhaps have been a respected headmaster, and Denis Browne established in the new world of media. As to Charles Lister, Patrick's closest – and most attractive – friend, if he had remained in the diplomatic service, I see him at his last post as our first post-Second World War Ambassador to Italy, writing trenchant dispatches about the Communist threat, and consistent as ever in his hatred of Russian tyranny.

In the First World War, destruction and death were largely confined to the battle zone and the fighting men: in the Second, terror bombing brought the conflict home to large numbers of cities and civilians also. So, despite being numbed by the endless lists of dead and wounded, the public in England was largely insulated from the horrors of the trenches. It was only in the 1920s that memoirs and poems and photographs brought a wider realization of the bestiality of modern warfare, spreading pacifism. At the time of Patrick's death, most people saw the glorious dead in battle as a necessary sacrifice. That, after all, was a strong theme in a classical education, as also in the history of the nation. Besides, death stalked the land more immediately before the era of modern medicine. Babies, children, and the young often died natural deaths, and few people lived to old age. Premature death was accepted as part of the human condition, and religion served to soften the blow. Several of Patrick's close friends had siblings who died in infancy or childhood.

A century later, after a long period of peace and prosperity in Europe, and with ever increasing longevity, we view the slaughter of millions of young men as scarcely credible. Patrick was indeed swept up in a holocaust, one which was only to be extinguished after a Second World War. Although not the 'war to end all wars', as was at first supposed, at least Europe itself is no longer a crucible for internecine warfare. We are now nearly as far in time from the Great War as that event was from the Napoleonic Wars. The last of the veterans who fought in it have died. Hardly anyone living can even remember any of the fallen. But our understanding of it in human terms can be enhanced, in however small a way, by individual experiences, such as those of Patrick Shaw Stewart.

Bibliography

Asquith, Cynthia, *Remember and be Glad*, J Barrie 1952

Asquith, Raymond, *Life and Letters*, ed John Jolliffe, Collins 1980

Bonham Carter, Violet, *Lantern Slides*, ed Mark Pottle, Weidenfeld and Nicolson, 1996

Card, Tim, *Eton Renewed*, John Murray 1994

Cooper, Diana, *The Light of Common Day*, Hart-Davis 1959

Cooper, Duff, *Old Men Forget*, Hart-Davis 1953

Davenport-Hines, Richard, *Ettie,* Weidenfeld and Nicolson, 2008

Glendinning, Victoria, *Vita*, Weidenfeld and Nicolson 1983

Hassall Christopher, *Edward Marsh*, Longmans 1959

Hassall, Christopher, *Rupert Brooke*, Faber 1964

Jones, John, *Balliol College*, OUP 1997

Jones, Lawrence, *An Edwardian Youth*, Macmillan 1956

Lascelles, Alan, *The End of an Era*, Hamish Hamilton, 1986

Lees Milne, James, *Harold Nicolson*, Chatto and Windus 1981

MacKenzie, Jeanne, *The Children of the Souls*, Chatto and Windus 1986

Moorehead, Alan, *Gallipoli*, Hamish Hamilton 1956

Mosley, Nicholas, *Julian Grenfell*, Weidenfeld and Nicolson 1976

Page, Christopher, *Command of the Royal Naval Division*, Staplehurst Spellmount, 1999

Palmer, Alan, *The Gardeners of Salonica*, 1965

Sellers, Leonard, *The Hood Battalion*, Leo Cooper 1995

Tree, Viola, *Castles in the Air*, Hogarth Press 1926

Waugh, Evelyn, *Ronald Knox*, Chapman and Hall 1959

Ziegler, Philip, *Diana Cooper*, Hamish Hamilton, 1981

Ziegler, Philip, *The Sixth Great Power*, Collins 1988

Index

Souls, 119, 121, 123; death in action, 182

Reid, Elizabeth: engaged as Patrick's nurse, 20; devotion to Patrick, 22, 24; admonishments to Patrick, 33, 49, 81, 99-100; criticizes Patrick's mother, 87; domestic life, 23, 41, 77, 143; sends food parcels, 187-8, 205-6

Revelstoke, 2nd Baron, 112, 115, 116, 117, 120, 151, 129, 221

Ribblesdale, 4th Baron: as a figure in society, 45, 64, 90, 195; welcomes Patrick as a friend of his children, 78-9, 81, 89, 97, 106, 130; writes memoir of his son, 15

Rodd, Lady (later Rennell), 137, 141

Royal Naval Division: inception, 152-3; in camp at Blandford, 154-6; dispatched to the Dardanelles, 157, 159; in Egypt and the Aegean, 160-2, 166-8, 175, 193; on Gallipoli, 170-1, 173-4, 183; reorganisation after Gallipoli, 193; on the Western Front, 225-6, 234-5, 239

Sackville West, Vita (later Nicolson), 134-6, 140-1

Sassoon, Sir Philip, 75, 85, 102, 211

Shaw Stewart, Lady Alice, 34, 69, 74, 87

Shaw Stewart, Brigadier General Basil: as Patrick's brother, 18, 20, 21, 22; marriage, 214, 221; meets Patrick at the front, 184, 239

Shaw Stewart, Sir Hugh, 7th Bt, 33, 34, 75

Shaw Stewart, General Jack, 18-22, 87

Shaw Stewart, Katherine, 18, 20, 22, 59, 65, 87

Shaw Stewart, Mary, 19, 20, 21, 87, 105

Shaw Stewart, Patrick: ambitions, 36, 48, 73, 240-1; appearance, 55, 72, 118, 184; as a banker, 116, 128, 136, 139-40, 144; birth, 18; character, 15, 71, 83, 93, 119, 127, 164; death in action, 239-40; hedonism, 43, 55, 99, 102, 103, 196, 222; love for Classical Greek, 38, 110, 161, 172, 176-7; his oration at Balliol, 84-5; his poem, 176-8; relationship with older women, 14, 44, 71, 118-9, 163; relationship with younger women, 71, 88, 91, 112, 125, 135-6, 146, 227-9; on religion, 26, 31, 37, 108, 189-90; scholarships, 24, 30, 36-7, 43, 77, 83, 119; social exclusivity, 80, 133-4, 144, 199, 210,

215-6; unmusicality, 96; unpunctuality, 33, 53, 134; on war, 76-7, 150-1, 172, 178, 202; as a warrior, 171-2, 175, 180, 208-9, 227, 229-30, 237-9

Shaw Stewart, Winifred, 18, 20, 22, 23, 87

Smith, F.E., (later 1st Earl of Birkenhead), 58

Stanley, Venetia (later Montagu): at social events with Patrick, 59, 64, 78, 90, 130, 236; during the War, 186, 188

Sutherland, Duchess of, 131, 224, 231

Tavistock, Marquess of (later 12th Duke of Bedford), 53, 102, 114

Tree, Sir Beerbohm, 64

Tree, Viola (later Parsons), 66, 71, 82, 95-6, 104, 138

Urquhart, Francis, 52, 55

Vernon, 8th Baron: among the Coterie, 139, 142, 143; death in action, 213

Vilmorin, Jean de, 205, 214

Wellington, 4th Duke of, 124-5

Wyndham, George, 96